D0855453

oday liberal feminism is a mix of several orientations. Although all liberal feminists adopt the ideas of freedom of choice, individualism, and equality of opportunity, they differ on how self-conscious they are about the patriarchal, economic, and racial bias of these ideas. The set of ideas identified as liberal feminist has remained strikingly similar in both its nineteenth- and twentieth-century formulations. What is interesting to note is that the position this set of ideas holds within the political spectrum of alternatives has changed considerably. Whereas the feminist demands of Wollstonecraft, Mill, Taylor, and Stanton stood as radically liberal in their day, they are now part of the established ideology of the state. Whereas these early feminists were utterly progressive in demanding education, the vote, and property rights for women, today these formal legal equalities exist. As a result, those who narrowly define women's equality in terms of citizen rights believe women have attained equality with men. My purpose is to identify the radical feminist tendencies that exist within significant sectors of liberal feminist politics and by so doing clarify the basis for building a revolutionary feminist politics. . . .

(from the text)

Longman Series in Feminist Theory

THE
RADICAL
FUTURE
OF
LIBERAL
FEMINISM

ZILLAH R. EISENSTEIN

JUN 0 5 1981

Longman
New York & London

THE RADICAL FUTURE OF LIBERAL FEMINISM

Longman Inc., 19 West 44th Street, New York, N.Y. 10036
Associated companies, branches, and representatives
throughout the world.

Copyright © 1981 by Zillah R. Eisenstein

All rights reserved. No part of this publication may be
reproduced, stored in a retrieval system, or transmitted
in any form or by any means, electronic, mechanical,
photocopying, recording, or otherwise, without the prior
permission of the publisher.

Developmental Series Editor: Nicole Benevento
Assistant Series Editor: Carol Camper

Editorial and Design Supervisor: Joan Matthews
Interior Design: Angela Foote
Manufacturing and Production Supervisor: Robin B. Besofsky
Composition: Book Composition Services, Inc.
Printing and Binding: Fairfield Graphics

Library of Congress Cataloging in Publication Data

Eisenstein, Zillah R
  The radical future of liberal feminism.

  Includes index.
  1. Feminism. 2. Liberalism. 3. Radicalism.
I. Title.
HQ1154.E44   305.4'2   80-19464
ISBN 0-582-28205-5
ISBN 0-582-28206-3 (pbk.)

Manufactured in the United States of America

9 8 7 6 5 4 3 2 1

for Giah and Julia
and the memories of our sister
Sarah

Acknowledgments

I learned the full meaning of the social content of ideas while writing this book. My debt to those who helped me clarify my ideas is enormous. Miriam Brody, Beau Grosscup, Rosalind Petchesky, and Isaac Kramnick contributed to this process endlessly. They read, criticized, and tirelessly commented on the entire manuscript. Beyond this, Miriam Brody shared her research and her most recent thoughts about Mary Wollstonecraft; Beau Grosscup shared his research on the liberal democratic state; Ros Petchesky shared her knowledge of seventeenth-century England and eighteenth-century France; Isaac Kramnick shared his work on bourgeois radical thought, which had a profound impact on my thinking about feminism.

I also wish to thank Nancy Chodorow, Ellen Dubois, Laura Englestein, and Mary Katzenstein for commenting on particular chapters. Attorney Elisabeth Yanof and Rosalind Kenworthy, planned parenthood and sex counselor, supplied me with much needed information on the ERA and abortion rulings. Camille Tischler helped me keep abreast of the literature on wage-earning women. Julie Mastoberti and Dorothy Owens graciously typed the many versions of the manuscript. My editors at Longman, Nicole Benevento, Carol Camper, Irene Glynn, and Joan Matthews, made important contributions in the last stages of the book's production.

Lastly, the work of this book has been shared with my students at Ithaca College for the past five years. Their probing questions often pushed me to a new level of analysis. And, if one must believe in what one writes about, I must thank the women's group of the First Unitarian Church of Houston, Texas, for organizing the Women and Power Conference in 1978. Many of the ideas of this book were given new life in the dialogue that took place at this meeting.

The writing of this book was completed with the aid of an American Council of Learned Societies grant. Several of the ideas in Part III of the book have been published as "Reform and/or Revolution: The Houston Conference and the ERA," in *Women and Revolution*, ed. by Lydia Sargent (Boston: South End Press, 1980); "El Estado, la familia patriarcal y las madras que trabajan," *En Teoria*, no. 1 (Abilunio de 1979): 135–168; and "The State, The Patriarchal Family and the Working Mother," *Kapitalistate*, 1980.

I wish, too, to thank these publishers for their kind permission to reprint from the following:

"Discourse on the Origin and Foundations of Inequality Among Men," in *The First and Second Discourses* by Jean-Jacques Rousseau, translated by Roger D. Masters, © 1964 by St. Martin's Press, Inc., New York.

Emile, or Education by Jean-Jacques Rousseau, translated by Barbara Foxley, an Everyman's Library Edition, © 1911. Reprinted by permission of the publisher in the United Kingdom, D. M. Dent & Sons Ltd., London, and by permission of the publisher in the United States, E. P. Dutton and Company, New York.

It Changed My Life: Writings on the Women's Movement by Betty Friedan, © 1977 by Random House, Inc., and Alfred A. Knopf, Inc., New York.

The Social Contract and Discourses by Jean-Jacques Rousseau, translated by G. D. H. Cole, an Everyman's Library Edition, © 1955. Reprinted by permission of the publisher in the United States, E. P. Dutton and Company, New York, and by permission of the publisher in the United Kingdom, D. M. Dent and Sons Ltd., London.

Zillah R. Eisenstein

Contents

ACKNOWLEDGMENTS   vii

PART

I INTRODUCTION   1

  1 / Placing Liberal Feminism in the Dialectic   3

  2 / Patriarchy, Motherhood, and Public Life   14
      Patriarchal Motherhood as Childbearer and
        Rearer   14
      The Historical Continuity of Patriarchy   18
      Patriarchy and Public-Private Life   22

PART

II THE HISTORICAL ORIGINS OF LIBERAL
FEMINISM   31

  3 / John Locke: Patriarchal Antipatriarchalism   33
      Rationality and Women   35
      The Liberal Attack on Divine-Right Patriarchy:
        Paternal vs. Political Power   37
      The Feminist Critique of Divine-Right Rule:
        Paternal vs. Parental Power   40
      Property and Rationality   44
      Liberal Individualism and the Family   47

  4 / J. J. Rousseau and Patriarchal Ideology:
    Liberal Individualism and Motherhood   55
      The Problem of Sexual and Economic Class   57
      The Family and the State   58
      Rousseau's Ambivalence Toward Women   60
      The Potential Power of Women   62
      The Virtuous Woman   64
      A Patriarchal View of Motherhood   67

The Embrace of Liberal Values 68
The Critique of the Bourgeois Market 70
Political Freedom 74
Freedom, Independence, and the Contradictions
of Patriarchy 76

5 / Mary Wollstonecraft: The Feminist Embrace
and Criticism of Liberalism 89
The Liberal Assault Against Aristocratic and Male
Right 90
Woman, Rationality, and Bourgeois Society 93
Woman, Work, and Economic Class in
Eighteenth-Century England 96
✓The Middle-Class Woman as Mother 99
Liberalism vs. Radical Feminism 102

6 / J. S. Mill and Harriet Taylor: Liberal
Individualism, Socialism, and Feminism 113
The Problem of Individuality and Liberal
Individualism 114
The Problem of Liberal Individualism 116
Liberal Individualism and the Working Class 119
On Socialism 122
Liberal Individualism and Women 127
Woman's Work at Home and in the Marketplace in
the Victorian Age 129
The Patriarchal Bias of Liberal Feminism 132

7 / Elizabeth Cady Stanton: Radical Feminist
Analysis and Liberal Feminist Strategy 145
The New Femininity vs. Liberal Ideology 146
Women's Rights Against "The Aristocracy of
Sex" 149
Liberal Individualism and Feminism 152
Stanton as a Radical Feminist 155
The Enfranchisement of Women as Liberal
Feminist Strategy 162

PART
III THE CONTEMPORARY PRACTICE OF
LIBERAL FEMINISM 175

8 / Friedan's Liberal "Feminist Mystique"
and the Changing Policies of NOW 177

Feminist Politics and a Liberal Theory of
  Power   179
The Liberal Feminist Mystique   184
A Conception of Individuality vs. Liberal
  Individualism for Feminism   190
The Practice of Liberal Feminism and the Politics
  of NOW   192

9 / The Contradiction Between Liberal
  Individualism and the Patriarchal Family:
  The "Working Mother's" Double-Day and
  Her Sexual Ghetto in the Labor Force   201
The Contradictory Needs of Patriarchy and
  Capitalism   204
The "Working Mother" and the Sexual Ghetto in
  the Labor Force   206
The "Working Mother" and Feminism   212

10 / The Capitalist Patriarchal State and
  the Politics of Liberal Feminism   220
The State, Patriarchy, and Capitalism   222
Toward a Feminist Theory of the State   225
Contemporary Liberal Feminism   229
THE ERA as a Necessary but Not Sufficient
  Strategy for Feminists   232
Reproductive Rights: Pregnancy Disability and
  the Politics of Abortion   236
Current Political Struggles: New Right vs.
  Feminists   241
Liberal Feminism and the State: The Houston
  Women's Conference and Abzug's
  Dismissal   244
Intrastate Conflict: Carter and Abzug   246

INDEX   254

PART

I INTRODUCTION

1

Placing Liberal Feminism in the Dialectic

I t is important for feminists of different political persuasions to recognize that mainstream feminism has the potential for radicalism. Because the politics of American society seems to be moving to the right with the renewal of the cold war, contradictory state policies on abortion, the so-called crisis of the family, and the probable reinstatement of the military draft for men (and, possibly, women), it is imperative that feminists see the radical tendencies within mainstream feminism. Feminists—radical, socialist, black, anarchist, and lesbian —must recognize this tendency toward radicalism and begin to build a mass-based feminist politics for the 1980s.

This book documents the radical potential of feminism reflected in the writings of Mary Wollstonecraft, John Stuart Mill, Harriet Taylor, and Elizabeth Cady Stanton that grows out of the contradictory base of liberal feminism. In other words, the contradiction between liberalism (as patriarchal and individualist in structure and ideology) and feminism (as sexual egalitarian and collectivist) lays the basis for feminism's movement beyond liberalism. The book also examines the non-radical feminist politics of Betty Friedan to better understand how the potential radicalism of feminism is not always actualized.

If we look at liberal feminist theory and its present politics, we find that its political practice has been inhibited by its theory. At the same time, we see that liberal feminist politics has moved beyond its own theory. The result is that liberal feminism lacks a theory to help guide and inform its political strategy. As Nancy Hartsock has stated:

> Forming theory out of practice, articulating what is taking place, does not come quickly or easily, and it is rarely clear what direction the theory will finally take. It requires close attention to practice, and to what diverse groups of people are doing.

> Contemporary feminism in the United States finds itself in a
> situation in which the very substantial struggles of women have
> not yet been "theorized." . . . Theory itself, then, can be seen
> as a way of taking up and building on experience.[1]

In Part 2 of this book I examine liberal feminism for its theoretical
content and then I examine the practical content of liberal feminist
theory in Part 3. My purpose is to clarify the difference between liberal
feminism as a political perspective and its oversimplified description as
a white middle-class reform-oriented politics.

Liberal feminism is but one form of feminism, although both
feminists and nonfeminists often mistakenly assume that it *is* feminism.
Therefore, the first thing to be done is to identify the specific theory and
politics of liberal feminism. Liberal feminism is best understood as
what Betty Friedan calls "mainstream" feminism. The position of liberal feminism, at center stage, reflects the broader and more general
liberal bias of American politics. When liberal feminism is equated
with feminism, other forms of feminist theory—be they radical,
socialist, lesbian, black, anarchist, or some blending of these—are ren-
dered nonexistent. The equation of liberal feminism with feminism also
reflects the fact that liberal feminists identify themselves as feminists
with little or no consciousness about the particular liberal political
theory they adopt. Nor, for that matter, have feminists of other political
persuasions really understood the history of liberal feminism. Even less
do they recognize the origins of their own feminism in this tradition.
The argument put forward here is that all feminism is liberal at its root
in that the universal feminist claim that woman is an independent
being (from man) is premised on the eighteenth-century liberal conception of the independent and autonomous self. All feminism is also
radically feminist in that woman's identity as a sexual class underlies
this claim. What this book argues is that both the history and the present formulation of liberal feminism is more complicated than the usual
and perfunctory description it elicits.[2]

"Liberal" in this book is used in its more historical sense and not in
the everyday usage suggesting open-minded or receptive to change.
Liberal ideas are the specific set of ideas that developed with the
bourgeois revolution asserting the importance and autonomy of the
individual. These ideas, which originated in seventeenth-century England and took root in the eighteenth century, are now the dominant
political ideology of twentieth-century Western society. Because the
liberal values of independence, equality of opportunity, and individualism are the predominant and accepted values of Western society,
they have lost their "particular" identity and history for most members
of liberal society. They are accepted as the norm rather than as a specific

ideology. Until liberalism is viewed as a political ideology by (liberal) feminists, they will be unable to identify the contradiction inherent in liberal feminism. As long as the liberalism in feminism parades invisibly, it cannot be assessed as contradictory with feminism, nor can dimensions of it be self-consciously reworked.

Liberalism is discussed in this book as a specific ideology seeking to protect and reinforce the relations of patriarchal and capitalist society. The particular relationship between liberalism as a political ideology and capitalism as an economic system has been made elsewhere and is not a central concern here.[3] Instead, the purpose is to explain the contradictory base of liberalism that lies in its patriarchal roots, a contradiction that comes to define the limits of liberal feminism as a radical force for social change even though liberal feminism develops as a reaction to the patriarchal bias of liberalism. The ideology of liberal individualism is used to criticize the rule of men as the "aristocracy of sex." The history that explains this critique is complex and often contradictory, but what emerges in the end is the possibility of building a sounder feminist politics.

One of the major contributions to be found in this study is the role of the ideology of liberal individualism in the construction of feminist theory. Today's feminists either do not discuss a theory of individuality or they unself-consciously adopt the competitive, atomistic ideology of liberal individualism. There is much confusion on this issue in the feminist theory we discuss here. Until a conscious differentiation is made between a theory of individuality that recognizes the importance of the individual within the social collectivity and the ideology of individualism that assumes a competitive view of the individual, there will not be a full accounting of what a feminist theory of liberation must look like for Western society.

A central concern of this study, then, is to examine the role of liberal thought in the development of feminist theory. Throughout, this book argues that while the liberal underpinnings of feminist theory are essential to feminism, the patriarchal underpinnings of liberal theory are also indispensable to liberalism. This is the contradictory reality that defines the problem. The very notion of citizen is male supremacist, as will be pointed out in the next chapter. This bias of liberal democratic theory is reflected in the inability of John Locke and Jean Jacques Rousseau to understand the patriarchal structuring of society as antithetical to the practice of democracy. The division between the public and private realms of social activity is the starting point for their analyses, a division that understands the realm of the family as the woman's sphere and the realm of the public world as the man's. The liberal feminists in this study often argue to include women within the public world without recognizing that the split between public and private life is reproduced in their own political strategies. They challenge what they understand to be the patriarchal elements of democratic theory, while they accept the specifically liberal interpretation of the patriarchal division between public and private life.

Nevertheless, when Wollstonecraft, Taylor, J. S. Mill, and Stanton applied to women the arguments for the rights of individual freedom, personal independence, achievement through merit, and equality of opportunity, they had to step outside the boundaries of established liberal thought, which were intended for men only. Understanding how they criticize liberalism and at the same time remain bound to it uncovers for us the complex beginnings of Western feminist theory.

Liberal feminism involves more than simply achieving the bourgeois male rights earlier denied women, although it includes this. Liberal feminism is not feminism merely added onto liberalism. Rather, there is a real difference between liberalism and liberal feminism in that feminism requires a recognition, however implicit and undefined, of the sexual-class identification of women as women. Early liberal feminists argued for the individual rights of woman on the basis that she was excluded from citizen rights as a member of a sexual class. Her *ascribed* sexual status prevented her from partaking in individual *achievements* promised by liberal society. This recognition of women as a sexual class lays the subversive quality of feminism for liberalism because liberalism is premised upon woman's exclusion from public life on this very class basis. The demand for the real equality of women with men, if taken to its logical conclusion, would dislodge the patriarchal structure necessary to a liberal society.

The analyses of Wollstonecraft, J. S. Mill, Taylor, and Stanton recognized the collective position of women in relation to men and therefore stood outside the liberal categories of individualist power. The early liberal feminists had a sense of woman's collective existence; they did not view women merely as individuals but as individuals differentiated from men in terms of the power men had. They used the ideology of liberal individualism to uncover the collective subjugation of women. Although these feminists were unable to develop a theory of oppression rooted in this sex-class system, they utilize one to criticize the liberal paradigm, even if, in the end, they are limited by the liberal paradigm. Without the beginnings of this conception of sexual class, they would not have had the feminist base with which to attack liberalism.

The discussion of eighteenth- and nineteenth-century theory and twentieth-century practice reveals the difficult process of women developing a consciousness of themselves as a sexual class. *Uncovering the patriarchal bias of liberalism expresses the political process of trying to understand how one's own life as part of a sexual class is part of the structure and needs of patriarchy. It expresses the developing consciousness of women as a sexual class. This historical development of sexual-class consciousness is uneven and contradictory.* Different conceptions of sexual-class oppression reflect the elusive nature of patriarchy—a highly mystified political form of domination that is yet to be fully understood. Examining these contradictions should expose a fuller understanding of the political force of patriarchy.

According to Wollstonecraft, men had power because they were educated and economically independent. According to Taylor and Stanton, men had power because they were recognized as citizens and were not restricted to a "sexual sphere." Within both views, women lacked power as a class because they were not allowed to compete as women in the public male world. The category "sexual class" applied, biologically, to the female gender, but early liberal feminists did not make much of this point. Women were sexually distinguished from men, but the theory of woman's subjugation was not explicitly tied to this reality.

Contemporary radical feminism emerged with a theory of woman's oppression rooted in the sexual-class system. Simone de Beauvoir[4] in the early 1950s was the first to document the significance of woman's biological difference from man. Shulamith Firestone in 1970 articulated a theory of sex class based on woman's biological function as a childbearer. She understood the sexual imbalance of power to be biologically based.[5] Ti Grace Atkinson built on this analysis by clarifying the difference between a biologically determinist theory of sex class and one that recognizes the cultural and political determinants of biology. As such, one's sexual class reflects the political relations of patriarchy that define woman's biology in specifically oppressive ways. She interprets the class nature of female oppression through the patriarchal relations that manipulate woman's childbearing capacities. The problem, according to Atkinson, is not childbirth itself but the patriarchal relations of society, which transform this capacity into woman's life function.[6] Christine Delphy has sought to further understand the sex-class nature of woman's oppression through woman's patriarchal exploitation[7] in marriage. Women's domestic work and childrearing responsibilities express the root of sexual-class relations in this case.

Atkinson's and Delphy's visions of sex class are different from the earlier biologically determinist radical feminist position of Firestone. They also differ from the early liberal feminist view that woman's oppression primarily reflects her "disenfranchised position" in bourgeois society. In their view, sex class is understood as the way the political system of patriarchy manipulates and uses woman's biology as a childbearer and childrearer. In spite of the apparent dissimilarities within the view of sex class, it is important to understand that the roots of contemporary radical feminist sex-class theory (i.e., the recognition of the collective-class position of women) are in part liberal feminist in origin. This recognition is necessary if radical feminists are to play a role in radicalizing contemporary mainstream feminist politics.

Therefore, Part 3 of this book establishes the radical feminist tendencies within factions of liberal feminism today. I hope to show how the theory of women as a sex class can be more fully understood.

Although women have become more politically conscious as a sexual class as a result of feminist struggle, liberal feminist theory does not recognize this sufficiently. Yet women have continued to emerge as a sexual class as they learn and become conscious of the patriarchal structuring of Western liberal society. There is a greater potential today than ever before for women to become more fully conscious of themselves as a sexual class, given the post–World War II phenomena of the married wage earner and the "working mother" alongside the subsequent struggles with the state on abortion, the ERA, and the draft. These struggles have begun to uncover the way patriarchy functions through the law, through ideology, and through woman's assignment to the double-day of work. Out of the struggles for greater equality, the mystified form of patriarchal rule is uncovered. It is in this sense that women's identity as a sexual class reflects political and historical processes and cannot be predefined statically as merely a biological class. This predefinition is true only in its most elemental form.

Although E. P. Thompson's statement applies to a discussion of economic class, it is helpful in mapping out a way to think about a feminist theory of sex class:

> . . . classes do not exist as separate entities, look around, find an enemy class, and then start to struggle. On the contrary, people find themselves in a society structured in determined ways . . . they identify points of antagonistic interest, they commence to struggle around these issues and in the process of struggling they discover themselves as classes, they come to know this discovery as class consciousness.[8]

By thinking about sexual class in such a way, it becomes a political process to be understood by the political struggles women engage in. It is not merely a construct reflecting woman's oppression. The contours of sexual class become defined through the fight against oppression.

I have purposely used "patriarchy," as opposed to "men" or "male privilege," to designate the system women choose to fight against. The sex-class structure defined in terms of men and women (although it is this initially) presents a biological and individualistic conception of sex class. Patriarchy is a political structure that privileges men, but it uses much more complex forms of political manipulation to do this than mere biology. Individual men, although a part of the problem of patriarchy, do not encompass the totality of the politics discussed here. Betty Friedan's characterization and dismissal of the theory of sex class as man-hating, as we shall see, reflects the way this construction of sex class can be misinterpreted and used against radical feminist politics. Because of the confusion here between individual (biological) and collective (political) identity, the structural and social nature of patriarchy can be simply ignored.

This volume offers an analysis of liberal feminism that uncovers its contribution to the development of feminist theory and political struggle, and at the same time suggests its limitations as a theory of liberation. The political argument of this book is addressed most specifically to two audiences. The liberal feminist reader will, it is hoped, become more self-conscious about the contradictory nature of her politics, which asks for sexual egalitarianism from within a structure that is patriarchal. Once she recognizes this contradiction, she will understand why the liberal state cannot meet the demands of woman's equality, and she can move beyond the liberal and patriarchal constraints of liberal feminism. Liberal feminism, containing the seeds of its own transformation in the contradictory nature of it as a political theory and practice, sets into motion this heightened political understanding. The radical and socialist feminists can recognize from this book the radical roots found within liberal feminism, so that they can begin to work with liberal feminists to actualize its radical core. At the same time, these feminists can become refocused on the issues raised by the individualist content of feminism. This would be a crucial step in building a mass-based women's movement.

Another issue critical to this study of liberal feminism is the identification of the middle-class woman and the role she has played in the development of liberal feminism.[9] It is often assumed by feminists—Marxists, radicals, and liberals—that liberal feminism is a middle-class woman's movement, a movement that reflects her economic privilege. It is certainly true that the relationship between liberal feminism and middle-class women's needs has existed, often to the exclusion of working-class and minority women. But much is confused in this statement. Although the middle-class woman in relation to the working-class woman was and is privileged, feminism was not developed from a middle-class position of privilege. As we shall see, Wollstonecraft's concern with the middle-class woman derived from the fact that women were losing their economically productive role as industrial capitalism undermined the household-based domestic economy. The development of the middle-class woman, whose distinctive characteristic was her purported idleness and her real economic dependence, is what gave rise to feminism. Our discussion points to the critical relationship between the historical creation of the middle-class woman, the ideology that surrounds her, and the development of feminism.

A related argument of the book is that the married woman, and the middle-class ideology that surrounds her, has been a major tool of political control within the system of capitalist patriarchy. Through the image of the married middle-class woman, capitalism enforces patriarchy by presenting woman as dependent on man. In the last chapters of this book, I argue that a major form of patriarchal control is undermined by the entrance of married women, especially those identified as middle class, into the labor force. The contradictions between capitalism and patriarchy become embodied within the married woman's everyday life when she becomes a "working mother."

The concept of ideology is critical to this analysis.[10] "Ideology" is defined here as a set of ideas that help mystify reality. It has this potency because it reflects enough of reality to appear persuasive. Because ideological statements are always partially true, they cannot be dismissed as utterly false but need to be understood in terms of the way they mystify the real relations of social power by presenting only parts of them, which become distorted in their piecemeal form. To the extent that ideology seems to describe some part of one's life correctly, it can pressure, direct, and affect people. "Ideology is not effective or credible unless it achieves resonance with people's experience. And to remain credible it must continually incorporate the new, responding to changes in people's lives and social conditions."[11]

The origin of an ideology is different from its life force. An ideology may remain static and therefore restrain change. The force of patriarchal ideology remains within the consciousness of individual women as it does within the social and political structuring of political society. Ideology is not located in one or the other. And there is no linear causal relationship between political ideology and individual consciousness. In the true sense of the dialectic, they affect each other. Ideology can intervene and limit one's consciousness of one's real conditions. Consciousness can obstruct the affects of ideology. Life conditions can obstruct consciousness. As such, the realms merge, and actual conditions come to include individual consciousness and ideology. Ideology becomes a part of the relations of power. "Thus any analysis of ideology is an analysis of *social relations* themselves, not a reflection of social relations in the world of ideas."[12] If consciousness is central to the understanding of ideology and its political force, and hence politics and political change, then we need to give the role of consciousness its due importance when we think about social change.

The issue of the nature of the relationship between reform and revolution is crucial here. If changing consciousness is part of the process of political change, then many activities written off by some socialist feminists and radical feminists in the past as reformist, because they only change consciousness, will have to be reexamined. If part of building a feminist revolution is building a feminist consciousness, then activities that attack patriarchal ideology and consciousness are a part of the process to fundamentally reorganize and restructure society.

The potentially subversive nature of liberal feminist reform that derives from the self-contradictory nature of liberal feminism necessitates a rethinking of the issues defining valid political struggle. Given the sex-class base of liberal feminist theory, reforms that grow out of this concern have the potential to expose the patriarchal bias of the state. Once one recognizes the role of patriarchy on the state level, one can understand the *potentially* subversive quality of liberal feminist reforms. I am not arguing that there is anything automatic about actualizing this potential for building a mass-based feminist politics. However, never before in history has the potential been so great for feminism to *utilize* and *transcend* its liberal origins.

NOTES

1. Nancy Hartsock, "Feminism, Power and Change: A Theoretical Analysis," in *Women Organizing*, ed. Bernice Cummings and Victoria Schuck (Metuchen, N.J.: Scarecrow Press, 1979), pp. 11–12.

2. An important exception to this treatment of the history of liberal feminism is Ellen Dubois, *Feminism and Suffrage, The Emergence of an Independent Women's Movement in America, 1848–1869* (Ithaca, N.Y.: Cornell University Press, 1978). See a fuller account of her work in chapter 7. For important discussions of the various politics of feminism that help elucidate the political context out of which liberal feminism has operated, see Sara Evans, *Personal Politics, The Roots of Women's Liberation in the Civil Rights Movement and the New Left* (New York: Knopf, 1979); and Redstockings, *Feminist Revolution* (New Paltz, N.Y.: Redstockings, 1975); reprint ed., N.Y.: Random House, 1978.

3. The contradictory nature between the promises of liberalism and the practice of capitalism has been documented by numerous Marxist scholars. See C. B. MacPherson, *Democratic Theory, Essays in Retrieval* (Oxford, England: Clarendon Press, 1973); and idem, *The Political Theory of Possessive Individualism, Hobbes to Locke* (London: Oxford University Press, 1962); for an excellent discussion of how the economic class system contradicts the promises of liberal ideology. Also see Daniel Bell, *The Cultural Contradictions of Capitalism* (New York: Basic

Books, 1976) for a different and interesting critique of how the crisis of liberalism reflects the conflict between the culture of hedonism and the capitalist marketplace.

4. Simone de Beauvoir, *The Second Sex* (New York: Bantam, 1952).

5. Shulamith Firestone, *The Dialectic of Sex* (New York: Bantam, 1970), pp. 9–12. For other contemporary radical feminist discussions of sex class, see Germaine Greer, *The Female Eunuch* (New York: McGraw-Hill, 1970); Susan Griffin, *Woman and Nature* (New York: Harper & Row, 1978); Anne Koedt, Ellen Levine, and Anita Rapone, eds., *Radical Feminism* (New York: Quadrangle, 1973); Kate Millet, *Sexual Politics* (New York: Avon, 1971); Robin Morgan, *Going Too Far, The Personal Chronicle of a Feminist* (New York: Random House, 1977); and *Papers on Patriarchy, Patriarchy Conference, London, 1976* (Brighton, England: Women's Publishing Collective, 1976).

6. Ti Grace Atkinson, *Amazon Odyssey* (New York: Links, 1974), p. 5.

7. Christine Delphy, *A Materialist Analysis of Women's Oppression* (London: Women's Research and Resources Centre, 1977), p. 13.

8. E. P. Thompson, "Eighteenth-Century English Society: Class Struggle Without Class?" *Social History* 3, no. 2 (May 1978): 149.

9. This reflects the much larger problem of the identification of women within particular economic classes to begin with. Most economic class analysis defines woman's class in relation to her husband, to her father, or to her son. We still do not have an economic class analysis that treats woman as an autonomous being or recognizes her particular place within the family structure *and* the market. The sexual bias of economic class analysis is a significant problem that limits the usefulness of such an analysis for this study. For the sexual bias of economic class theory, see the various articles in the following volumes: Zillah Eisenstein, ed., *Capitalist Patriarchy and the Case for Socialist Feminism* (New York: Monthly Review Press, 1978); Annette Kuhn and Ann Marie Wolpe, eds., *Feminism and Materialism* (London: Routledge and Kegan Paul, 1978); and Lydia Sargent, ed., *Women and Revolution* (Boston: South End Press, forthcoming).

10. For the discussion in this book, liberalism is fundamentally treated as an ideology in that it seeks to mystify its patriarchal structure. In this particular sense, all liberal theory is ideological. Nevertheless, there is important content within liberal ideology that should be re tained for feminist theory in its nonpatriarchal form. It is in this sense that an examination of the content of liberal feminist theory is so necessary. See Antonio Gramsci, *Selections from the Prison Notebooks*, ed. and trans. Quintin Hoare and Geoffrey Nowell Smith (New York: International, 1971), for an intriguing discussion of ideology.

11. Douglas Kellner, "Ideology, Marxism and Advanced Capitalism," *Socialist Review* 8, no. 42, 6 (November–December 1978): 53. Also see Todd Gitlin, "News as Ideology and Contested Area: Towards Theory of Hegemony, Crisis and Opposition," *Socialist Review* 9, no. 48 (November–December 1979): 11–54.

12. Roisin McDonough and Rachel Harrison, "Patriarchy and Relations of Production," in Kuhn and Wolpe, *Feminism and Materialism*, p. 17. The argument that ideology becomes part of the social relations themselves should be distinguished from the idealist vision that ideology fully represents the material world.

2

Patriarchy, Motherhood, and Public Life

The reality that underlies the patriarchal bias of liberalism is that women have been defined by their reproductive capacities in Western society. Woman's distinguishing biological characteristic is her ability to reproduce the species through her body. On the basis of this capacity she has been excluded from other human activities and contained within a sphere defined as female. This reduction of woman to her biology is at the core of Western liberal ideology. The divorce of reason and passion, mind and body, thought and action, virtu and nonvirtu, public and private, reflects the patriarchal division of male *from* female. My particular concern here is with the phase of patriarchal development that has defined the institution of motherhood specifically in terms of child*rearing* as opposed, for instance, to the formulation of mother in ancient society, which emphasized woman as a vessel to bear the male seed. My concern is to elaborate the historical formulation of motherhood that equates childbearing with childrearing and as a result assigns woman a place outside the public sphere of life. In this study, we shall see woman's exclusion from public life operating on two levels. Woman is relegated to childrearing by biological fiat on an individual level, which is then reformulated through the formation of the state and the institutionalization of public-private domains on a political level.

Patriarchal Motherhood as Childbearer and Rearer

Patriarchy as a political structure seeks to control and subjugate women so that their possibilities for making choices about their sexuality, childrearing, mothering, loving, and laboring are curtailed. Patriarchy, as a system of oppression, recognizes the potential power of women and the actual power of men. Its purpose is to destroy woman's consciousness about her potential power, which derives from the necessity of society to reproduce itself. By trying to affect woman's consciousness and her life options, patriarchy protects the appropriation of women's sexuality, their reproductive capacities, and their labor by individual men and society as a whole. The sexual organization to control women reflects the priorities of patriarchy. According to Roisin McDonough and Rachel Harrison, "the characteristic relation of human reproduction is patriarchy, that is, the control of women, especially of their sexuality and fertility, by men." [1]

Although there is much variety in the sexual arrangements of society, Dorothy Dinnerstein emphasizes the fact that the prevailing arrangements today place woman in the position of primary responsibility for the care of infants and young children. [2] Nancy Chodorow also documents the importance of women as mothers in society. Women not only bear children but they rear them. They love and care for them and sustain society by creating emotional bonds that appear nowhere else. This is what Chodorow describes as women's mothering role:

> Women mother. In our society, as in most societies, women not only bear children. They also take primary responsibility for infant care, spend more time with infants and children than do men, and sustain primary emotional ties with infants. When biological mothers do not parent, other women, rather than men, virtually always take their place. Though fathers and other men spend varying amounts of time with infants and children, the father is rarely a child's primary parent. [3]

Adrienne Rich identifies the caretaking of the young and the old by women as institutional motherhood that "revives and renews all other institutions" [4] and reflects the politics of patriarchy. Institutional motherhood is not merely premised on woman's ability to biologically bear and nurture children. Institutional motherhood, instead, locks woman into a limited set of choices and alternatives. At the same time that society writes women off *as* mothers, it requires women to be mothers. "The institution of motherhood is not identical with bearing and caring for children, any more than the institution of heterosexuality is identical with intimacy and sexual love. Both create the prescriptions and the conditions in which choices are made or blocked; they are not 'reality' but they have shaped the circumstances of our lives." [5]

Women can sexually reproduce and they lactate. These are biological facts. That women are defined as mothers is a political fact and reflects a political need of patriarchy, which is based partially in the biological truth that women bear children. The transformation of women from a biological being (childbearer) to a political being (childrearer) is part of the conflict expressed in the politics of patriarchy. Patriarchy seeks to maintain the myth that patriarchal motherhood is a biological reality rather than a politically constructed necessity. I will argue later in this book that the state's embodiment of the public and private division, which is fundamentally a male/female division, aids in this process. The state legitimates the notion that women function outside the public realm as noncitizens and nonrational beings. They are mothers. Patriarchy tries to enforce this vision so that the equation between childbearing and rearing is seen as natural or inevitable.

Any system of power must have a purpose, and in this case it is the creation of newborn children and the mothers to rear them. Patriarchy, then, expresses the struggle to control women's options in order to keep their role as childbearer and rearer primary. Power reflects the activity of trying to limit choices. The priorities of patriarchy are to keep the choices limited for women so that their role as mothers remains primary. Trying to understand the force of patriarchy is basically trying to understand what it does. And ultimately what it does is reproduce a new generation of mothers. Because early child care is female dominated, boys and girls alike learn that it is women who rear children. This reproduction of gender roles supplies society with the most basic form of hierarchical social organization and, hence, order. The woman as mother reveals woman's role in the reproduction of the species most easily. Derived from this are the more subtle forms of patriarchal organization: the sexual division of labor in the labor force, the division between public and private life, and the divorce of political and family life. The separation of male from female constructs a dichotomous world view that limits insight into the structure of patriarchal organization itself. Woman defined as mother structures the "either/or" mentality. Therefore, when I argue that patriarchy seeks to maintain the idea and reality of woman as mother, I mean this in the broad political sense of the term as well as in the narrower biological sense. The biological definition of mother grasps only a small part of the meaning of motherhood in patriarchal society. Motherhood also involves the notion of woman as a caring, emotional, dependent being. This reflects the political construction of motherhood, which means that there is nothing natural about it; it is consciously organized and socially constructed.

By relegating woman to her supposedly biological role, as a mother, she is sidelined into the private sphere of home and family. Because patriarchal ideology presents motherhood as natural, woman's assignment to the private sphere and dismissal from the public realm is argued as a defense of the natural order of things. The logic derives from patriarchal needs. The confusing issue is that the politics of assigning woman a sphere different from men can be mystified by using woman's biology. This complicated reality reflects that women bear children; but until this biological fact is distinguished from the political motivations of patriarchy, one cannot recognize the role of patriarchy in the assignment of woman to the private sphere, man to the public.

Patriarchy erases the evidence of its presence on this individual level through the manipulation of woman's biology. We shall see that it puts this to use on the state level as well.

Patriarchal power is based in the political controls developed to limit women's alternatives in relation to motherhood and mothering, and presents politics as nature. These relations exist historically and therefore are always changing, although the concept of motherhood is presented by patriarchal ideology as a determined, static category. Woman defined as mother is therefore both a universal political condition in Western history and a specific, historically constructed reality.[6] Women reproduce; yet changes in contraception change their relationship to reproduction. Women, as mothers, have constantly borne and reared children; yet this reality changes as the culture, economics, and medical health of a society change. The mother of the sixteenth century was a different kind of mother from the mother of the eighteenth century. The woman who labored in the fields and in the house in the seventeenth century was different from the mother of the Victorian era. The middle-class mother of the nineteenth century was a different mother from the sweatshop laborer/mother of the early twentieth century. And yet they were all mothers—all responsible for bearing children and raising them in many different ways—but the main responsibility was still the reproduction of a new generation.

It is important to understand that struggles around abortion rights, pro-choice reproductive-rights planks, and lesbianism take place within a political arena that defines woman as mother in the first place. A lack of choice and alternative is necessary to maintain woman's primary activity as childbearer *and* rearer. This does not mean that women cannot or do not exercise reproductive choice through infanticide, self-induced abortion, the use of contraceptives, and so forth, but ultimately in a society where one's major worth as a woman is judged as a mother, the choice is curtailed.

The struggle for reproductive control[7] and lesbian motherhood is a struggle directly at odds with patriarchal motherhood, as is nonfemale childrearing, because they undermine the system that relegates woman to the different and specific tasks of the family and the home. The challenge to patriarchal motherhood is a challenge to the political ordering that exists between public and private, male and female worlds. In order to understand Western patriarchy, one must understand the way it politically structures women's lives through motherhood, because the destruction of patriarchy does not mean the destruction of motherhood but rather the destruction of the patriarchal relations of it. I argue in later chapters that the married woman wage earner, by transversing home and market, has begun to uncover this patriarchal organization of contemporary American society.

The Historical Continuity of Patriarchy

There are, to be sure, certain problems with the term patriarchy. It is used in differing and contradictory ways as (1) a legalistic concept involving the historical period of father-right from antiquity to the demise of feudalism [8] and (2) as an all-encompassing view of human culture that spans recorded history to the present. Although I argue for the usage of the term, I adopt neither of these views because I wish to emphasize both the historical framework of the first view and the recognition of patriarchy's universality in the second view. My conception recognizes the transformations patriarchy makes to accommodate the needs of particular economic systems without losing its original impetus to control the reproductive power of women and their place in the political structure.

Mary Daly gives an example of the latter version, which argues that "patriarchy appears to be 'everywhere.' Even outer space and the future have been colonized." [9] She has no specific historical analysis of patriarchy. Patriarchy is patriarchy, whether in Nazi Germany or in tribal rites in Africa or in capitalist America. Daly collapses all history into its patriarchal roots instead of threading the presence of patriarchy through particular economic and political forms. In the end, patriarchy seems static because we are not shown *how it changes* or how women have fought to change it.

In the legalistic view of patriarchy, which identifies its demise with the end of feudalism, there is no recognition of patriarchy as a continuous force in history, especially after feudalism. This assumes that when the law that codified father-right significantly changed, so did men's rule as fathers. According to this view, the man in patriarchy, as the father, codified through law, had supreme authority over the family (i.e., over the wife and children). Ownership lay with the head of the household, and women and children were considered to be owned by the husband and father. [10] When the laws of father-right changed, it is argued that patriarchy was replaced by liberal society. Nevertheless, Blackstone's statement on woman's status, made as late as the eighteenth century, demonstrates how patriarchal power can be eroded without being removed: "By marriage, the husband and wife are one person in law: that is, the very being or legal existence of the woman is suspended during the marriage, or at least is incorporated and consolidated into that of the husband; under whose wing, protection, and cover she performs everything. . . ." [11]

Adrienne Rich more accurately emphasizes the fact that rule by the father is not merely a legalistic construct: "Patriarchy is the power of the fathers: a familial-social, ideological, political system in which men—by force, direct pressure, or through ritual, tradition, law and language, customs, etiquette, education and the division of labor, determine what part women shall or shall not play, and in which the female is everywhere subsumed under the male." [12] Patriarchy in this sense means male control of life and property ownership. [13] Men, as husbands and fathers, have the means for maintaining their privilege outside of the law.

Patriarchy as a system of sexual hierarchical relations is not fully embodied within the law. The law defines and protects particular male privileges in marriage law, family law, domestic law, but many of the privileges derived from sexual hierarchy remain in practice without laws to define them as such. There is no specific law that says women will bear children or rear them. Only the economic dimension of patriarchy—woman's relationship to property, possessions, income—is openly embodied in bourgeois patriarchal law. Laws controlling women's lives sexually are more implicit and indirect, as in the case of rape, although there are instances of more direct interference on issues of abortion and homosexuality. The issues of motherhood and sexuality are not directly present in the law because they are defined by the state as private. Laws that deal directly with sexuality, like laws regarding prostitution or homosexuality, are developed on the premise that they affect the public realm and therefore fall within the purview of the law.

Patriarchal privilege is therefore most often protected by its indirect presence in the law. Whether a woman chooses to bear a child is supposedly her private affair. That the law does not give her an alternative is not understood as a reflection of indirect patriarchal control. Even with the changes that have occurred in the law from the thirteenth century, with the transition of feudalism, many statements of patriarchal privilege are still within the law today, as attested to in the struggle for the ERA. To cut these struggles off from the historical struggle against patriarchal control is to destroy a sense of the continuous power relations of patriarchy and the struggle against them. History reflects the process of changing needs; and patriarchy, as it attempts to organize to defend itself, changes and develops.

If the system of patriarchy is not fully encompassed within the law, a legalistic definition of patriarchy is limited and insufficient. Changes in the law will not substantially alter or weaken the relations of power men derive from sexual hierarchy. The modernization of the law, or the liberalization of it, reflects a transition within patriarchy, instead of its demise. In this view it should be clear that feudal society was patriarchal and the transition to capitalism did not destroy patriarchy but only redefined it in liberal terms. Further changes in patriarchal law have reflected the transition from feudal to capitalist patriarchy.

As will be evident in the next chapter, John Locke attacks the absolutist conception of father-right as a basis for political rule, without undermining patriarchy. Lawrence Stone in *The Family, Sex and Mar-*

riage, In England 1500–1800 assumes that Locke's dismissal of paternal rule in the state is the same as a rejection of patriarchal rule in the family. Stone argues that by the eighteenth century, the egalitarian, individualistic, and companionate family replaced the patriarchal family, a view of the feudal family as the last vestige of patriarchal life held by most historians today, liberal and Marxist alike. Earlier, John Stuart Mill gave voice to the same theory: "But the feudal family, the last historical form of patriarchal life, has long perished, and the unit of society is not now the family or clan, composed of all the reputed descendants of a common ancestor, but the individual; or at most a pair of individuals, with their unemancipated children." [14] We shall see that although Mill dealt with the inequities between men and women as citizens, he was unable to understand the patriarchal underpinnings of this inequality. This was possible because he failed to understand patriarchy as a continuous political system.

The society and the family have presumably become liberal. Liberalism has supposedly replaced patriarchy. On the contrary, feudalism was and capitalism still is patriarchal. In fact, liberalism as the *ideology* of bourgeois society cannot fully replace the patriarchal structure of society. To assume liberalism has replaced patriarchy is to collapse history into economic class history instead of recognizing two systems, one economic, the other sexual, which are relatively autonomous from each other. [15] It also reduces the problem of patriarchy to one of ideology.

In order to demystify patriarchy as a system of power and its use by particular economic modes, one needs to understand that patriarchy is a relatively autonomous system operating alongside the economic mode of society rather than simply derived from it. Neither is the mere instrument of the other, yet they are completely intertwined. In the transition from feudalism to capitalism, patriarchy changed in relation to these economic changes, but it also set the limits and structure of this change. Patriarchy alters itself in order to preserve itself, and these changes reflect real political struggles. This conception of patriarchy focuses on it as a dynamically changing political system rather than a static one. The changes and processes one sees are part of the system of patriarchy and actually define it. They express its historical formulation. Patriarchy is no longer protected through as repressive a legal system structured around the male as father as it once was. The redefinition of the father's power speaks to the changing nature of patriarchy, not to its erosion. These changes signal the presence of new modes of patriarchal control, the loss of former methods of control, and the modernization of patriarchal law. Women's struggles against patriarchal domination have been a part of this process, as we shall see.

What one calls the system of patriarchy is less important than how one understands it.[16] Reflecting the particular longevity of woman's oppression, "patriarchy" can comprehend two important ideas: the notion that sex-gender relations are intrinsically neutral and the notion that these relations have an oppressive history. Important feminist scholars like Gayle Rubin[17] object to the term patriarchy because they believe the term inhibits understanding of the possibility for "neutral" sex-gender relations. The term collapses the history of sexuality into a history of oppression.[18] I argue that part of describing Western society as patriarchal describes the oppressive relations of the sex-gender system at the same time it points to the possibility of changing them. Rubin defines a sex-gender system as "a set of arrangements by which the biological raw material of human sex and procreation is shaped by human, social intervention and satisfied in a conventional manner, no matter how bizarre some of the conventions may be."[19] The "sex-gender system" is a preferable term to Rubin because it is neutral. It "refers to the (sexual) domain and indicates that oppression is not inevitable in that domain."[20]

The problem with this dismissal of the term patriarchy is that it ignores that patriarchy, like any system of oppression, lays the roots for its own transformation. The fact that any system of oppression has the capacity to transform itself necessitates the oppressive structuring of these relations. The reason patriarchy exists is because a nonpatriarchal sex-gender system could exist if allowed to. If one thinks about potential power and oppression as part of the same process, one sees patriarchy as a concept that explicitly connotes oppression and also specifies the possibility of its transformation.

The sex-gender system in Western society and political thought is not neutral. Rubin's analytic distinction between sex-gender system and patriarchy as an oppressive statement of sex-gender is an important contribution to feminist theory. But when the sex-gender system is patriarchal, we think it is not only appropriate but important to use the term. Rubin fears that the term will be used for inappropriate cases and will obliterate the differences within sex-gender systems. This seems like an insufficient reason not to use the term patriarchy. Any concept can be misused, and it is part of the responsibility of feminist scholarship to see that this does not happen. Instead of dismissing the concept, we need to better understand why it is feared. Rubin helps elucidate the problem when she states that patriarchy as a concept does not recognize change: "Its use is analogous to using capitalism to refer to all modes of production, whereas the usefulness of the term 'capitalism' lies precisely in that it distinguishes between different systems by which societies are provisioned and organized."[21]

The problem with Rubin's analogy is that patriarchy is not a parallel reality to capitalism. Although patriarchy changes, it has never undergone a revolutionary upheaval. There is a continuity to patriarchal history that has not existed in economic history. There should be a term that expresses the continuity of women's oppression, which has existed through different economic systems. Patriarchy is not as historically specific a system as any economic system we have known. It changes historically, but universal qualities of it are maintained even if they are specifically redefined. The continuity of woman's oppression must be understood alongside the specificity of it, without being afraid that the universal qualities will be interpreted as inevitable. Only as we come to understand the historical continuity of patriarchy can we begin to see what must be done to end the seeming inevitability of woman's oppression.

Patriarchy, as a concept, expresses the great durability of the hierarchical sexual organization of Western society. To be sure, defined in this way, it remains an abstract and somewhat distorted concept because it never actually exists by itself. Its full definition always takes place alongside ancient, feudal, capitalist society. As I have written elsewhere: "Any understanding of the relations of patriarchy has to treat them in their particular historical frame and any statement of the universal or unifying elements becomes an abstraction, albeit a necessary level of abstraction if we are to understand the universal elements of patriarchal history."[22]

Patriarchy and Public-Private Life

The universality of patriarchy in Western society is expressed in the sexual assignment of private and public life, to woman and man, respectively. Although the meaning of "public" and "private" changes in concrete ways, the assignment of public space to men and private space to women is continuous in Western history. To speak in such sweeping terms of so pervasive a category as public and private spheres in the Western world is indeed to run the risk of oversimplification. But no student of history can fail to be impressed with the consistency with which societies have organized themselves into public realms considered male and private realms considered female. The narrative that follows is intended only to chart the bare outlines of this course.[23]

Sarah Pomeroy discusses the separation of the sexes in classical Athens. Women were tied to the home by their household duties, their husbands, and their infants.[24] Public areas like the marketplace were the male domain. "The separation of the sexes was spatially emphasized. While men spend most of their day in public areas such as the marketplace and the gymnasium, respectable women remained at home."[25] The urbanization of Athens made women's lives even more isolated by moving their activities and their labor indoors. Their lives became less visible, and less valued.[26] The division between men and women could be characterized in terms of living inside or outside in the world.[27] In Plato's *Republic,* Isomachus, when speaking with Socrates, assigns indoor tasks to women and outdoor tasks to men.[28] Civic space dominates the household; men and women are separate and unequal. Aristotle (384–322 B.C.) articulates a view of woman as noncitizen that is premised on the division of male and female space. "The male is naturally fitter to command than the female."[29] Man is more deliberative and reasoned. Woman's place is the domestic sphere. Different capacities of deliberation define different forms of rule. "The rule of the freeman over the slave is one land of rule; that of the male over the female another; that of the grown man over the child still another."[30] The relation of male to female is naturally that of the superior to the inferior.[31]

It is this classical vision of male and female separation that Rousseau envisions to replace the decadence of the bourgeois order, which has allowed women to think that they can be like men. Ancient society is based on the separation of citizens and noncitizens, the reasoned and the passionate, the city and the household, the public and the private. These distinctions all arise from the fundamental conception of the difference and ultimate inequality between men and women. They replicate the dichotomy of masculine/feminine. Virtue derives from the word meaning man. In this republican vision, virtue represents the male public domain of reason and citizenship: ". . . virtue is the passion for pursuing the public good. . . ."[32] The separation between public and private life in ancient society reflects the antagonism between male and female domains. Nancy Schwartz states this somewhat more hesitantly: "To be sure, ancient society is based on a real separation, if not an antagonistic contradiction, between the citizens and noncitizens. To the extent, then, that the citizen represents public life and the slave (and woman) represents private life, there is indeed an antagonism between the public and the private."[33]

This patriarchal division of society into male and female "spheres" is retained in feudalism, although it is redefined in terms of the feudal economy and its relation to the state. The particular integration of political and economic power, which characterizes feudal society, belies the not yet developed bourgeois conditions and liberal distinction of public and private life rooted in this differentiation. But feudal society still recognizes the public domain as male, the private as female, even though the *political* differentiation of the family and the state does not develop until bourgeois society is established. Feudal patriarchal law established the public militaristic domain as male and the home as female. Woman was characterized as the *private* property of her father or her husband in the family.

The feudal patriarchal family[34] was an integral part of the system of production. With the development of the capitalist wage-labor system, the feudal home, as a self-sufficient unit supplying its own needs, disappeared.[35] In the same way that the needs of capital required the destruction of the self-sufficient worker, it required the destruction of the self-sufficient home. "The collapse of the feudal economy meant the decline of the domestic and family industry upon which it was based."[36] The worker who could maintain his or her family through the household economy would not enter into the market relations of society. The unity of the feudal patriarchal household was rooted in the unity of capital and labor. "The common basis of the feudal family—that its members jointly made a living from the land—had rested in the unity between capital and labor."[37]

The decline of the family and domestic industry and its replacement by wage labor lays a different historical basis for liberal ideology's division of public and private life, home and work, male and female domains. Liberal ideology and bourgeois society each represent work performed in the household as no longer a part of the same work process carried on outside the home for wages. Women's lives, within the family, become redefined by liberal, as well as patriarchal, ideology. It redefines their place in the world of work while the actual world of work comes to be defined in terms of the wage-labor process. Whereas the feudal patriarchal family was an integral part of the system of production, the capitalist patriarchal family is based on the distinction between domestic and wage labor. It therefore is represented ideologically as separate and apart from the world of work (wage labor).

Although in this (over)generalized sense, the family in feudal society was defined by the integration of work and home, both practically and ideologically, it was still structured by the political differentiation between men and women that maintained a system of female reproduction and mothering. Women were the private property of men, and men represented the public sphere, which was simultaneously economic, political, militaristic. Therefore, even though women were an integral part of the work process in their homes in feudal society, they were not viewed as the equal to men.

The gentleman's wife of sixteenth-century England was responsible for making her country house self-supporting. This involved her in year-round planning, especially in preparation for winter. Bread was made and butter was churned all year round. Ale was brewed once a month. Fats were saved for the candlemaker. Soap was made from leftover fat and lye. Feathers from the poultry yard were cured for mattresses and pillows. Spinning was constant, and vast laundries would be done every three months.[38] Although the Elizabethan countrywoman worked alongside her husband in the household, she was defined as the "subject" to man. A hierarchical sexual division of labor operated. "The father and husband was the acknowledged and accepted head of the family. The wife and mother, though actively employed in assisting to win the family livelihood with her dairy and poultry, her spinning and weaving, her preserving and distilling, accepted her subjection to her husband."[39]

The feudal patriarchal family was more integrated into the society than the capitalist patriarchal family because of the nature of agrarian household labor; the lack of a child-oriented existence; and because the feudal family existed before the development of a whole culture of privacy, intimacy, and individualism—a development partially rooted in the political differentiation of the state and the family. The family in this sense was more public both ideologically and practically because its private role in the bourgeois sense of the term had not yet been developed.

Patriarchy, as a system of power, structures and manipulates this relationship between what is private and public and what seems to be public or private. During feudal society, the family is characterized as public, and as such, one does not ask whether relations of power other than feudal class relations are operating here because no differentiation is made between patriarchal family and feudal economic relations. The relations of sexual hierarchy are totally mystified through the economic relations of society. With the development of capitalism and the differentiation of the family from the economy, the distinction is manipulated once again to interfere with understanding the patriarchal base of the family. This time the family is characterized as disconnected from the economy and the public world and therefore protected *from* political or state interference. Either way, the family is not understood in terms of its patriarchal base and the relations of power that define it.

The distinction between public (male) and private (female) life in Western thought, a preliberal patriarchal distinction, has been inherent in the formation of state societies. The formation of the state institutionalizes patriarchy; it reifies the division between public and private life as one of sexual differences. Rayna Rapp elaborates this point: "The radical separation of home and work place in industrial capitalism transforms and buttresses the distinction between private and public domains that has long had ideological legitimacy through state formation."[40] The domain of the state has always signified public life, and this is distinguished in part from the private realm by differentiating men from women. It is not accidental that heads of state are men. They represent this public space as male. This is a vital part of the authority and power the state receives and institutionalizes for men.[41] *The state formalizes the rule by men because the division of public and private life is at one and the same time a male/female distinction.* Rapp substantiates this point, though somewhat more cautiously: "Within the variation of male-female relations, there is a strong tendency for state societies to consider public functions as male and private ones as female."[42] The state's purpose is to enforce the separation of public and private life and with it the distinctness of male and female existence.

Patriarchy enforced as a political system appears to exist nowhere. As I argue in the final chapter of this book, the state mystifies its patriarchal base by not only constructing but also manipulating the ideology describing public and private life. The state is said to be public (by definition) and therefore divorced from the private realm, which is the area of women's lives. The state can appear, through its own ideology, to be unrelated to the family as the private sphere, when in actuality this sphere is both defined and regulated *in relation* to the state realm. As such, patriarchy becomes mystified on the state level whereas it is at this level that patriarchy, in fact, becomes institutionalized. Unable to see how patriarchy has set itself into motion, we are left with explanations of male supremacy as natural and/or inevitable. Rather than depend on a biogenetic inevitability, the state institutionalizes patriarchy by establishing the public and private domains of sexual hierarchy between men and women as an ideology at the same time that the ideology erases the existence of patriarchy. Part of the power of patriarchy is this capacity to mystify itself. Its ideology masks its political base.

One should not overemphasize the abstracted patriarchal qualities of state societies. Because all state forms institutionalize economic systems as well, it is a distortion to discuss the state as simply patriarchal. There is no such thing as "the" state or "the" patriarchal state. There are particular, specific forms of the patriarchal state—feudal, Nazi, racist, capitalist, and so on. Yet the level of theoretical abstraction of the patriarchal definition of public and private life is necessary in that this force weaves its way repeatedly through history. Nevertheless, there is no constant meaning to the terms *public* and *private* other than their sexual identification, and even this identity takes on particular meaning within the specific culture and society one is examining. Sex is not a determined category that can just be plastered onto history in order to understand it. And yet sex does predefine the way history has been structured.

It is the changing and yet constant quality of the nature of patriarchy alongside its constancy that becomes so confusing in understanding the history of Western theory. The presentation of patriarchy through its ideology makes patriarchy elusive. With the coming of bourgeois society and its protective liberal theory, the values of egalitarianism, independent selves, and individual achievement were to replace the patriarchal and aristocratic values of hierarchy, inequality, and ascription. It is time now to examine how the patriarchal bias of feudalism and capitalism is maintained in the ideology of liberalism.

NOTES

1. Roisin McDonough and Rachel Harrison, "Patriarchy and Relations of Production," in *Feminism and Materialism,* ed. Annette Kuhn and Ann Marie Wolpe (London: Routledge and Kegan Paul, 1978), p. 26.

2. Dorothy Dinnerstein, *The Mermaid and the Minotaur, Sexual Arrangements and Human Malaise* (New York: Harper & Row, 1976), p. 4.

3. Nancy Chodorow, *The Reproduction of Mothering, Psychoanalysis and the Sociology of Gender* (Berkeley: University of California Press, 1978), p. 3.

4. Adrienne Rich, *Of Woman Born, Motherhood as Experience and Institution* (New York: Norton, 1976), p. 45.

5. Ibid., p. 42.

6. This discussion focuses on motherhood in Western society. Recent work by Michelle Zimbalist Rosaldo cautions against applying this conception of motherhood cross-culturally, particularly in simple societies. See her "The Use and Abuse of Anthropology: Reflections of Feminism and Cross-Cultural Understanding," *Signs,* forthcoming, Spring 1980; and Michele Zimbalist Rosaldo and Jane Collier, "Politics and Gender in Simple Societies," unpublished, 1980.

7. See Linda Gordon, *Woman's Body, Woman's Right: A Social History of Birth Control in America* (New York: Grossman, 1976), for a full historical account of woman's struggle for reproductive control.

8. Two recent examples of this position are Lawrence Stone, *The Family, Sex and Marriage, In England 1500–1800* (New York: Harper & Row, 1977); and Randolph Trumbach, *The Rise of the Egalitarian Family: Aristocratic Kinship and Domestic Relations in Eighteenth-Century England* (New York: Academic, 1978).

9. Mary Daly, *Gyn/Ecology, The Metaethics of Radical Feminism* (Boston: Beacon, 1978), p. 1. Daly represents one of the contemporary radical feminist conceptions of patriarchy that can be termed ahistorical. Although I agree with the emphasis on the continuity and centrality of patriarchy as an historical force, I argue that the continuity can really be understood only by understanding the way patriarchy *changes* in different historical and political periods. It functions similarly and differently in Victorian England and post–World War II America. By un-

derstanding how it is different, one can examine how patriarchy changes and does not change. This helps elucidate the *nature of power* in patriarchy and the kinds of political struggles that have forced it to change. Such a view also helps explain how women as a sex class develop into a self-conscious class, which focuses on the politics that define women as a sex class. This is quite different than Daly's static representation of patriarchy.

10. Trumbach, *The Rise of the Egalitarian Family*, p. 119.

11. Frances Gies and Joseph Gies, *Women in the Middle Ages* (New York: Crowell, 1978), p. 30.

12. Rich, *Of Woman Born*, p. 57.

13. Ibid., p. 61.

14. John Stuart Mill, "From the Political Economy, Bk. 2, chap. 3," in *Socialism*, ed. W. D. P. Bliss (New York: Humboldt, 1890), p. 39.

15. See Annette Kuhn, "Structures of Patriarchy and Capital in the Family," in Kuhn and Wolpe, *Feminism and Materialism*, for a somewhat different discussion of patriarchy and capitalism as relatively autonomous. There has been much dispute among feminists about the usage of the term patriarchy. Barbara Ehrenreich and Deirdre English in *For Her Own Good, 150 Years of the Expert's Advice to Women* (New York: Doubleday, 1978) distinguish between patriarchy as "a specific historical organization of family and social life" (p. 11) and male dominance, which they understand as a more general term. They argue that the scientific spirit of the bourgeois market defeated patriarchal ideology, although the new world view remains masculinist (p. 16). The problem with their differentiation between patriarchy and male dominance is that the continuity in the sexual ordering of society between these two periods is lost. I think it more helpful to understand male dominance as an aspect of patriarchal social structure. Ehrenreich and English, in their differentiation of these two concepts, assume that the economic system replaces or fundamentally changes the sexual ordering of society. I argue that without a revolutionary assault against patriarchy, this cannot and has not been the case.

16. Although the purpose of this chapter is to spell out the importance of patriarchy as a political force in history, I do not wish to create an endless debate on the importance of the term itself. The significant issue is that one recognize the structural presence of sexual hierarchy as a relatively autonomous system within political history. The ultimate political issue is the centrality of sexual class oppression in history. It is this reality that is important to identify. If one recognizes this, the term itself is less important. For a discussion of the different meanings within patriarchy, see Veronica Beechey, "On Patriarchy," *Feminist Review* 1, no. 3 (1979): 66–82; and Joseph Interrante and Carol Lasser, "Victims of the Very Songs They Sing: A Critique of Recent Work on

Patriarchal Culture and the Social Construction of Gender," *Radical History Review* 20 (Spring–Summer 1978): 25–41.

17. Gayle Rubin, "The Traffic in Women: Notes in the 'Political Economy' of Sex," in *Toward an Anthropology of Women*, ed. Rayna Reiter (New York: Monthly Review Press, 1975).

18. This is Sheila Rowbotham's major objection to the term as well. See her "The Trouble with 'Patriarchy,' " *New Statesmen*, 21/28 December 1979, pp. 970–71.

19. Rubin, "Traffic in Women," p. 165.

20. Ibid., p. 168.

21. Ibid., p. 167.

22. Zillah Eisenstein, "Some Notes on the Relations of Capitalist Patriarchy," in *Capitalist Patriarchy and the Case for Socialist Feminism*, ed. Zillah Eisenstein (New York: Monthly Review Press, 1978), p. 46.

23. For a discussion of the particular relationship between public and private life in historical context, see Joan Kelly, "The Doubled Vision of Feminist Theory: A Postscript to the 'Women and Power' Conference," *Feminist Studies* 5 (Spring 1979): 216–28; Nannerl Keohane, "Female Citizenship: The Monstrous Regiment of Women," prepared for the Conference for the Study of Political Thought, New York, 6–8 April 1978; Carole Pateman, "Sublimation and Reification: Locke, Wolin and the Liberal Democratic Conception of the Political," *Politics and Society* 4 (1975); Rayna (Rapp) Reiter, "Men and Women in the South of France: Public and Private Domains," in Reiter, *Toward an Anthropology of Women*; Michelle Zimbalist Rosaldo, "Women, Culture and Society: A Theoretical Overview," in *Woman, Culture and Society*, ed. Michelle Z. Rosaldo and Louise Lamphere (Stanford: Stanford University Press, 1974); Sherry Ortner, "Is Female to Male as Nature Is to Culture?" in Rosaldo and Lamphere, *Woman, Culture, and Society*; and Nancy Schwartz, "Distinction Between Public and Private Life, Marx on the Zoon Politikon," *Political Theory* 7 (May 1979): 245–66.

24. Sarah Pomeroy, *Goddesses, Whores, Wives and Slaves, Women in Classical Antiquity* (New York: Schocken, 1975), p. 79.

25. Ibid.

26. Ibid., p. 71.

27. Gies, *Women in the Middle Ages*, p. 229. Also see Eileen Power, *Medieval Women*, ed. M. Postan (Cambridge, England: Cambridge University Press, 1975).

28. For a discussion of women in classical political thought, see Francis Cornford, ed., *The Republic of Plato* (New York: Oxford University Press, 1945); Eric Havelock, *The Liberal Temper in Greek Politics* (New York: Yale University Press, 1957); Mary Briody Mahowald, *Philosophy of Woman, Classical to Current Concepts* (Indianapolis: Hackett, 1978); Martha Lee Osbourne, ed., *Woman in Western Thought* (New

York: Random House, 1979); Susan Moller Okin, *Women in Western Political Thought* (Princeton: Princeton University Press, 1979); Plato, *The Laws* (London: Penguin, 1970); Sarah Pomeroy, "Feminism in Book V of Plato's Republic," *Apeiron* 8, no. 1 (1974): 33–35; and F. A. Wright, *Feminism in Greek Literature, from Homer to Aristotle* (London: George Routledge and Sons, 1923).

29. Ernest Barker, ed., *The Politics of Aristotle* (New York: Oxford University Press, 1962), p. 32.

30. Ibid., p. 35.

31. Ibid., p. 13.

32. J. G. A. Pocock, *The Machiavellian Moment, Florentine Political Thought and the Atlantic Republican Tradition* (Princeton: Princeton University Press, 1975), p. 472.

33. Schwartz, "Distinction Between Public and Private Life," p. 250.

34. The abstracted notion of the "feudal patriarchal family" is used to focus on the general trends of patriarchy in this period and not the specific and differentiated forms of family structure. See E. P. Thompson's "Happy Families," *Radical History Review* 20 (Spring–Summer 1979): 42–50, for a discussion of the problems with abstract theories of "the" family.

35. For an excellent discussion of the breakup of the self-sufficient family as a unit of production with the advent of capitalism, see Roberta Hamilton, *The Liberation of Women, A Study of Patriarchy and Capitalism* (London: Allen and Unwin, 1978).

36. Ibid., p. 16.

37. Ibid., p. 20.

38. Christina Hole, *The English Housewife in the 17th Century* (London: Chatto and Windus, 1953), p. 15.

39. G. E. and K. R. Fussell, *The English Countrywoman, A Farmhouse Social History 1500–1900* (London: Melrose, 1953), p. xv.

40. Reiter, "Men and Women in the South of France," p. 281.

41. Female heads of state do not really contradict the notion of male-dominated public spheres. Gandhi and Thatcher do more to remind one that the public sphere is male than they allow one to think it is female.

42. Reiter, "Men and Women in the South of France," p. 273.

PART

II THE HISTORICAL ORIGINS OF LIBERAL FEMINISM

The chapters that follow outline the historical development of liberal feminism in the seventeenth century with the coming of the bourgeois marketplace and the beginnings of liberal ideology. I examine both the radical content of liberalism for feminism and the feminist critique of the male bias within liberalism. What emerges is the political perspective of liberal feminism as a radically important indictment of liberalism and yet an insufficient conception of woman's emancipation.

3

John Locke: Patriarchal Antipatriarchalism

The contemporary relationship between liberalism and feminism is rooted in the history of developing capitalist relations in seventeenth-century England and the earlier patriarchal order of feudalism. It is no surprise, then, that one finds in the writings of John Locke[1] (1632–1704) both the defense of the new property relations of bourgeois society and the criticism of the absolutist patriarchal justification of political rule: the assumption that political power is identical with the power of fathers.[2] Locke replaced the increasingly outdated absolutist patriarchal model of Sir Robert Filmer[3] with a liberal redefinition of patriarchal rule. Whereas for Filmer familial authority had been divine, natural, and unlimited, for Locke politics was based on convention and contract[4] and had to be distinguished from the rules regulating familial life.

While Locke differentiates between the family and the state, he continues to assume the patriarchal bias of Filmer and feudal society, but in a new liberal form. This involves the investigation of Locke's motives in offering a new justification for political rule other than "rule by the father ordained by God." What we shall find is that Locke differentiates between family and political rule in order to free the market from paternalist, aristocratic relations, rather than to free the family from paternal rule. He recognizes that the new relations of bourgeois society require a new definition of patriarchal rule to replace the equation of God, the father, and the king. The politics of the family and the politics of the state, he will conclude, are not one and the same thing. It will be a conclusion rooted in the actual historical changes of seventeenth-century England as the home becomes distinguished from the market and the family from the state. This change will partially redefine the basis for the ideological distinction between the private and public worlds of male and female reality in particular liberal terms.

In offering this new perspective, Locke is in fact invoking the earlier notion of Aristotle that fatherly rule, like monarchical power, cannot define the polity. A patriarchal father-son relation in the political world negates part of the individualism inherent in bourgeois society and is therefore relegated to the activity of the family, but the hierarchical relations between male and female are still deemed necessary to the smooth operations of the "free market." Locke assumes this to be part of the *natural* order of things.

In examining this patriarchal bias of liberalism in Locke, I look at his redefinition of divine-right theory contained in the liberal distinction between familial and political authority offered in his *Two Treatises of Government*.[5] Basic to this distinction is Locke's view of the independent, active, rational individual who may choose to undertake voluntary contractual associations. The power of the king is transferred to individual men as independent actors. We are presented with bourgeois man, and we see clearly the economic class and sexual class bias involved here. Locke is working from a theory of rationality that excludes the laboring classes and excludes women.

> The greatest part of mankind have not leisure for learning logic, and super-fine distinctions of the schools. Where the hand is used to the plough and the spade, the head is seldom elevated to sublime notions, or exercised in mysterious reasonings. 'Tis well if men of that rank (to say nothing of the other sex) can comprehend plain propositions, and a short reasoning about things familiar to their minds, and nearly allied to their daily experience.[6]

There are two levels of analysis here. First, I examine Locke's development of the ideology of the public/private dimensions of life out of the real changes that have taken place in the seventeenth century between the home and the bourgeois marketplace and the marketplace and the state. One concern of this chapter, then, is how Locke does this with his distinction between familial and political rule.

On a second level, I am interested in investigating how Locke's theory promises an equality that in actuality is impossible. Implicit in this concern is understanding the relationship between Locke's liberal idealism and its expression in a language that divorces reality from the relations of society. He speaks of a generalized equality without specifying the contradictions posed by society. The split between ideas and reality is part of the mystification of power itself in that the ideas of Locke are developed in the service of a new political order—capitalist patriarchy.[7] *In reality*, his ideas are not disconnected from power at all. They explicate the liberal patriarchal paradigm that sets the context in which liberal feminism develops.

Rationality and Women

The seventeenth century inherited the view of woman as both intellectually and morally inferior to man. Woman's inequality to man was a prevalent precapitalist vision.[8] Her inferiority was rooted in the presumption of her moral weakness as described by the church fathers. The book of Genesis establishes woman's responsibility for the existence of sin in the world. Woman, by her fall, brought sin into the world.[9] She is responsible for the evil in society by the law of nature and the law of God. Woman represents the passionate, irrational element in life.

The new relations of the developing capitalist market in seventeenth-century England utilize this vision of woman while redefining it. According to Peter Laslett, ". . . patriarchalism has always been an essential, perhaps the essential, presupposition of capitalism."[10] For him this particularly means that "all these assumptions about the transference of property are the assumptions of patriarchalism."[11] In the end, "God is still the father, the Pope is still Papa. . . ."[12] Alice Clark views the subjugation of woman as the foundation of capitalism also: ". . . we must remember that the subjection of women to their husbands was the foundation stone of the structure of the community in which capitalism first made its appearance."[13] This vision of subjugated woman is rearticulated in the domestic literature of the seventeenth century to accommodate the changing relations of the economy. The home was beginning to be differentiated from the market,[14] and woman's subjugation would have to be rewired in terms of this.

The books dealing with domestic relations in this period assume the position held by the church, and their instructions reflect these ecclesiastical teachings: ". . . the church as a whole consistently maintained the inferiority of woman and sought to instill into her an entire submission and obedience to her husband in all family affairs."[15] Women are depicted as weak, sinful, and inferior to men. Bishop Aylmer, in a sermon delivered before Queen Elizabeth, articulates this view:

> Women are of two sorts, some of them are wiser, better learned, discreeter, and more constant than a number of men; but another and a worse sort of them and *the most part,* are fond, foolish, wanton, flibbergibs, tatlers, triflers, wavering, witless, without council, fable, careless, rash, proud, dainty, nice, talebearers, evesdroppers, rumour-raisers, evil-tounged, worse minded, and in every way doltified with the dregs of the devil's dunghill.[16]

The contents of a typical domestic book reflected these conceptions of most women. The chapter headings from Perkin's *Christian Oeconomie* include discussions of (1) the wife's inferiority and her subjection to her husband, (2) the necessity of a husband's consent in all family matters having to do with the management of the house as well as the disposition of property, (3) the fact that the husband's duties derive from his basic superiority, and (4) the importance of maintaining the authority the husband has to beat his wife.[17] As we shall see, these conceptions of domestic life reflected the new needs of bourgeois marriage as well as the old needs of patriarchy.

According to Powell's study, *English Domestic Relations,* few books were written for the instruction of women alone in domestic activity before the first part of the seventeenth century.[18] Books on domestic duties actually reached their height in the second quarter of this century, although books dealing with marriage started with the publication of William Harrington's *Commendacious of Matrymony* in 1528 and Richard Whitford's *A Werke for Householders* in 1531. This literature both reflects and tries to direct the changes in marriage and family life during this period.

The Puritan doctrine of this period reflected the changing nature of the married woman's position within this sexual system of subordination. She was defined as the helpmeet of her husband but within a family partnership in which she remained the subordinate.[19] This change in the absolutist power of the husband that existed in feudal society to woman's "junior partnership"[20] in marriage showed a partial transformation of patriarchal relations in marriage from feudal to capitalist society. In feudal society the power of the father as head of the household was absolute in that the family was the economic, social, and political unit. "Since the acting head of the household is not merely the head of a social unit, the family, but also simultaneously the head of a small firm, in other words the work boss, he can appeal to two systems of authority."[21] Woman's subordination in capitalism reflected the differentiation of home and market, state and family. The home became her domain, which instigated a reformulation of men's power within this realm. Christopher Hill argues that the Puritan view of women reflected this: "The Puritan attitude toward women assumes the world of small household production, in which the wife had a position of authority over servants, apprentices and children, though in subordination to her husband."[22] The feudal notion of marriage as a property transaction was replaced by the Puritan conception of free choice and marriage for love. Cromwell's establishment of marriage as a civil institution in 1653 also spoke to the changing nature and conception of marriage. Nevertheless, the rigidity of marriage was still found within the divorce laws of this period.

Seventeenth-century England was characterized by domestic, family, and capitalist industry.[23] Although married women continued to labor within the home, this work became less visible from the male vantage point of the market system.[24] Alice Clark argues that this period was still characterized by "independent hard-working families living under the conditions provided by Family and Domestic Industry."[25] But the work done in the home, which remained necessary to the subsistence of the family and the worker, became separated and differentiated (from the market and male activity) and increasingly was defined as woman's sphere. Most homes were still characterized by the production of necessary goods, whereas the market was an arena of exchange.

This definition of the home as a differentiated sphere was reflected on many levels. Activities within the home took on a more particular identity. The architecture of the home dwelling changed significantly in the seventeenth century with kitchens as well as bedrooms appearing.[26] Pottery and glass began to replace pewter and wood at the table, and many families began using knives and forks to eat with. "The modern arrangement of meals—breakfast, lunch, dinner—dates from the seventeenth century."[27] The activity and daily patterns within the home began to take on their own particular shape and flavor in this period. And as this happened, the man's sphere as the world of the marketplace and the married woman's sphere as the world of the home took on their particular seventeenth-century color. Women and men were separate and unequal—which was nothing new—but there was a changing set of relations operating.

What we see in the domestic literature of this period is the *re*articulation of woman's subjection, particularly of the married woman, but now within the (unequal) partnership of bourgeois marriage. The *re*articulation of woman's evil nature is necessitated, as we shall see, by the differentiation of familial and political power within liberal ideology. Woman will still be restricted from the public world of citizenship and rationality. A reification of the ideology of woman's subjection within the home establishes a patriarchal base of power for the family, and at the same time the bourgeois limits to this power are defined.

The Liberal Attack on Divine-Right Patriarchy:
Paternal vs. Political Power

The accepted view of political society in sixteenth- and seventeenth-century England had men and women assigned their places in the hierarchical order of things ordained by God.[28] When Locke spoke of government deriving legitimacy from the consent of the governed, this challenged the rule "of God in his bequest of authority to Adam."[29] Locke did not think that the power of rulers on earth was derived from "Adam's private Dominion and Paternal Jurisdiction."[30] In other words, Adam had no authority over his children or dominion over the world by the natural right of fatherhood or by the gift of God. Locke rejected Filmer's equation between the power of fathers and the power of kings, the power of kings and the power of God. "For as Kingly power is by the law of God, so it hath no interior law to limit it."[31] The dominion of Adam is the source of all government and propriety.[32] Hence, power and the right of government become the ordinance of God—as the Father. Locke interprets Filmer: "to confirm the Natural Right of Regal Power, we find in the Decalogue, that the Law which enjoys obedience to Kings, is delivered in the Terms, Honour thy Father."[33]

Filmer assumed that fatherhood began in Adam and criticized the notion of natural freedom among individuals by maintaining the natural and private dominion of Adam. "And all Power on Earth is either derived or usurped from the Fatherly Power, there being no other original to be found of any Power whatsoever."[34] Filmer's equation between religious life, family life, and political life is seen in his assertions that all authority derives from the Fatherhood of God. There is no differentiation between political authority, paternal authority, and Divine authority. Kingly power is the same as the law of God or the law of Adam, as the father. The hierarchical relations of the family structure the relations of society as well. "Men are not naturally free. . . . Men are born in subjection to their parents, and therefore cannot be free."[35] The authority of parents is understood as interchangeable with royal and fatherly authority.

This model of political power no longer made sense in a bourgeois society where society was supposedly made up of free, equal, rational individuals who were capable of owning property. The bankers, traders, and manufacturers who were beginning to comprise society sought a theory of individual freedom that characterized *their* lives and needs.[36] The relationships of master-servant, teacher-student, employer-worker, landlord-tenant, and magistrate-subject could not all be understood as identical to the father-child relation within the family.[37] Societal relations were being differentiated from the relations of the family. "Fatherhood and Property together, which are distinct titles that do not always meet in the same person."[38]

The ascribed hierarchical relations of feudalism experienced by birthright were outdated by the new market relations and the promise of the equality of opportunity. The reorganization of home life itself made the distinction between family and politics and private and public life plausible and even necessary. This, of course, was not true under feudalism. "James was still expected to 'live of his own,' to finance government from crown lands, feudal dues, and the customs: no distinction was drawn between the public and private capacity of the King." [39]

This equation between "the public and private capacity of the King" was the paradigm of power that best suited the power of the aristocracy. Their hereditary claims to power were understood as one and the same with their economic and political power; as was patriarchal power understood as one and the same with feudal relations of power. This equation of political spheres of power can be found in feudal law. It is with the advent of the market and eventually wage labor that we begin to see the economic and political spheres develop their own identity. As Laski states: ". . . public law begins to be sharply differentiated from private law with which, under the feudal system, it had been closely confounded." [40] These changes did not push Locke to redefine the family in nonpatriarchal terms, but it allowed him to differentiate paternal power within the family from political power outside the family. "Paternal power is only where minority makes the child incapable to manage his property; Political where men have property in their own disposal; and Despotical over such as have no property at all." [41]

Locke rejects Filmer's equations because they do not recognize the differing purposes or requirements of familial and political life. Family life is organized around the *inequality* of parent and child, whereas political society must be organized around the *equality* of individuals in their activity in the market. Whereas in Locke's mind the purpose of the family is procreation and the care of dependent infants, the state is organized to coordinate independent individuals. Parents must care for children until they are capable of reason, whereas the state assumes the reasonableness of its citizens. Parental power is based on the caring and affection of the parent for the child [42] and is merely the requisite for political life: "the paternal as a natural Government but not at all extending itself to the Ends, and Jurisdictions of that which is Political." [43]

Another problem that arises from Filmer's equation of paternal with political power is that, according to Locke, you will have as many rulers as you have fathers. If the rights of royal authority are derivative of fatherhood, then ". . . everyone that has Paternal Power has Royal Authority . . . there will be as many Kings as there are Fathers." [44] If each father or grandfather has sole sovereign power, how does this relate to the power between fathers? The only answer, according to Locke, is that one cannot equate familial and political rule. If one has not distinguished between these different activities, one has laid the *democratic* basis of *despotic* rule. The contradictions are clear to Locke, even if they were not clear to Filmer.

Political activity is then best reserved for the activities of the market and the protection of private property rights. The family, with the advent of capitalism, is defined as separate and apart. "Political Power then I take to be a Right of making Laws with Penalties of Death, and Consequently all less Penalties, for the Regulating and Preserving of Property, and of employing the force of the Community, in the Execution of such Laws, and in the defence of the Common-wealth from Foreign Injury, and all this only for the Public Good."[45]

Absolute monarchy is inconsistent with civil society[46] because absolute monarchy rejects the notion of a state of perfect freedom and independence. For Locke, power and jurisdiction were to be reciprocal, much like the contract agreements wage laborers found themselves involved in. "The Natural Liberty of Man is to be free from any Superior Power on Earth, and not be under the Will or Legislative Authority of Man. . . ."[47] One is subject to the political power of another only if one consents to it. The purpose of entering political society is the enhancement of one's freedom, and individual freedom is defined in terms of the laws that protect one's property. One enters political society in order to protect property. This is the essence of freedom, to Locke. The rule of law creates the possibility of individual freedom: ". . . where there is no Law, there is no Freedom."[48] Locke has defined the liberal notion of freedom. "The great and chief end therefore, of Men's uniting into Commonwealths, and putting themselves under *government, is the Preservation* of their Property."[49]

Locke's liberalism focuses on the importance of the role of bourgeois law in the attempt to establish individual freedom. Also bound up here is the theory of rationality and individualism mentioned earlier, which undercuts the arbitrariness and absolutism of Divine Right Rule. "But Freedom of Men under Government, is to have a standing Rule to live by, common to every one of that Society, and made by the Legislative Power erected in it. . . ."[50] A government existing for the welfare of the individuals who have agreed to it operates as long as it has the approval of the governed. Power is no longer arbitrary. Consent is the only legitimate basis of government.

The Feminist Critique of Divine-Right Rule:
Paternal vs. Parental Power

Locke's attack on Filmer's divine-right rule challenges the absolutist nature of patriarchal power derived from the sole power of Adam. By dislodging the power of Adam, Locke shows the illogic of Filmer's equation of God, the father, and political rule. Locke argues that Adam has always shared his power with Eve, thus proving Adam's power is not absolute. Instead of paternal power, Adam shares parental power with Eve, although, as we shall see, Locke retains paternal power *within the family* with respect to mothering, property, and inheritance.

Locke argues that God did not give Adam dominion over inferior creatures, but only rights in common with all mankind. Filmer's position was that man, as the father, has sovereignty because he is the principal agent in generation.[51] Filmer thought God's creation of Adam and the dominion Adam had over Eve was the dominion he had as father over his children. But according to Locke, men and women share the honor and obedience due them as parents equally; nowhere in the Bible is it stated that the man has sovereignty over the woman: "For if Adam had any such Regal Power over Eve . . . it must be by some other title than that of begetting."[52]

For Locke, man and woman, together, are responsible for the procreation of the child. The father, at best, has a joint share in bringing the child into the world. According to Locke, the woman carries the child in her body for nine months, and out of her lifeblood the child grows.

> For nobody can deny but that the woman hath an equal share, if not the greater, as nourishing the child a long time in her own Body out of her own substance . . . it must certainly owe most to the Mother: But be that as it will, the mother cannot be denied an equal share in begetting of the child, and so the *Absolute Authority of the Father will not arise from hence.*[53]

The *absolutist* rule of patriarchy is challenged here by attacking the **supposed supremacy of Adam over Eve on the basis of parenting the child. Although Locke does not argue his point to conclusion—the woman, in terms of begetting the child, as the mother has the greater power.**

Locke further documents his case by noting the commandment to "honour thy father and mother."[54] This commandment gives the father no supremacy over the mother. The mother and father share authority here: ". . . the mother having by this law of God, a right of Honour from her children which is not Subject to the Will of her Husband, we see *this Absolute Monarchical Power of the Father, can neither be founded on it. . . .*"[55] Filmer leaves out "thy mother" in his reading of the commandment because, as Locke notes, it is helpful to his argument. Parenthood involves mothers and fathers for Locke, and this destroys Filmer's argument of the *origins* of political power.

But once again Locke does not take his argument to its explicit and logical conclusion: that at the base of political power is parental power which would destroy the paternalist base of Filmer's thought as well as its absolutist dimension. Parental power never dislodges paternal power for Locke. He, instead, uses the equality between men and women in parenting to debunk only the despotic absolutist nature of paternal power between husband and wife. The power of the father and husband still applies within the home. It is just that in its liberalized form, the patriarchal power of the husband over the wife is not absolute. There are limits defined by the law.

> Or that either of our Queens Mary or Elizabeth, had they married any of their Subjects, had been by this Text put into a Political Subjection to him: or that he thereby should have had *Monarchical Rule* over her? God, in this Text, gives not, that I see, any Authority to Adam and Eve, or to Men over their Wives, but only foretells what should be the Womans Lot, how by his Providence he would order it so, that she should be subject to her husband, as we see that generally the Laws of Mankind and customs of Nations have ordered it so; and there is, I grant, a Foundation in Nature for it.[56]

Woman still is subject to her husband, and this is derived from nature. Locke is simply denying that this subjection should be used to justify the "original grant of government" or the "foundation of monarchical power." Adam has conjugal power and not political power.[57] The power this does define for the husband is "the Power that every Husband hath to order the things of private Concernment in his Family, as Proprietor of the Goods and Land there, and to have his Weill take place before that of his wife in all things of their common Concernment; but not a Political Power of Life and Death over her, much less over any body else."[58]

When differences of opinion arise between husband and wife, "the last determination" is the husband's. It falls naturally to the man as the abler and stronger. But this must be distinguished from the absolutist rule of the father and the husband that feudal England embraced. The husband has no more power over the life of the woman than she has over his. "The *Power of the Husband* being so far from that of an absolute monarch, that the *Wife* has, in many cases a Liberty to separate from him. . . ."[59] In seventeenth-century England, marriage was indeed to become more of a civil contract, as was government itself; indeed, it changed from an ecclesiastical institution to a civil one.

Although man and woman share in the process of procreation and therefore share the authority of parenthood, the father has the added power since he controls the inheritance of the family. "And this is the Power Men generally have to bestow their Estates on those, who please them best."[60] Children have a title to the property of their parents and a right to inherit their possessions, but it is the father who continues to control this process.[61] Although Locke has earlier distinguished between fatherhood and property, he now reconnects them in their particularly liberal patriarchal form. It is still fathers who will exercise power—this time through the specific control of the property line of inheritance and with it the definition of rationality. To the extent that rationality was a male prerogative in the seventeenth century, given the existing patriarchal religious and ideological views of woman, she was *in reality* excluded from the new radical bourgeois view of the individual on the basis of her sex and on the basis of her exclusion from the market.

The bourgeois system of property reasserts the patriarchal basis of the society by redefining the subjugation of woman in particularly bourgeois terms. Woman's subjection to man is reinforced by the relations of property and inheritance. Her definition as mother, both as childbearer and rearer, has no status within the new market values and yet she is utterly necessary to the functionings of society. Woman's activity in the begetting of children and the preparation of children for political life are both recognized by Locke. Nevertheless, these dimensions of women's lives have been relegated to the "private sphere" by liberal patriarchal ideology, and she is maintained and limited to this sphere by her exclusion from the market, which has become a new tool of patriarchal control. The married woman has no title to money or right to litigation.

The redefinition of patriarchal power within the family is based partially on the new distinctions being drawn between religion, civil society, the family, and the state. Paternal power within the family is not challenged by Locke. He does, however, reject paternalism as the model of power for an economy that requires that individuals shift and take responsibility for themselves. The bourgeois economy contradicts the familial notion that someone else will take care of you. It asserts the necessity of independence rather than the dependent relations inherent in the paternalism of the aristocratic order.

In bourgeois society, the notion of equality of opportunity replaces the aristocratic conception of ascribed hierarchy. Achieved status displaces the ascribed status of hereditary birth. The concept of the "equality of opportunity" challenges the reality of ascribed privileges by virtue of its celebration of "meritorious attainment." [62] It is based on the recognition of the self-made individual, "a society disinterestedly rewarding people of merit and talent, people of hard and useful work." [63] Liberal ideology dislodges the privilege of birth and replaces it, not with egalitarianism, but with equality of opportunity in the marketplace, for men only. The ascribed status of womanhood is left intact. Equality of opportunity does not apply to her yet.

In order to understand the full significance of bourgeois society and liberal ideology for women's lives, it is important to note that Locke opens up the conception of individuality for women as well as men, even if he does not follow through on this potentiality. In Locke's defense of the new individual—independent, free, and rational—he provides a political language that can be applied to all equally. The ideology sets forth a commitment to all alike. The promise of this potential freedom in liberal ideology may be denied by the political realities of society, but it still stands as a model on which later feminists can call.

Property and Rationality

It is important to examine the exclusion of woman on the basis of her sex, as well as her position in the market along with the exclusion of the laboring poor from Locke's conception of the rational individual. Locke's negation of the laboring man's citizenship is more explicit (than that of woman's) because all men qualified initially for citizenship *as male*. Locke, therefore, had to clarify how the vulgar activities of the laboring masses excluded them from the achievement of a rational life and hence from citizenship. The exclusion of women is, however, assumed more than it is explained. C. B. MacPherson is correct when he writes that seventeenth-century liberalism was radical in that it presented and asserted the free rational individual, yet was limited in that it denied this individualism to a majority of the people given the economic class inequities of the time.[64] But it must be added that it denied this individualism to all women as well on the basis of the equation of rationality and maleness. In the name of personal freedom, Locke's theory reinforces the patriarchal relations of the family via his theory of rationality. One is left questioning whose freedom and individuality Locke is speaking about as he reifies the distinction between familial and political life.

The differential rationality that Locke describes is not understood as inherent in men but is socially acquired by virtue of their different economic positions.[65] Locke defines rationality in terms of property in the sense that property is understood as a reflection of one's personality and the control one has over one's life and activity: ". . . private property is a natural right anterior to the State, and to protect which; inter alia, the State came into existence. Private property is the outcome of human personality; it is founded on the dominion which man has over his own exertions; it represents the fruits of his labour."[66] Private property expresses Locke's thoughts on personal freedom, individuality, and rationality simultaneously. It is the possession of private property that allows individuals to enjoy their freedom or to be viewed as rational. But this right to private property is also proof that individuals are rational or free. It determines one's chances and reflects one's life chances at the same time.[67] To the degree that the right to private property excludes the working classes and women, they are excluded from the realm of free and rational activity.

Property, for Locke, as it will be for Hegel, is the external expression of one's freedom. It asserts one's individuality in that it expresses one's personality. Property becomes a means toward freedom and rationality. "God, who hath given the World to Men in common, hath also *given them reason* to make use of it to the advantage of Life and convenience." [68] It is only natural and rational that one seek to appropriate and utilize what God has so generously given "men in common." But "since he gave it [to] them for their benefit, and the greatest Conveniencies of Life they were capable to draw from it, it cannot be supposed he meant it should always remain common and uncultivated. He gave it to the use of the *Industrious and Rational. . . .*" [69]

This notion of property presents the new liberal idea of property in democratic terms compared with the previous aristocratic relations of feudal society. The authority of property replaces the authority of God: ". . . that it be difficult to make out Property, upon a supposition, that God gave the World to Adam and his Posterity. But I shall endeavour to shew, how Men might come to have a property in several parts of that which God gave to Mankind in common. . . ." [70] Property was the right of each person found in *his* capacity to labor, to appropriate nature and land for his needs. "Though the Earth, and all inferior Creatures be common to all Men, yet every Man has a Property in his own Person. This no Body has any Right to but himself. The Labour of his Body, and the Work of his Hands, we may say, are properly his." [71] But this is where the *practical* realities of labor and property, defined as private property, become clearly exclusionary. Locke speaks of *each* man having the right to property in his capacity to labor.

C. B. MacPherson's discussion in *The Political Theory of Possessive Individualism* draws attention to Locke's equation of labor and property and his failure to understand that they are in an antagonistic relation to each other. According to MacPherson, "the more emphatically labour is asserted to be a property the more it is to be understood to be alienable." [72] For Locke, a man's labor is so much understood as his own property that he can do anything with it—even "freely" sell it for wages.[73] Labor's new bourgeois definition was that it could be freely exchanged, and this is at the base of Locke's equation between labor and property. It also constructs the equation between property, rationality, and freedom.

It is important to remember that Locke believed the right to property to be a natural one that all men share—equally. He did not understand that private property is an exclusive right, that, by definition, it excludes everybody but the owner from the rights or usage of it. The very meaning of the term derives from the *relations* between owners and nonowners of the property. Private property at one and the same time reflects private ownership; the two realities give meaning to each other.

According to MacPherson, the estimated size of the propertyless wage-earning and unemployed class in England in 1688 was no less than half the population. This reality does not intervene in Locke's equation between labor and property. As a matter of fact, he instead offers an argument in which the natural right to property lays the basis for the natural right to equality. In doing so, he asserts the freedom of the marketplace with no assurance of equality because the equality is assumed as a natural right. "No mans labour could subdue, or appropriate all: nor could his Enjoyment consume more than a small part; so that it was impossible for any Man, this way, to intrench upon the right of another. . . ." [74] Locke's theory of private property assumes the rationality of those who are successful at appropriating it and does not explain how or why some are unsuccessful at it. He does not understand that it is in the nature of private property to exclude the laboring masses. Society, in reality, has two economic classes: the industrious, rational, and propertied, and those who are not.[75] Yet in his theoretical formulations, Locke depicts this reality as a society composed of atomistic individuals, equal and free. Locke's "ideal" presentation stands in stark contrast to the "real" social relations of society. This idealized discussion takes the form of the language of rationality. The propertyless classes are spoken of, instead, as the immoral, irrational laboring classes. Locke even applauds Christianity for being a religion written for the laboring classes because it can be understood by those who are illiterate and vulgar: ". . . and the all-merciful God seems herein to have consulted the poor of this world, and the bulk of mankind; these are articles that the labouring and illiterate man may comprehend. This is a religion suited to vulgar capacities. . . ." [76]

By dismissing those of vulgar capacity and equating individual rights with property rights, Locke believes the individual rights (of the property class) to be coterminous with that of the majority. The propertied individual is equated with the idea of the generalized electorate, and the laboring class is subsumed into this category. This presents a notion of individuality that excludes the propertyless at the same time as it presents the individuality of the propertied class as the preferred model. Even the Levellers assumed some of this bias: "Thinking in terms of small household industrial and agricultural units, the Levellers held that servants—apprentices and labourers as well as domestic servants—were represented by the head of the household no less than were his womenfolk and children." [77]

It should be clear from this discussion of rationality and property that the economic class bias of seventeenth-century England was integrally linked with the patriarchal bias of feudal society. Women were not understood as politically autonomous beings within seventeenth-century England in terms of their exclusion from the propertied class and their exclusion on the basis of patriarchy from the world of rationality. Both the bourgeois relations of property and the preexisting sexual inequality of patriarchy denied woman a full part in enjoying the radical dimensions of the liberalism of Locke. His concerns with the new individualism of bourgeois society required that he strike down the absolutist dimensions of familial feudal patriarchy and redefine it in terms of the developing bourgeois one.

Liberal Individualism and the Family

The ideology of liberal individualism and personal freedom applied only to men in the market. The bourgeois attack on the class hierarchy of the aristocracy did not extend to the sexual hierarchy of patriarchy within the family. And as woman was confined to these hierarchical relations within the family, she was also restricted within the political society. The differentiation between paternal and political power, which is at the base of liberalism for Locke, did not apply to woman. In this sense, she was excluded from the liberal individualist revolution. It was a revolution for the propertied *males* of the seventeenth century.

This should not be taken as overstating the patriarchal bias of Locke's thought. In the light of this, Locke's statements on the education of children are particularly interesting. His basic assault against the rule of arbitrary power is clearest in his discussions on the cultivation of the rational individual. In his correspondence with Clarke,[78] Locke advises him to cultivate a friendship with his son. "But whatever he consults you about, unless it lead to some fatal and irremediable mischief, be sure you advise only as a friend of more experience; but with your advice mingle nothing of command or authority, no more than you would to your equal or a stranger."[79]

Locke's argument is that one should try to use reason as the source of one's authority rather than force. Although a boy of three is not able to be reasoned with as a grown man, he is potentially reasonable.[80] The tutor's role, then, is to teach the art of reason, which involves the love of knowledge and human improvement: ". . . his tutor should remember, that his business is not so much to teach him all that is knowable, as to raise in him a love and esteem of knowledge; and to put him in the right way of knowing and improving himself, when he has a mind to it."[81]

Locke articulates a theory of education that coincides with the needs of bourgeois society and liberal ideology. All are potentially rational and potentially virtuous. "I place virtue as the first and most necessary of those endowments that belong to a man or a gentleman, as absolutely requisite to make him valued and beloved by others, acceptable or tolerable to himself."[82] This conception of education undercuts the need for force and absolutist authority in daily activity. It places the responsibility to "improve oneself" on the individual. And, according to Locke, there should be no significant differences in the education of boys and girls. Allowances will have to be made in consideration of woman's beauty, but otherwise their breeding should be quite similar: ". . . wherein there will be some though no great difference, for making a little allowance for beauty, and some few other consideration of the s(ex), the manner of breeding of boys and girls, especially in their younger years, I imagine should be the same."[83]

He believes that boys and girls both need appropriate amounts of exercise; otherwise men will be left with frail wives. Nevertheless, the exercise should be done with care to protecting the girl's beauty from wind and drying. "But since in your girls, care is to be taken too of their beauty, as much as health will permit, this in them must have some restriction. . . ."[84] At the same time Locke restricts women for the sake of their beauty, he is critical of the hard bodices that pinch and pressure the lungs and the binding of women's feet in China:

> Narrow breasts, short and stinking breath, ill lungs, and crookedness, are the natural and almost constant affects of hard bodice and clothes that pinch. That way of making slender waists, and fine shapes, serves but the more effectually to spoil them. . . . It is generally known, that the women of China (imagining I know not what kind of beauty in it) by bracing and binding them hard from their infancy, have very little feet.[85]

Against the backdrop of the existing ideology of woman as passionate and primarily responsible for the evil in society, Locke's inclusion of women in his theories of education is interesting. Although most of his discussion of education seems preoccupied with the training of little boys, he says in his correspondences to Mrs. Clarke that this training applies to girls as well. In this case, the ideology of rationality and individuality appears to be extended to women by Locke. But little is said on behalf of women's education. The education of girls takes place within the societal context of the division between home life and political life for men and their equation for women. In liberal patriarchal ideology, woman has no political life. Her life in the home is her life. Whereas the family is differentiated from political life for men, these spheres are still equated for women. Her education will find its expression within the home politically organized by liberalized patriarchal values, which in actuality exclude women from the "rational" life by virtue that they are women. This develops into the mystifying anomaly that woman, as a mother within the family, exists separate and apart from political life. In the end she is excluded from political life. Men are freed from familial patriarchal rule; women are relegated to it.

Liberalism depicted a new category of free man. Bourgeois society was not able to actualize the demand for all men because of the exclusionary nature of private property. It was not able to actualize the demand for women, nor did it even understand this as a demand in the seventeenth century because of the exclusionary bias of patriarchy.

Liberalism explicitly espouses a commitment to rationality, individualism, and property and the inherent freedom involved here, while implicitly it embraces the paternalism and patriarchal values of the family that were a part of the foundation of bourgeois society. The point is not to hold Locke accountable in terms of a twentieth-century feminist consciousness, but rather to explicate the contradictions built into liberalism. It is patriarchal in its foundation and therefore can never meet the demand for equality for women although it can promise it.

Liberal ideology would demystify the nature of government by specifying the importance of the individual in relation to the political contract. It would do this while mystifying the place of the family in terms of politics and, hence, the patriarchal bias of liberalism. It does not replace the patriarchal dimensions of society, but rather redefines them in liberal terms. This means that the explicit new model of politics presents the model of the bourgeois market at center stage. The paternalist familial relation is no longer presented as the paradigm of political power. According to liberal ideology, familial patriarchy no longer needs to be duplicated by the state. This relegates the relations of the family to the private realm. Capitalism and liberal ideology have displaced the family. The model of father and son has been displaced by a model of liberal equality. Bourgeois society still needs the mother-child relation, however, and the system of patriarchal power is intended to mystify this familial and political necessity.

This is where the contradictions involved in women's equality with men become clearest. Women, in terms of the needs for family life and mothering, are still viewed in the passive and dependent terms of paternal patriarchy. The public realm is still structured by this patriarchal hierarchy, but in bourgeois form. Liberal ideology misrepresents these political realities by its particular differentiation of familial and political life. Although this distinction is used in a progressive effort by Locke to lay the basis for a more egalitarian society, it simultaneously lays the basis for the particularly liberal mystification of patriarchal power. The market does not displace the patriarchal family in terms of the liberal notion of politics, but in actuality merely redefines it.

NOTES

1. Locke was born to a Puritan family and was brought up amid lawyers, officials, and merchants. He trained first as a cleric and then as

a doctor. He lived during the Interregnum (1649–60) and took part in the debates over the nature of political rule in this period. After 1660 he became preoccupied with the constitutional struggles between Charles II and Parliament. Locke was the leading theoretician who argued for parliamentary sovereignty and in favor of the Glorious Revolution. For a discussion of Locke's personal and political life, see Maurice Cranston, *John Locke, A Biography* (London: Longman's, Green, 1957). Also see Christopher Hill, *The Century of Revolution, 1603–1714* (Edinburgh, Scotland: Nelson, 1961), for an analysis of the political debates in this period.

2. Gordon Schochet, *Patriarchalism in Political Thought* (Oxford, England: Blackwell, 1975), p. 269. In Schochet's impressive and important book, he defines patriarchal thought as the familial premodern political tradition that posits "that human relationships were the natural outgrowths of the familial association and its paternal authority" (p. 55). He argues that patriarchalism, as a theory, declined after 1690 and was eventually replaced by the contract theory of the eighteenth century. In line with this argument, also see Melissa Butler, "Early Liberal Roots of Feminism: John Locke and the Attack on Patriarchy," *American Political Science Review* 72, no. 1 (March 1978): 135–50.

3. Sir Robert Filmer was born in 1588, the year of the Spanish Armada, and died in 1653, thirty-five years before his *Patriarcha* was published and used in the Royalist defense of James II. This debate between Locke and Filmer is part of the constitutionalist debate that centered around the authority of Parliament in relation to the king. It was a debate that continued into the eighteenth century, as can be seen in the writings of Lord Bolingbroke. See Sir Robert Filmer, *Patriarcha and Other Political Works*, ed. Peter Laslett (Oxford, England: Blackwell, 1949); Isaac Kramnick, "An Augustan Reply to Locke: Bolingbroke on Natural Law and the Origin of Government," *Political Science Quarterly* 82, no. 4 (December 1967): 571–94; and idem, *Bolingbroke and His Circle, The Politics of Nostalgia in the Age of Walpole* (Cambridge, Mass.: Harvard University Press, 1968).

4. Locke is not the first to argue for the importance of a contract in the formation of the state. According to Harold Laski in *The Rise of European Liberalism* (London: Unicorn, 1936), Protestantism aided in the development of the liberal notion of the political contract by facilitating the growth of the secular state (p. 23). See Max Weber's discussion of Protestantism, especially in its Puritan form, in influencing the "spirit of capitalism" in *The Protestant Ethic and the Spirit of Capitalism* (New York: Scribner's, 1958). Also see Christopher Hill, *Society and Puritanism in Pre-Revolutionary England* (New York: Schocken, 1964), and his *Puritanism and Revolution* (London: Secker and Warburg, 1958); and R. H. Tawney, *Religion and the Rise of Capitalism* (London: Penguin,

1938). Other earlier currents in political thought aided Locke in the related question of the relationship between the state and the family. See Ernest Barker, ed., *The Politics of Aristotle* (New York: Oxford University Press, 1962); and Jean Bodin, *The Six Books of a Commonweale*, ed. Kenneth McRae (Cambridge, Mass.: Harvard Political Classics, 1962).

5. John Locke, *Two Treatises of Government*, ed. Peter Laslett (London: Cambridge University Press, 1960). The original title page, published in 1698, reads: "Two Treatises of Government, In the Former, The Falfe Principles and Foundation of Sir Robert Filmer, and his Followers, are Detected and Overthrown. The Latter is an Essay Concerning The True Original, Extent, and End of Civil Government." An earlier discussion of these ideas can be found in Edward Gee's *The Divine Right and Original of the Civil Magistrate from God* (London, 1658). See Schochet, *Patriarchalism*, for a discussion of this. Nevertheless, the changes within the seventeenth-century market and the family made divine-right rule an anachronistic doctrine.

6. John Locke, *The Reasonableness of Christianity*, ed. I. T. Ramsey (Stanford: Stanford University Press, 1958), p. 76.

7. See Zillah Eisenstein, "Developing a Theory of Capitalist Patriarchy and Socialist Feminism," in *Capitalist Patriarchy and the Case for Socialist Feminism*, ed. Zillah Eisenstein (New York: Monthly Review Press, 1978), for an explication of the concept capitalist patriarchy.

8. Christopher Hill, *Milton and the English Revolution* (New York: Penguin, 1977), p. 120.

9. Chilton Latham Powell, *English Domestic Relations, 1487–1653* (New York: Columbia University Press, 1917), p. 149.

10. Filmer, *Patriarcha*, p. 23. Laslett's use of the term patriarchalism applies to the familial base of political power and not the political relations between men and women *within* the family.

11. Ibid.

12. Ibid.

13. Alice Clark, *Working Life of Women in the Seventeenth Century* (New York: Kelley, 1968), p. 300.

14. This differentiation of home and market in capitalism affects the economic classes of this period differently. For further study of this question, see Rose Bradley, *The English Housewife in the Seventeenth and Eighteenth Centuries* (London: Arnold, 1912); G. E. and K. R. Fussell, *The English Countrywoman, A Farmhouse Social History, 1500–1900* (London: Melrose, 1953); Roberta Hamilton, *The Liberation of Women, a Study of Patriarchy and Capitalism* (London: Allen and Unwin, 1978); Christina Hole, *The English Housewife in the Seventeenth Century* (London: Chatto & Windus, 1953); and idem, *English Home-Life, 1500–1800* (London: Batsford, 1947).

15. Powell, *English Domestic Relations,* p. 171.

16. Ibid., p. 147.

17. Ibid., pp. 235, 236.

18. Ibid., p. 154.

19. Christopher Hill, *The World Turned Upside Down* (New York: Viking, 1972), p. 249.

20. Hill, *Milton and the English Revolution,* p. 119.

21. Alan Macfarlane, *The Origins of English Individualism, The Family, Property and Social Transition* (New York: Cambridge University Press, 1978), p. 26.

22. Hill, *Milton and the English Revolution,* p. 119.

23. Clark, *Women in the 17th Century.*

24. David Levine, *Family Formation in an Age of Nascent Capitalism* (New York: Academic, 1977), argues that the proletarianization of agriculture characterizes England from 1550 on. "Thereafter to be sure, small independent landowners and farmers persisted, but within an economic universe in which the classic triad of landlord, tenant farmer, and wage laborer exercised hegemony" (p. 2). I would argue that in the seventeenth century wage workers were primarily occasional day workers and seasonal workers, who mainly survived by cultivating their own plots of land.

25. Clark, *Women in the 17th Century,* p. 301.

26. See Christopher Hill, *The Century of Revolution, 1603–1714* (Edinburgh, Scotland: Nelson, 1961), for this discussion.

27. Ibid., p. 3.

28. See John Neville Figgis, *The Divine Right of Kings* (New York: Harper Torchbooks, 1965); and Joseph Strayer, *On the Medieval Origins of the State* (Princeton: Princeton University Press, 1970).

29. John Dunn, "The Politics of Locke in England and America," in *John Locke—Problems and Perspectives,* ed. J. W. Yolton (London: Cambridge University Press, 1969), p. 50. Also see John Dunn, *The Political Thought of John Locke: An Historical Account of the Argument of the "Two Treatises of Government"* (London: Cambridge University Press, 1969).

30. Locke, *Two Treatises of Government,* 2:285.

31. Filmer, *Patriarcha,* p. 96.

32. Ibid., p. 71.

33. Locke, *Two Treatises of Government,* 1:202.

34. Ibid., p. 213.

35. Ibid., p. 162.

36. See Laski, *European Liberalism,* for a discussion of the role of science, religion, and rationalism in seventeenth-century liberalism. Also see his *Political Thought in England* (London: Oxford University Press, 1920).

37. Schochet, *Patriarchalism,* p. 66. His discussion of the role patri-

archalism has played within political thought is particularly important here.

38. Locke, *Two Treatises of Government*, 1:217.

39. Hill, *Century of Revolution*, p. 2.

40. Laski, *European Liberalism*, p. 38. It is interesting to note that liberal ideology presents these spheres as *separate* from one another rather than differentiated and still interrelated. Also see J. G. A. Pocock, *The Ancient Constitution and the Feudal Law* (New York: Norton, 1957), for an in-depth discussion of this issue. For a discussion of this historical period, see Joseph and Frances Gies, *Merchants and Moneymen* (New York: Crowell, 1972); Henri Pirenne, *Medieval Cities* (New York: Doubleday, 1956); and L. F. Salzman, *English Life in the Middle Ages* (New York: Appleton-Century-Crofts, 1955).

41. Locke, *Two Treatises of Government*, 2:402.

42. Ibid., p. 399.

43. Ibid.

44. Ibid., 1:211.

45. Ibid., 2:286.

46. Ibid., p. 344.

47. Ibid., p. 301.

48. Ibid., p. 324.

49. Ibid., pp. 368–69.

50. Ibid., p. 302.

51. Ibid., 1:198.

52. Ibid., p. 214.

53. Ibid., p. 198 (italics mine).

54. Ibid., p. 204.

55. Ibid. (italics mine).

56. Ibid., p. 192.

57. Ibid.

58. Ibid.

59. Ibid., 2:339.

60. Ibid., p. 333.

61. Ibid., 1:225.

62. Isaac Kramnick, "Religion and Radicalism, English Political Theory in the Age of Revolution," *Political Theory* 5, no. 4 (November 1977): 519.

63. Ibid., p. 513.

64. C. B. MacPherson, *The Political Theory of Possessive Individualism, Hobbes to Locke* (New York: Oxford University Press, 1962), p. 262. Also see his *Democratic Theory, Essays in Retrieval* (Oxford, England: Clarendon Press, 1973), and his edited volume *Property* (Toronto, Canada: University of Toronto Press, 1978).

65. MacPherson, *Possessive Individualism*, p. 246.

66. Paschal Larkin, *Property in the Eighteenth Century with Special Reference to England and Locke* (Cork, Ireland: Cork University Press, 1930), p. 1.

67. For a critique of this theory of property, see Karl Marx, *The Economic and Philosophic Manuscripts of 1844*, ed. Dirk Struik (New York: International Publishers, 1964); and MacPherson, *Possessive Individualism*.

68. Locke, *Two Treatises of Government*, 2:304 (italics mine).

69. Ibid., p. 309 (italics mine).

70. Ibid., p. 304.

71. Ibid., pp. 305–6.

72. MacPherson, *Possessive Individualism*, pp. 214–15.

73. Ibid

74. Locke, *Two Treatises of Government*, 2:310.

75. C. B. MacPherson, "The Social Bearings of Locke's Political Theory," in *Life, Liberty and Property*, ed. Gordon Schochet (Belmont, Calif.: Wadsworth, 1971), p. 77.

76. Locke, *Reasonableness of Christianity*, p. 76.

77. Hill, *Century of Revolution*, p. 131.

78. See Benjamin Rand, ed., *The Correspondence of John Locke and Edward Clarke* (Cambridge, Mass.: Harvard University Press, 1927).

79. Ibid., p. 158.

80. John Locke, *On Education*, ed. Peter Gay (New York: Columbia University Press, 1964), p. 65.

81. Ibid., p. 161.

82. Ibid., p. 99.

83. Rand, *Correspondence*, p. 121.

84. Ibid., p. 103.

85. Locke, *On Education*, p. 23.

4

J. J. Rousseau and Patriarchal Ideology: Liberal Individualism and Motherhood

Jean Jacques Rousseau (1712–78) raises interesting problems in a study of the history of liberal feminism. He most definitely is not a feminist. His importance rather stems from his explicit statement of patriarchal ideology.[1] An understanding of Rousseau's presentation of patriarchal ideology will help one comprehend the liberal feminism of Wollstonecraft and Stanton better. It will also help one see how liberal feminists adopt part of the patriarchal bias of Rousseau at the same time they think they are criticizing it. In the same vein, one needs to examine how Rousseau's patriarchal thought remains a predominant part of present-day liberal ideology.

Rousseau's importance for a study of liberal feminism also derives from his commitment to the new liberal values of freedom, individualism, and independence that flourished in eighteenth-century France. He embraces the same view of private property as did Locke and sees it as an expression of an individual's freedom, although he criticizes the extremes of rich and poor on the basis of the dependence these relations create. His criticism of the market is bourgeois in itself; Rousseau is antimarket, antimoney, and against inequality because he is the liberal individualist par excellence. He embraces the liberal notions of freedom, independence, merit, and individualism and uses them to critique the bourgeois market for not actualizing the freedom and independence it promises. His thought represents the ultimate conflict between bourgeois society and liberal democratic commitments. Rousseau understands that the conflict exists, which is more than Locke does, but he does not understand that the problem of equality lies in the relations of the family and its relationship to private property.

Rousseau's commitment to equality directs him to questions about individual domination and submission. We shall see that these questions involve the sexual and economic class nature of society for him. He wishes to transform the inequalities of civil society, which encompass the realm of artificiality and egoism, into a moral society where men will be citizens and women will be virtuous mothers. In order for this transformation to take place, the sexual passions of society and the excesses of private property must be curtailed.

Women are the source of sexual passion for Rousseau and therefore must be controlled. Amid the flux and change of feudal rural France and bourgeois Paris, Rousseau seeks to control the artificial, empty, sensuous, luxurious tendencies of Paris, which he identifies with the feminine world.[2] The inequalities he fears arise as much out of the potential sexual power women have over men as they do from the economic market. Freedom lies in the control and rule of self,[3] and this involves the ability of men to rule their passions, as Saint-Preux must do with Julie in *La Nouvelle Heloise*.[4] Although Rousseau contends that freedom requires economic equality, this is only a small part of his theory of moral freedom. For men to be free, they must be rational rather than passionate. And for men to be rational, women must be patriarchically controlled. Women must be curbed and limited and then men can be free. The patriarchal ideology of Rousseau is as much directed against the feminine part of society as it is simultaneously critical of the excesses of the aristocracy and the new bourgeois market system. As a result, he often equates sexual and economic class. As such, his concerns with sexual submission and economic class domination form his complicated study of freedom and patriarchal individualism.

We explore Rousseau's position on women—the family, sexuality, virtue, and motherhood—as it both constructs patriarchal ideology and impinges on his conception of liberal individualism. His concern with restructuring the inequalities of the market is curtailed by his conception of "woman's sphere." In other words, the argument shows the contradictory nature between Rousseau's commitment to liberal individualism, which is not supposed to be limited by an ascribed status, and his devotion to the patriarchal family, which is. It shows that Rousseau's individualism for men is rooted in a patriarchal and, hence, dependent existence for women; that the promise of independence and equality for man *requires* the subordination of woman. In trying to deny woman her "natural" power, Rousseau renders her powerless. In trying to strengthen man, he seeks to weaken woman.

The crucial question here is, What is the political impact of Rousseau's ideas about women on women and men, and as such, on society as a whole? Does his view of the naturally dependent woman invalidate the notion of the naturally independent man? Does the dependent woman in society negate the independence of man? Wollstonecraft understands the dilemma these questions raise, as does the twentieth-century liberal feminist women's movement. This tension between liberalism and patriarchy is actually a part of the crisis of twentieth-century liberalism. But this is not how it is seen in patriarchal France with the coming of the bourgeois market.

The Problem of Sexual and Economic Class

Eighteenth-century France was still primarily a rural society, but it saw a rapid development of urban centers and a bourgeois market. Feudal arrangements were technically operative and a part of many people's lives until the decree of the Convention of July 17, 1793.[5] According to Olwen Hufton, the home, an integral part of agricultural production, was being transformed by the rise of wage labor among agricultural workers. The economy was primarily a family economy "dependent upon the efforts of each individual member and one in which the role of both partners was equally crucial."[6] Fifty to 90 percent of the holdings (depending on the region) of most farmers were insufficient to maintain a family. Many of the women of these households looked for industrial work, and many became agricultural laborers. Women who needed to work for wages often worked in some part of textile production. Women who were spinners and lacemakers worked in the putting-out system. Women who turned to the towns for work usually were involved in glove production, ribbon manufacture, lacemaking, and silk manufacture, the very industries Rousseau criticizes as artificial, wasteful, and feminine.

The earning power of single women was very limited. Wages earned by women were not enough to live on if that was their only source of maintenance:

> Falling as low as four sous for a day's lacemaking in parts of the Massif central (the price of two or two and a half pounds of bread) and rarely rising above eight to ten sous except in certain favoured industries at very restricted periods, such sums might feed her and possibly, if they rose to eight or ten sous, might purchase the candles and fuel necessary to work into the night, but emphatically they would not both feed her adequately and keep a roof over her head.[7]

Marriage was an economic necessity and was seen as an economic partnership for those dependent on some combination of wage labor and home industry. The agricultural worker's wife made the difference between subsistence and destitution. As Olwen Hufton has noted, ". . . the difference they made to the composite family economy was the difference between subsistence and destitution."[8] The woman who worked as an agricultural laborer, or in the towns, or at both, was not a homemaker in the modern sense of the term. Cleaning, mending, and even cooking were only marginal activities for her.[9]

It would appear, then, that the economy of France required more and more women to labor for wages, although this was most true for unmarried women. In contrast to the woman who worked for wages was the new woman of the bourgeoisie. This is the economic class of women Rousseau is mainly concerned with. It is a small group of women, and he does not want it to grow larger. Their seeming idleness and movement into male circles distresses him. He rather thinks they need to invest their energy and activity toward *useful* enterprise. The particular useful enterprise he has in mind is motherhood. Motherhood becomes the sole liberal patriarchal vision for this new woman, who is the wife of the financier, industrialist, merchant, lawyer, or law clerk.[10] But she does not represent the majority of women in France. Rather, she is the picture of woman, given patriarchal ideology, that emerges while the market relations of society are in transition and need to be stabilized. As Eileen Power notes in discussing the medieval woman, "the position of women is one thing in theory, another in legal position, yet another in everyday life."[11] What in fact is happening is that Rousseau is intimidated by the new bourgeois woman and believes she will destroy society. He nevertheless champions the new ideology of liberal individualism for men. The free society will require the repression of women and their sexuality at the same time that it requires that no man be rich enough to control another. As such, Rousseau's views on women and the patriarchal family lay the basis for his liberal democratic male state.

The Family and the State

The family, for Rousseau, is the first form of society and is necessitated by the struggle for survival. Interestingly enough, Rousseau discusses the need children have for their fathers (rather than their mothers) in this elemental stage. He states in *The Social Contract*: "The most ancient of all societies, and the only one that is natural, is the family; and even so the children remain attached to the father only so long as they need him for their preservation. As soon as this need ceases, the natural bond is dissolved."[12]

Once the need is dissolved, father and child return to their independent status. The state is also based upon need. Individuals alienate their liberty for their advantage. "The family then may be called the first model of political societies; the ruler corresponds to the father, and the people to the children; all, being born free and equal, alienated their liberty only for their own advantage."[13] The difference between the family and the state is the love that exists between father and child.

Therefore the family requires a different kind of regulation than the relations of the state do. According to Rousseau, the rules of conduct proper to one sphere are not proper to the other.[14] Besides love, the family is organized around the physical strength of the father. Paternal authority is established by nature for as long as the children need protection. The laws governing the family and the state must be different because the duties and rights deriving from each sphere are not the same. Therefore the activities and obligations also differ. Rousseau self-consciously rejects Filmer's patriarchalism, while defining his own.

> From all that has just been said, it follows that *public* economy, which is my subject, has been rightly distinguished from *private* economy, and that, the State having nothing in common with the family except the obligations which their heads lie under of making both of them happy, the same rules of conduct cannot apply to both. I have considered these few lines enough to overthrow the detestable system which Sir Robert Filmer has endeavoured to establish in his *Patriarcha*. . . .[15]

Rousseau distinguishes between the state as the public economy and the activity of the family as the private economy, much like Locke does. These spheres are understood as different, separate, and apart in function and purpose. Once again we see the patriarchal distinction between home life and public life extended to the bourgeois differentiation of the state and the family.[16]

> The word Economy, or Oeconomy . . . meant originally only as the wise and legitimate government of the house for the common good of the whole family. The meaning of the term was then extended to the government of that great family, the State. To distinguish these two senses of the word, the latter is called *general* or *political* economy, and the former domestic or particular economy.[17]

The prebourgeois patriarchal differentiation of home and public life comes to take on particular classical *and* liberal definition for Rousseau, as we shall see shortly. He sets the stage for this analysis by first articulating the importance of patriarchal rule of the father in the home. Authority should not be divided equally between father and mother. Power within the family must be concentrated and complete. He backpedals from Locke, who assigned parental power to both mother and father in order to undermine the notion of absolutist divine-right rule. Rousseau seeks to reestablish the power of the father over the mother because he fears women's usurpation of men's freedom.

> In the family, it is clear, for several reasons which lie in its very nature, that the father ought to command. In the first place the authority ought not to be equally divided between father and mother; the government must be single, and in every division of opinion there must be one preponderant voice to decide.[18]

The father needs ultimate and sole control over the sexual independence of the wife in order to assert his control over the children. Rousseau reinforces the renewed eighteenth-century emphasis on female chastity and monogamy. "Besides, the husband ought to be able to superintend his wife's conduct, because it is of importance for him to be assured that the children, whom he is obliged to acknowledge and maintain, belong to no one but himself." [19]

Rousseau's differentiation between family and public life reflects very different concepts of political rule. Whereas the public order will be organized around freedom and independence of the general will, the family is organized around the concentration of authority in the father and the dependence of the woman. Female subordination underpins the developing market society and the freedom of the liberal democratic state. The control of women within the family by the man as husband and father is to create independence for men, not women, in the political society. In Rousseau's estimation, for men to be really independent, women have to be made dependent.

Hence, at the same time Rousseau presents the liberal formulation of the separateness of the family and the state in *The Social Contract*, in *Emile* and *La Nouvelle Heloise* and a *Letter to M. d'Alembert*, he must explicate their complementary nature because the family is actually the structuring base of the moral (political) society for him. He therefore asks: "Can devotion to the state exist apart from the love of those near and dear to us? Can Patriotism thrive except in the soil of that miniature fatherland, the home? Is it not the good father, who makes the good citizen?" [20] The critical purpose of the analysis to which we now turn is to examine how and why Rousseau believes that it is in controlling women's passions and directing them toward virtuous motherhood and wifehood that society can become moral. If women would just be good mothers, men could be good citizens. Mothers are women and citizens are men—free, independent, self-sufficient men. The family structure creates the moral society; it transforms civil society.

Rousseau's Ambivalence Toward Women

Both personal and cultural origins help explain Rousseau's thoughts about women. There is much about his private life that uncovers the personal reasons why he articulates patriarchal ideology so explicitly, although these reasons do not resolve the contradictions he poses between liberal individualism and patriarchal thought. This is because his patriarchal analysis is not merely his "personal" problem. Nevertheless, Rousseau's position on women is often explained as though it were. Victor Wexler attributes Rousseau's thoughts on women partially to his mother's death in childbirth with him, partially to a urinary problem, and partially to an abnormally formed penis. "His mother died within a week of his birth, and he was abandoned at the age of ten by an indifferent father. Moreover, he was the victim of a congenital urinary disorder, which forced him to undergo frequent and painful catheterization and he apparently had an abnormally formed penis, which made intercourse awkward." [21] These individual peculiarities alone do not explain Rousseau's ideas about women. But by examining Rousseau's private thoughts, we are able to view a particular instance of the relationship between the psychic and social dimensions of patriarchal ideology. [22]

For Rousseau the devil was a woman [23] supplied with an endless energy of will and always demanding obedience. When speaking of Madame de Luxembourg in *The Confessions of Jean Jacques Rousseau*, he speaks of his feelings of subjugation to women: "I was excessively afraid of Madame de Luxembourg . . . but she was said to be malignant and this in a woman of her rank made me tremble. I had scarcely seen her before I was subjugated." [24] Rousseau particularly feared the sexual subjugation to women that was the source of all submission for him. The subjugation of men to their sexual desires made them dependent and unfree. Men's freedom requires the containment of sexual passion.

Rousseau's feelings for Madame de Warens reflect much of the ambivalence he had toward sexuality and, hence, women. She took him in first as a son and then as a lover. His first sexual experience was with her, the woman he called "Mama." The death of his own mother, just hours after his birth, left him seeking a mother for most of his life. He saw in most women their potential as a mother. It could be argued that this is why he sent his five children, conceived with Therese, to foundling homes. He is the eternal child. Woman is the eternal mother.

In the early days with Madame de Warens, he finds that he is unable to desire her. I "loved her too much to desire her. . . ." [25] When he finally makes love with her, he feels as though he has committed incest. Sexual "possession" for Rousseau simultaneously means his own subjugation: ". . . what really attaches us to a woman is not so much sensual enjoyment as a certain pleasure in living beside her." [26] In this sense, Rousseau believes he is virtuous in regard to Madame de Warens because he thinks of her as a mother, a sister; a nonsexual, nonpassionate being.

He fears woman's sexuality and believes it heightens men's passions, as it does his. From early childhood, he identifies sexual arousal with the physical beatings given him by Mlle. Lambercier. Sexuality and power are completely intertwined for him: "But when in the end I was beaten I found the experience less dreadful in fact than in anticipation; and the very strange thing was that this punishment increased my affection for the inflicter."[27] These childish punishments determine Rousseau's attitudes toward sex by his own admission: "Who could have supposed that this childish punishment, received at the age of eight at the hands of a woman of thirty, would determine my tastes and desires, my passions, my very self for the rest of my life. . . ."[28] Even in adulthood, Rousseau cannot be sensually aroused without connecting the arousal to this situation; woman as batterer, woman as powerful. Rousseau cannot experience sensuality with a woman without subjugating himself to her. Here lies his fear of the loss of self and freedom. "My own childish tastes did not vanish, but became so intimately associated with those of maturity that, I could never, when sensually aroused, keep the two apart. This peculiarity, together with my natural timidity, has always made me very backward with women."[29]

The above discussion uncovers the personal, private origins of the *individual* who seeks to reformulate the patriarchal organization of society. However, the psychic structure of the individual is not separable from the cultural and political structure. In a sense they are a part of each other. Therefore, our discussion has only begun to explain how Rousseau as an individual can be so completely committed to freeing men from the dependence and constraint in their lives while reconstructing it for women. We need still to understand how this contradiction is politically formulated in the system of patriarchy and used by bourgeois society.

The Potential Power of Women

Rousseau's fear of women stems from his equation of woman with sexual passion. Nature has made woman the stimulator of men's passions and, hence, men must try to please women if their desires are to be met. Men, in this sense, are dependent on women, although Rousseau usually speaks of woman's dependence on men:

> . . . that the stronger party seems to be master, but is as a matter of fact *dependent on the weaker*, and that, not by any foolish custom of gallantry, nor yet by the magnanimity of the protector, but by an inexorable law of nature. *For nature has endowed woman with a power of stimulating man's passions in excess of man's power of satisfying those passions*, and has thus made him *dependent on her good will*, and compelled him in his turn to endeavour to please her, so that she may be willing to yield to his superior strength.[30]

He believes that women capitalize upon this basic control they have by trying to cultivate the moral ingredient of love as well as the physical.

> The physical part of love is that general desire which urges the sexes to union with each other. The moral part is that which determines and fixes this desire exclusively upon one particular object; or at least gives it a greater degree of energy toward the object thus preferred.[31]

Women cultivate the moral part of love to establish their supremacy. By their cleverness, they "put in power the sex which ought to obey."[32] Emanating from this control is woman's ability to manage men. They coyly use their gentleness, their kindness, and their tears[33] to get what they want. And as long as men are dependent on women for love, women will get what they want. Therefore, Rousseau will guard Emile from women's trickery. "The only snares from which I will guard him with my utmost care are the wiles of wanton women."[34] The sole protection that men have from women is to repress women's sexuality and their passionate selves. Make mothers and wives of them and they will excite men less. In discussing this issue he asks:

> . . . when you enter a woman's room what makes you think more highly of her, what makes you address her with more respect—to see her busy with feminine occupations, with her household duties, with her children's clothes about her, or to find her writing verses at her toilet table surrounded with pamphlets of every kind and with notes on tinted paper?[35]

It is the purpose of patriarchal ideology along with the structures of the family and the state to enforce the position of patriarchal motherhood on women. But this is always done in mystified form to try to cover up the relations of power that are really involved. Rousseau usually does not speak of the power of women, but rather their dependence on men. Instead of explaining how men need women in order to become the moral citizens he so desires, he presents woman as dependent on man:

> Men and women are made for each other, but their mutual dependence differs in degree; man is dependent on woman through his desires; woman is dependent on men through her desires and also through her needs; he could do without her better than she can do without him. She cannot fulfill her purpose in life without his aid, without his goodwill, without his respect. . . .[36]

But we shall see that for Rousseau, man *needs* woman to be virtuous. He *needs* her to be a mother and a wife, to nurture and care for him. Given the sexual structuring of society Rousseau puts forth, men *need* women. Without a mother and a wife, a man cannot be a citizen. Rousseau's citizen is not as free as he likes to present him. He *needs* the family, and the basis of the family is the mother.

The Virtuous Woman

The virtuous woman is the woman who can control her sexual passions and put this newly controlled energy to use. In *La Nouvelle Heloise,* Julie is to be modest and industrious. "Modesty and virtue were dear to me; I hoped to cherish them in a life of simplicity and industry." [37] In this novel written by Rousseau, Julie's passionate love for Saint-Preux in the end is controlled, and she devotes herself as a wife and mother to her husband Wolmar: "it is the result of an unparalleled victory. People stifle great passions; rarely do they purife them." [38] She becomes virtuous with this triumph over her passions; "that is a real triumph of virtue." [39] The moral woman is timid and chaste and modest.[40] She is defined by her duty. "But you, virtuous, and Christian woman, you who see your duty and respect it, you who know and follow rules other than public opinion, your foremost honor is that which your conscience gives you. . . ." [41]

Sophy, the woman who is to be educated to match the moral man Emile, is also educated to love virtue. "Sophy loves virtue. . . ." [42] Emile as well is educated to be the virtuous man who will be able to conquer his feelings and allow reason to prevail as long as Sophy remains virtuous. He will be free because he will be his own master: "He who can conquer his affections; for then he follows his reason, his conscience: he does his duty; he is his own master and nothing can turn him from the right way. . . . Now is the time for real freedom; learn to be your own master; control your heart, my Emile, and you will be virtuous." [43]

Romantic love represents artificial social relations for Rousseau. As such, it constructs false dependencies in men's lives. They become slaves to passion and, hence, women. This is why Rousseau structures the liberal patriarchal morality of his time around the law of duty and reason. This will breed virtue and with it freedom. Locke defines this freedom for the marketplace, whereas Rousseau sees it as important to define this law of reason for the sexual marketplace as well. The spirit of love must be sacrificed to duty.[44] The law of duty rather than passion must reign between men and women. "Chastity is sustained by itself; desires constantly repressed become accustomed to remaining at rest, and temptations are multiplied only by the habit of succumbing to them." [45] Duty wins out over passion as a theory of sexuality. This theme is continued as love and marriage are distinguished from each other. Love does not necessarily form a happy marriage as much as duty, virtue, and honor do.[46] Marriage enables two people to fulfill their duties to society and govern the house and care for the children; it is not an institution of sexual passion and love. "People do not marry in order to think exclusively of each other, but in order to fulfill the duties of civil society jointly, to govern the house prudently, to rear their children well."[47] Love represents uncontrolled passion, and women have the upper hand in this. Marriage is virtuous and dutiful and reasonable. Men have the upper hand here. They then can have their freedom as well.

Marriage requires chasteness because it is an inviolable contract.[48] Emile must therefore be educated in the "horrors of debauchery."[49] Chastity is part of virtue; it reflects the control of one's passions: ". . . on a desire for chastity depends health, strength, courage, virtue, love itself, and all that is truly good for man. . . ."[50] The virtuous woman is not only reasonable in sexual matters but also applies reasoned simplicity to her style of dress and her home as well: ". . . what a pleasant and affecting sight is that of a simple and well regulated house in which order, peace, and innocence prevail, in which without pomp, everything is assembled which is in conformity with the true end of man."[51] She does away with show; all that is in the house is useful. She will dress simply, not in excess. She will be useful and will learn the details of housekeeping and keeping accounts. "She has also studied all the details of house keeping; she understands cooking and cleaning, she knows the price of food, and also how to choose it; she can keep accounts accurately."[52] The virtuous woman adopts the liberal values of reason, simplicity, and usefulness as opposed to the opulence and idleness of the aristocracy. The liberal values of independence and personal freedom are not, however, extended to her. For the small number of women married to financiers, industrialists, merchants, doctors, clergy, or law clerks,[53] their homes become the center of activity for them. "To the bourgeois, domesticity or life *in the home* with his family had greater emotional significance than it did for the nobility."[54]

It is important to note that Rousseau's definition of woman in terms of these liberal values is rooted as much in the patriarchal forms of classical antiquity as it is in the new bourgeois relations of France. The patriarchal division of home and public life as female and male worlds, respectively, is utilized by him to set up his vision of the ideal family order. This conception is then reconceptualized in terms of the liberal values of usefulness, reason, and virtue. As we shall see, Wollstonecraft does not think it has been redefined fully enough, particularly in terms of woman's capacities for a rational and independent life.

The desire for this simplicity, virtue, and dutiful citizenry requires that society become more masculine and less feminine, more reasonable and less passionate. This is to be done by instituting the clear divisions of male and female worlds of ancient Greece. "When the Greek women married, they disappeared from public life; within the four walls of their home they devoted themselves to the care of their household and family. This is the mode of life prescribed for women alike by nature and reason." [55] Women are to devote themselves to their homes and the rearing of their families. Rousseau remembers fondly that these Greek women "gave birth to the healthiest, strongest, and best proportioned men who ever lived. . . ." [56]

The divisions between public and private life in Greek society were rigid. Women were relegated to the home and were allowed to make few appearances in public.

> Amongst all the ancient civilized peoples they led very retired lives; they appeared rarely in public; never with men, they did not go walking with them; they did not have the best places at the theatre; they did not put themselves on display; they were not even always permitted to go; and it is well known that there was a death penalty for those who dared to show themselves at the Olympic games. [57]

Within their homes, women had private apartments, which men never entered. When husbands entertained, women remained out of sight. "There was no common place of assembly for the two sexes; they did not pass the day together." [58] Rousseau envisions this period as a time of domestic peace and tranquility.

Rousseau wishes to reestablish the separate spheres of classical antiquity to aid in the development of the moral male citizen. A woman belongs in the private sphere of the home. "Whatever she may do, one feels that in public she is not in her place. . . ." [59] Women, according to Rousseau, have had too much effect on society already. "What fatal splendour has succeeded the Ancient Roman simplicity? What is this foreign language, this effeminacy of manners?" [60] He is unable to distinguish the course of history from the sexual character of that history. The problem with bourgeois society is that it is effeminate. "It is thus with man also; as he becomes sociable and a slave, he grows weak, timid, and servile; his effeminate way of life totally enervates his strength and courage." [61] The sexual character of society is reflected in luxury, falseness, and men's lack of freedom: ". . . it is necessary to abolish, even at court, the ordinary amusements of court, gambling, drama, comedy, opera; all that makes men effeminate; all that distracts them, isolates them, makes them forget their fatherland and their duty. . . ." [62]

The separation of the sexes is necessary, otherwise men will become like women—passionate and effeminate: ". . . for this weaker sex, not in the position to take on our way of life, which is too hard for it, forces us to take on its way, too soft for us; and no longer wishing to tolerate separation, unable to make themselves into men, the women make us into women."[63] This is what the men of Paris are to Rousseau—womanish and foppish. Hence, woman's effect on society must be controlled by limiting her sphere of activity, and she must help create the moral society from within that sphere. The moral woman is the mother in the home. And she will help create the moral society *for* men. "But if I add that there are no good morals (manners) for women outside of a withdrawn and domestic life; if I say that the peaceful care of the family and the home are their lot, that the dignity of their sex consists in modesty. . . ."[64]

A Patriarchal View of Motherhood

Julie's virtue triumphs when she is able to identify herself primarily as a wife and mother, and has repressed her passions for Saint-Preux. "The rank of wife and mother elevates my soul and sustains me against remorse for my former condition."[65] As a mother and wife she disassociates herself from romantic love and sensuality. Duty and obligation guide her; she is both close to nature and has transcended her natural passions. She represents, for Rousseau, the authentic self in this sense.[66] Her life is simple and controlled.

As a mother, woman nurtures. She cares for and nurses others, especially children and husbands. "The real nurse is the mother and the real teacher is the father."[67] As a wife, Sophy is trained to be the guardian of Emile. Hers is a labor of love according to Rousseau. It is her care that unites and preserves the family.

> The consequences of sex are wholly unlike for man and woman. The male is only a male now and again, the female is always a female, or at least all her youth; everything reminds her of her sex; the performance of her functions requires a special constitution. She needs care during pregnancy and freedom from work when her child is born; she must have a quiet, easy life while she nurses her children; . . . what loving care is required to preserve a united family! And there should be no question of virtue in all this, it must be a *labour of love*, without which the human race would be doomed to extinction.[68]

It is the mother who sustains the family: ". . . the right ordering of the family depends more upon her and she is usually fonder of her children."[69] It is she who transforms bourgeois civil society into a moral order.

Without a loving home, persons learn to think only of themselves. Woman as the mother and architect of the emotional life of the home begins with her nursing her own children. "But when mothers deign to nurse their own children, there will be a reform in morals; natural feeling will revive in every heart. . . ."[70] Rousseau's position on nursing mothers reflects the privileged-economic-class aspect of his discussion. Most women who sought wet nurses were women "in fulltime employment, particularly townswomen who worked full time in industry."[71] His conception of motherhood defines nursing *as* the central aspect of women's work; he conceives of women as having no other work. "These gentle mothers, having got rid of their babies, devote themselves gaily to the pleasures of the town."[72]

According to Judith Shklar, the child-centered family was first articulated in *Emile* and *La Nouvelle Heloise.*[73] As home life was defined around the mother-child relationship, a conception of childhood developed that reflected this. "Love childhood, indulge its sports, its pleasures, its delightful instincts . . . why rob these innocents of the joys which pass so quickly."[74] If children are to be defined as children, there must be mothers to care for them. "Mankind has its place in the sequence of things; childhood has its place in the sequence of human life; the man must be treated as a man and the child as a child. Give each his place, and keep him there."[75]

The woman who does not care for her children and her husband destroys the family. If she is faithless to her husband ". . . her crime is not infidelity but treason."[76] She maintains the familial order necessary for the political, public world. The private realm of the family is her domain. It is a "haven" from civil society, and is necessary to create the moral society. For Rousseau, these spheres are separate and equal. Each does its part to create the moral order. That this division between private and public life both reflects and constructs dependent and unequal relations is beyond his understanding. Patriarchy is understood as natural and therefore does not raise problems for his vision of the free, independent, and moral man. But the excesses of the bourgeois market create problems for his independent man. The market creates false dependencies between men *and disrupts the male-headed household of an agrarian subsistence economy.* It is for both these reasons that Rousseau criticizes the excesses of the bourgeois market and embraces a vision of a nonmarket society. Other times he envisions an ideal society of petit-bourgeois artisans. Both visions are to protect the patriarchal household for Rousseau.

The Embrace of Liberal Values

Rousseau reacted simultaneously to both the aristocratic and bourgeois qualities of eighteenth-century France. Feudalism, he felt, was an absurd and corrupt system.[77] In prescribing a government for Poland, Rousseau speaks of freeing their people, "to make the serfs who are to be freed worthy of liberty and capable of enduring it."[78] Presently "the nobles, who are everything; the burghers, who are nothing; and the peasants, who are less than nothing"[79] define the corrupt relations of Poland. Feudal society in transition is still corrupted by luxury. "In proportion, as arts and industry flourish, the despised husbandman, burdened with the taxes necessary for the support of luxury and condemned to pass his days between labour and hunger, forsakes his native field to seek in town the bread he ought to carry thither."[80]

These artificial relations of ascribed status even define the social life of Paris. "Merit is respected, I agree; but here the talents which lead to fame are not those which lead to fortune. . . ."[81] When Rousseau describes the ideal education of Emile, which will create the moral citizen, he indicts the shallowness of inherited rank and stresses the importance of industry rather than idleness. Instead of training Emile to be a lord or a marquis or a prince, "I want to give him a rank which he cannot lose, a rank which will always do him honour. . . ."[82] The civilized man is the bourgeois man defined as industrious, hard-working, and meritorious.[83] As the bourgeois man is, so Emile should be. "Emile is industrious, temperate, patient, steadfast, and full of courage."[84] He will be independent of others and they will be independent of him. "He thinks not of others but of himself, and prefers that others should do the same. He makes no claim upon them, and acknowledges no debt to them. He is alone in the midst of human society, he depends on himself alone, for he is all that a boy can be at his age."[85]

Given the nature of society, all men must work. Anyone who remains idle is a thief. The aristocracy was idle; the bourgeoisie is active.[86] Emile must thus be taught a trade, but he must not be an embroiderer or gilder like Locke's gentleman.[87] He must be taught an honest and useful trade: ". . . there can be no honesty without usefulness."[88] Part of this training will require that he become active and aggressive in the competitive nature of life. "He will have pride enough to wish to do well in everything that he undertakes, and even to wish to do it better than others; he will want to be the swiftest runner, the strongest wrestler. . . ."[89]

In this struggle to achieve, one's talents and one's merits take precedence over one's birthright and rank: ". . . the country in the world where merit is most respected is that which is best for you and that you only need to be known to be employed."[90] Rousseau discusses this question of rank vs. talent explicitly in La Nouvelle Heloise: ". . . I should be very sorry to have no other proof of my merit than the name of a man dead for five hundred years."[91] After Julie's father has refused Saint-Preux entry to their home, claiming that he lacks birthright and hence social understanding, his wife questions his judgment. "I did not think . . . that intelligence and merit might constitute reasons for exclusion from society. To whom, then, must we open your house, if talent and manners may not obtain admittance?"[92] The letters between Julie and Saint-Preux are a continual discussion of talent and merit. Julie laments to Saint-Preux that his "talents" are being ignored and wasted. She asks Saint-Preux to "try to revenge yourself for neglected merit."[93]

In the end, Rousseau wishes that men would ignore the forms and the artificiality that govern polite society. Simplicity is the key to virtue and individual freedom. Men must disengage themselves from the show and artifice of the aristocracy. Emile will have learned to ignore these things, which are merely for show. Furniture should be simple. Showy dress will be abandoned for its inconvenience.[94] Emile will come to despise useless things.[95] By doing so, he will have gained his liberty. He will be removed from the falsity of life, wherein lies much of men's dependence.

In his attempt to develop the possibility of liberty, Rousseau also articulates a theory of equality. He is distressed by the extremes of the very rich and the very poor and offers instead a theory of economic moderation—of the small propertied owner.

> I have already defined civil liberty by equality, we should understand, not that the degrees of power and riches are to be absolutely identical for everybody; but that power shall never be great enough for violence, and shall always be exercised by virtue of rank and law; and that, in respect of riches, no citizen shall ever be wealthy enough to buy another, and none poor enough to be forced to sell himself; which implies, on the part of great, moderation in goods and position, and, on the side of the common sort, moderation in avarice and covetousness.[96]

No one shall be rich enough to oppress another. Beggars and rich men alike will be done away with. Then there will be the possibility of economic independence—artisan production, independent commerce, and agricultural work.[97]

The Critique of the Bourgeois Market

Rousseau's *Emile* is a discussion about the education of a young boy for virtuous manhood. At the root of his virtue is an understanding of private property and its value. Because Rousseau considers private property the foundation of civil society, he wishes Emile be taught to respect it and cultivate it. Emile is therefore taught by his tutor to plant a set of beans and to water them and to watch them grow. Then he must be taught that the beans belong to him because of the labor that he has expended and the time he has spent. They are an expression of him and his individuality. "To explain what that word 'belong' means, I show him how he has given his time, his labour, and his trouble, his very self to it; that in this ground there is a part of himself which he can claim against all the world. . . ." [98]

Private property, however, must be limited. It should not rule society but should instead be controlled by public needs. Rousseau wishes that the state "owns everything, and for each individual to share in the common property only in proportion to his services." [99] If this formula were practiced, private property would not be destroyed, but it would be controlled; "to confine it within the narrowest possible limits; to give it a measure, a rule, a rein which will contain, direct, and subjugate it, and keep it ever subordinate to the public good." [100] This is the ideal that Rousseau maps out in the Constitution for Corsica. He is instead surrounded by the uncontrolled rule of private property and the inequalities it creates:

> . . . the origin of society and law, which bound new fetters on the poor, and gave new powers to the rich; which irretrievably destroyed natural liberty, eternally fixed the law of property and inequality, converted clever usurpation into unalterable right, and for the advantage of a few ambitious individuals, subjected all mankind to perpetual labour, slavery and wretchedness. [101]

The laborer becomes the dependent: ". . . it is impossible to make any man a slave unless he be first reduced to a situation in which he cannot do without the help of others. . . ." [102] The poor must be defended by the rich, and this becomes the purpose of a just government. However, "the greatest evil has already come about, when there are poor men to be defended, and rich men to be restrained." [103]

Rousseau criticizes bourgeois society because it is organized for the rich, not because it is organized around private property. He contends that the purpose of government should no longer merely be that of protecting property rights as it was for Locke. It now must protect the poor from the abuses of private property. "It is therefore one of the most important functions of government to prevent extreme inequality of fortunes; depriving all men of means to accumulate it; not by building hospitals for the poor, but by securing the citizens from becoming poor." [104] Taxes, according to Rousseau, can be used to create greater equality, to make more equitable the distribution of wealth. [105] Taxes should be used to limit luxury and useless professions. They should limit the very *aristocratic* or *idle* pleasures of the feudal past and the bourgeois future.

> Heavy taxes should be laid on servants in livery, on equipages, rich furniture, fine clothes, on spacious courts and gardens, on public entertainments of all kinds, on useless professions, such

> as dancers, singers, players and in a word, on all that
> multiplicity of objects of luxury, amusement, and idleness,
> which strikes the eyes of all, and can the less be hidden, as their
> whole purpose is to be seen, without which they would be
> useless. [106]

He wishes to curtail the excesses of the rich, who are corrupt and idle, and instead merge society into one middle class. He prefers to "bring all fortunes nearer to that middle condition which constitutes the genuine strength of the state." [107] "It is riches that corrupt men, and the rich are rightly the first to feel the defects of the only tool they know. Everything is ill-done for them, except what they do themselves, and they do next to nothing." [108] This attack on the rich is simultaneously one against the aristocracy and the sections of the developing bourgeoisie that mimic it. They are not totally distinct groups in France at this time, nor in Rousseau's discussion.

His vision of the just society requires a nonmarket economy. He embraces the artisan model as ideal. While writing on the economy of Poland, he describes agriculture, arts and crafts, and simplicity:

> . . . you must preserve and revive among your people simple
> customs and wholesome tastes, and a warlike spirit devoid of
> ambition; you must create courageous and unselfish souls;
> devote your people to agriculture and to the most necessary arts
> and crafts; you must make money contemptible and, if
> possible, useless, seeking and finding more powerful and
> reliable motives for the accomplishment of great deeds. [109]

When writing about Corsica, he advises that it should hold on to its rural origins as long as it can. It should only turn to industry and commerce when it must.

Rousseau is careful to point out that although it is important to reject the "idle arts," which cultivate nothing but luxury, it is necessary to support "those which are *useful* to agriculture and advantageous to human life. We have no need for wood-carvers and goldsmiths, but we do need carpenters and blacksmiths; we need weavers, good workers in woolens, not embroiderers or drawers of gold thread." [110] Rousseau supports the productive useful aspects of bourgeois society as he continues to condemn the idleness of the old aristocracy.

> Cities are useful in a country in so far as they foster commerce
> and manufacture; but they are harmful under the system we
> have adopted. Their inhabitants are either idlers or
> agriculturists. But tillage is always better performed by
> countrymen than by city-dwellers; and idleness is the source of
> all the vices which have thus far ravaged Corsica. The stupid

pride of the burghers serves only to debase and discourage the farm-worker.[111]

He maintains his criticism of money, commerce, industry, and luxury as a part of the market society. His ideal visions are of preindustrial society, of the artisans, of the nonmarket system. Money represents the negation of all these things to him, and the vision of independence he attributes to them. He asks the men of Poland to cultivate their fields rather than the market of money, hoping to show them "how important it is for a good economic system not to be a system of money and public finance." [112] An economy based on "natural" rather than "pecuniary" goods does not *depend* on trade, which subordinates the individual to the market.

His concern is not to ban the use of gold or silver but to make them less necessary, so that a person with none "can be poor without being a beggar." [113] Once again, Rousseau tries to limit the *excesses* of the market, as he wishes to control the *extremes* of private property relations. It is within the realm of these excesses and extremes that dependence is born. Money and hence the pursuit of profit represent this realm for Rousseau. "Financial systems make venal souls; and when profit is the only goal, it is always more profitable to be a rascal than to be an honest man. The use of money is devious and secret; it is destined for one thing and used for another." [114] Money makes the individual dependent on the market system. Independence is lost. "Money has never seemed to me as precious as people think it. Indeed it has never seemed to me very *useful*. For it has no value in itself and must be transformed to be enjoyed." [115] Rousseau criticizes money for not being useful in and of itself.[116] He is critiquing the epitome of the bourgeois market, money, according to the liberal value of "usefulness." The men who control money are not useful themselves either, as they try to covet more.

What is so interesting in Rousseau is that he criticizes the developing bourgeois market in terms of liberal values—independence, merit, usefulness. In this sense his articulation of liberalism is different from Locke's, which embraces both the new market and its values. Rousseau redefines the concepts of freedom and individualism that the new market relations have instigated and at the same time criticizes the excesses of the market that appear to reproduce the dependence, servility, and artificiality of the aristocracy, but this time in bourgeois form. "I love liberty, and I loath constraint, dependence, and all their kindred annoyances." [117] His attack is at one and the same time against the aristocracy and the new bourgeois market as they intersect in reproducing relations of economic dependence. The transitional nature of the French economy, as noted earlier, makes this critique all the more valid.

Rousseau's liberalism develops out of a more complicated critique than Locke's, which criticizes the aristocratic order and embraces the bourgeois. In trying to both protect and redefine the patriarchal family, Rousseau criticizes the bourgeois market for the false dependencies it creates among men. He also fears that it will release women from the controls within the patriarchal family. Hence his harkening back to classical Greece and its vision of family life. As he struggles to define freedom for men, he articulates a system of constraint for women that will aid men in their search for independence. Men, for Locke, have found their freedom in the bourgeois market. They have not for Rousseau, which forces him to search elsewhere. They must find it with the help of the family and the state. His preferred economic model of a society of petty craftsmen and farmers presupposes a particular form of patriarchy rooted in this economic mode. Rousseau prefers an economy based on small proprietors in order to ensure man's place as the head of the household. It is not clear what he fears most: the inequality of the economic market or the transition of the classical patriarchal family. Therefore, the economy, the family, and the state must combine for Rousseau to create independence and freedom for men—from women. Now that we have viewed Rousseau's theory of economic freedom, we need to examine the theory of political freedom he enlists to protect it.

Political Freedom

The new economic arrangements based on merit and the egalitarian spirit of commerce made the superiority of birth irrelevant [118] both economically and politically. Rousseau's vision of the preferred political community is organized around this new equality of merit.

> The fundamental law of your new constitution must be equality. Everything must be related to it, including even authority, which is established only to defend it. All should be equal by right of birth; the state should *grant no distinctions save for merit*, virtue and patriotic service; and these distinctions should be no more hereditary than are qualities on which they are based. [119]

This view, that people must be represented and be involved in the process of their rule, is rooted in Rousseau's unique conception of liberal individualism. It is this natural individual freedom and independence that he seeks to reestablish in his moral society. In order to do this, the egoism and dependence of civil society will have to be transformed by the state and the law. The *possibilities* of the individualism and independence of the bourgeois market must be protected by the state; otherwise the market of money and its resulting inequalities will destroy them.

Rousseau seeks to legitimate the authority of the state by requiring the participation of the citizenry.

> There is but one law which, from its nature, needs unanimous
> consent. This is the social compact; for civil association
> is the most voluntary of all acts. Every man being born free and
> his own master, no one, under any pretext whatsoever, can
> make any man subject without his consent. To decide that the
> son of a slave is born a slave is to decide that he is not born a
> man.[120]

The political authority of the state ultimately resides in its citizens.
Force does not create this right. "Let us admit that force does not create
right, and that we are obliged to obey only legitimate powers."[121] The
authority of the state resides instead in the way it promotes the individual's liberty. "What then is government? An intermediate body set
up between the subjects and the Sovereign, to secure their mutual correspondence shared with the execution of the laws and the maintenance
of liberty, both civil and political."[122]

With the rise of political society (the state), the individual loses
natural liberty (rule by strength) but gains civil liberty (rule by the
general will). Moral life becomes a possibility. The citizen also gains
proprietorship, which means one gains positive title rather than mere
possession based on force.[123] The moral society can be created if the
general will is fulfilled, because "while uniting himself with all, may
still obey himself alone, and remain as free as before."[124] This is Rousseau's attempt to deal politically with the question of the autonomy and
freedom of the individual. The individual must take part in the articulation of the general will, which is the collective will and hence part of *his*
will, in abstracted form. Henceforth, when one obeys the general will,
one is obeying oneself. The state is no longer ruling over citizens.
Hierarchical dependence is dismissed through the general will. The
independence of self is regained. Politics encompasses the *freedom* of
individual men. "Finally each man in giving himself to all, gives himself to nobody; and as there is no associate over which he does not
acquire the same rights as he yields others over himself, he gains an
equivalent for everything he loses, and an increase of force for the
preservation of what he has."[125] This model of independent and free
citizens becomes the political expression of the economic model of the
independent artisan and nonmarket society. It is to resolve the dilemma
between private and public life in that public life (general will) represents the private self but in a generalized form.

> There is often a great deal of difference between the will of all
> and the general will; the latter considers only the common
> interest while the former takes private interest into account,
> and is no more than a sum of particular wills: but take away
> from these same wills the pluses and minuses that cancel one

another, and the general will remains as the sum of the differences. [126]

The general will tries to reconcile private individual freedom with the public collective need. In the moral society, private individual life will not be totally differentiated from the public affairs of society. But Rousseau's concerns to integrate the private self and the public community operate alongside his acceptance of the developing bourgeois distinction of the family and the state, which builds on the preliberal patriarchal distinction between home life and public life. The use of this separation between private and public life stunts the possibilities of real independence and, hence, the possibilities for actualizing the general will.

Freedom, Independence, and the
Contradictions of Patriarchy

I have already shown that Rousseau does not believe the patriarchal statement that woman is dependent on man, but rather fears man's dependence on woman. He wishes to create her dependence because he knows it does not exist in the fashion that he presents it. I now want to argue that the contradictions between Rousseau's use of the patriarchal vision of the dependent woman and the independent man are irresolvable. His vision of the moral society collapses under the tension he creates.

Rousseau envisions the creation of a society that will respect the autonomy and freedom of individuals, and individuals are defined as men. He is interested in making the political economy more democratic for men while positing the patriarchal family and its inegalitarian relations at the base of this political economy for women. While Rousseau attacks the social inequalities that arise in society through the historical developments of agriculture, metallurgy, and the rise of private property because of the dependence they create, he condones the dependence of women on men. "Her dependence need not be made unpleasant, it is enough that she should realize that she is dependent." [127] The same theorist who articulates the ideas of autonomy and independence for men, embraces the ideas of connection and dependence for women. The contradictions involved here negate the possibilities of freedom for men and women alike.

Freedom for Rousseau means autonomy, radical self-independence, and self-sufficiency, which derive from his atomistic picture of the individual. However, his conception of the naturally free man falls into serious question if one posits his conception of the naturally dependent woman or his conception of the naturally passionate and powerful woman. How can man be absolutely free when freedom is defined as atomistic individualism, if woman is dependent on him? Or if he is naturally, sexually dependent on her? Woman's presence, let alone her dependence, negates atomistic autonomy. Dependence presupposes obligation and responsibility within a set of power relations rather than self-sufficiency and atomized independence.

> Let us conclude that wandering in the forests, without industry, without speech, without domicile, without war and without liaisons, with no need of his fellow men, likewise with no desire to harm them, perhaps never even recognizing anyone individually, savage man, subject to few passions and self-sufficient, had only the sentiments and intellect suited to that state; he felt only his true needs, saw only what he believed he had an interest to see; and his intelligence made no more progress than his vanity. If by chance he made some discovery, he was all the less able to communicate it because he had not recognized even his children. [128]

This description of radical autonomy precludes the relations of dependency of woman on man.

Rousseau has set up a model of individual freedom, meaning autonomy and independence in the state of nature, and tries to recreate this freedom by capturing it for his society of the social contract and general will. Women, as we have seen, are not a part of this vision of the responsible citizenry; but it is my argument that if the social contract were ever to envision the *real* autonomy of man, it would have to recognize the autonomy of woman. Rousseau has abstracted men from the relations with women, which is a part of his atomistic individualism, an abstraction in itself, and presented a vision of a moral political society as though it were and should be entirely male, supported by the private female familial structure.

Sexual Equality and the State of Nature

When Rousseau discusses men's freedom in the state of nature, we need to know if this statement includes women. Are women equally a part of the description of the natural freedom, autonomy, and near isolation from the needs of another as men are in the state of nature? Is Rousseau's use of the terms "man" and "men" generic? Are women part of the atomistic individual free life? Rousseau describes this state: ". . . it is impossible to enslave a man without first putting him in the position of being unable to do without another; a situation which, as it did not exist in the state of nature, leaves each man there free of the yoke, and renders vain the law of the stronger." [129] Within the state of nature, it is the physical needs of individuals that define human activity. This activity does not require the false dependencies that arise from artificial or social needs. To the degree that sexual needs are physical needs, they do not require an infringement upon men's or women's freedom in the state of nature.

> Hunger and other appetites making him experience by turns various manners of existing, there was one appetite that invited him to perpetuate his species; and this blind inclination devoid of any sentiment of the heart, produced only a purely animal act. This need satisfied, the two sexes no longer recognized each other, and even the child no longer meant anything to his mother as soon as he could do without her.[130]

According to Rousseau, then, the act of reproduction itself leaves men and women free of each other in the state of nature. Men and women in his description of the sex act are thus equal and equally free in the state of nature, although this clearly contradicts other strains of Rousseau's thoughts on sexuality. Childrearing itself appears to be limited and perfunctory. It is only with the progression of history that we have the development of the family and with it the artificial needs that arise.

> The first developments of the heart were the effect of a new situation, which united husbands and wives, fathers and children in a common habitation. The habit of living together gave rise to the sweetest sentiments known to men: conjugal love and paternal love. Each family became a little society all the better united benause reciprocal affection and freedom were its only bonds; and it was then that *the first difference was established in the way of life of the two sexes, which until this time had but one.*[131]

With the rise of the family the lives between the sexes become differentiated. According to Rousseau's discussion in "Discourse on the Origin and Foundations of Inequality Among Men," this differentiation is not part of the state of nature and in this sense not part of nature itself. It is a product of history. The position of woman as tied to the home and man as active in the public realm develops *through* history. "Women *became* more sedentary and grew accustomed to tend the hut and the children, while the man went to seek their common subsistence."[132] However, Rousseau chooses to treat the development of the family in history as natural, and he does this very clearly in *The Social Contract,* whereas the development of private property is seen as part of artificial history and therefore changeable. The process of history seems to begin with the development of the family as well as with the development of private property, although Rousseau does not connect the two processes nor does he say which came first. History becomes divided between the process of meeting natural needs and artificial needs. As such, the family becomes viewed as natural and necessary, private property as artificial and problematic, although both are developments in history.

Rousseau discusses the first division of labor as deriving from the establishment of individual households. Women tended the hut and men labored daily outside the hut for subsistence needs. The relationship remains an equal one, however, as each individual provides certain needs for both. Inequality arises only with the advent of private property, according to Rousseau. One would think that Rousseau's notion of private property as the source of inequality among men would point to the resulting equality between men and women. He then could understand that at this point, the man, in his work outside the home, gains property, which is not attached to the woman's work within the home. As a result, the woman is in the position of working outside the developing social network of property relations. Women's labor, which cannot appropriate any property, becomes valueless. But he does not see this. His analysis of the family lacks an understanding of the way it operates within the political economy. He rather reduces the history and the development of civil society to the developments leading up to the rise of private property, and the family becomes a static reality. Although Rousseau has elsewhere stated that the family was the first form of society, he now reduces civil society to its origins in private property. "The first person who, having fenced off a plot of ground, took it into his head to say *this is mine* and found people simple enough to believe him, was the true founder of civil society." [133]

The interesting point here is that Rousseau's political criticism is devoted to examining the artificial history constructed around the relations of property, and not the family. The family, in his discussions in *Emile*, is treated as a natural phenomenon as though defined in the state of nature, even though he has clearly stated in the "Discourse on the Origin and Foundations of Inequality Among Men" that it is a product of historical development. The sexual differentiation and inequality between man and woman is a major stabilizing force of the moral society for Rousseau, whereas, as noted above, he has stated this differentiation did not exist in nature. The contradictions are stark here because Rousseau makes clear that sex is not only undifferentiated but that it is not seen as either a natural or an aritificial inequality.

> I conceive of two sorts of inequality in the human species: one, which I call natural or physical, because it is established by nature and consists in the difference of ages, health, bodily strengths, and qualities of mind or soul; the other, which may be called moral or political equality, because it depends upon a sort of convention and is established, or at least authorized by

the consent of men. The latter consists in the different privileges
that some men enjoy to the prejudice of others, such as to be
rich, more honored, more. . . .[134]

Rousseau did not understand the role of the family and the sexual
dependency within it as part of the system of political inequality. His
basic understanding of inequality is tied to the notion of economic
dependence. "And what can be the chains of dependence among men
who possess nothing?"[135] He did not understand the chains of dependence between men and women as defining a problem of inequality.

Sexual Dependence and the Moral Society

In *Emile* we are presented with an education for a young boy,
Emile, and a young girl, Sophie, which will re-create the lost freedom of
their natural state. Nevertheless, we are met with the clear dilemma that
Emile's and Sophie's nature are said to be different and, as a result,
their education and training will have to be different as well. Whereas
Emile will have to be trained to reassert his independence, Sophie will
have to be taught (or retaught) dependence and passivity. Although the
nature of Emile coincides with the description of natural man in the
"Discourse on the Origin and Foundations of Inequality Among Men,"
Sophie's nature is not to be found there. Rather, we have a new construction of woman's nature that appears to be related to the discussion
of woman in the family rather than prefamilial (natural) woman. Rousseau collapses the two, and woman's nature becomes equated with
woman as she is in the patriarchally defined family. Sophie's nature is a
construction and description of femininity as it has been defined historically through the relations of the family. Rousseau has reified the patriarchal definition of the natural woman.

Rousseau designs the education of Emile so that he can recapture
his natural inclinations toward independence and free will. For men,
the transition from the state of nature to society has meant the shift from
freedom to dependency. Emile's education will have to counter this
tendency.

Sophie, as I have discussed, is reared to be a loving mother and
wife. Her very definition is in terms of others rather than an independent self. "The obedience and fidelity which she owes her children are
such natural and obvious consequences of her position that she cannot
sincerely refuse her consent to the sensibility which guides her, nor can
she mistake her duty unless her inclinations are already corrupted."[136]
Woman is seen as nonautonomous. Woman as a mother must be provided with a wage earner, her husband. By definition, this arrangement—which Rousseau often terms "complimentation"—defines
woman as an economic dependent, which negates her freedom, and

defines man as the income provider, which negates man's freedom as well, because freedom requires self-sufficiency and autonomy, not obligation and financial responsibility.[137]

> Rousseau claims there are two kinds of dependence: The first on things, which is that of Nature; the second on men, which is the effect of society. The former, being non-moral, does not destroy liberty nor give rise to vices: the latter, being unnatural, produces a rich crop: the relation of master and slave depraves both. . . .[138]

Yet he defines the dependence of women on men, which is a dependence on others, as natural and necessary. To the degree he does so, he never chooses to describe the relation between men and women as one of inequality. It rather is necessary and natural. Although men and women are different, this does not connote inequality in the "abstracted" discussions of Rousseau. Rousseau has no foundation to stand on when he declares that the *natural* disposition of women is to serve men because he has already argued the basic likeness of men and women in the state of nature. Sex is also not listed as a source of differentiation or inequality. And all natural inequalities are said to be quite unimportant in the state of nature. Nevertheless, Rousseau states: "Woman was made especially to please man; if the latter must please her in turn, it is a less direct necessity; . . . This is not the law of love, I grant; but it is the law of nature, which is antecedent even to love." [139] Rousseau does not acknowledge the conflict within his writing nor does he try to explain or justify it. He further states in *Emile* that "there is no sort of parity between man and woman as to the importance of sex." [140] This also negates the conception of radical freedom that existed in the state of nature described by Rousseau himself.

These statements raise questions about the validity of Rousseau's initial conception of the radically autonomous individual. This vision of absolute autonomy is at the base of the conflict he poses between individual autonomy and social community. Rousseau denies the validity of this picture of absolute self-sufficiency in his conception of the relationship between men and women as it is discussed in *Emile* and the general will in *The Social Contract*. The problem is that he does not recognize that he is describing utterly patriarchically defined social relationships for women, not natural ones. As a result, he defines the role of women as natural and inevitable rather than historical, societal, and political.

Rousseau is often unable to distinguish between the natural and the artificial in terms of the capacities and needs of women. And he is also unable to distinguish between the artificial relations of dependence that occur as a result of male/female relations, although he is acutely aware of the artificial dependence created by excessive inequality in property relations between men. Given his initial view of the autonomous atomized individual, he assumes all social relations are artificial. And yet the relations of male/female life are not understood as such by him.

The interesting point that Rousseau fails to acknowledge is that the very meeting of the needs of subsistence (food, shelter, and clothing) necessitates others. He therefore cannot distinguish between the social relations of *dependence* and *interdependence*. Social interdependence, which negates the view of atomized individuals and the ideology of liberal individualism by definition, recognizes the need of others without envisioning a loss of freedom or an acceptance of power relations. Rousseau did not understand this, and social life itself becomes a problem because individuals lose their freedom in it. Yet it is not the need of others that creates dependence in and of itself, but rather the relations of sexual and economic class domination.

Rousseau embraced the family and the sexual division of society within it as natural and necessary for the moral society. The moral society was to have free men, although some would be freer than others. Women were not defined in terms of their freedom but in terms of their nature, and this conception has been constructed haphazardly and contradictorily. Women's nature seems to be only what society needs her to be—a mother and wife. Rousseau in this sense accepted the existing definition of woman and the relations of dependence that are a part of it. As such, he stands as a protector of patriarchal society and the property values that are part of its connected existence.

He declares that there are no significant natural inequalities between the sexes, but structures society completely in terms of these so-called natural differences between men and women. He says he is committed to changing the artificial inequalities of society, but creates the greatest artificial distinction of all—separate spheres for men and women. Clearly, this is a restricted notion of the individualist freedom Rousseau cares so much for. And if this freedom does not encompass women, can it *effectively* apply to men? Either the self-sufficient autonomous individual is a liberal fallacy or the view of woman as naturally dependent on man is wrong. One need not accept either view to understand that both visions cannot *logically* be embraced within one theory. Rousseau tries, but, in the end, merely mirrors for us the internal contradictions between the ideology of liberal individualism and patriarchal society. If one's notion of freedom does not take into account human interconnectedness, how can it ever attempt to deal with the social reality of human existence? When persons' needs for one other are not recognized, as in the ideology of liberal individualism, human relations become defined in terms of dependence; and for Rousseau, the dependence is structured particularly along sex lines. In the end, Rousseau uses the ideology of liberal individualism to protect the social relations of patriarchy.

NOTES

1. Most studies of Jean Jacques Rousseau in political philosophy ignore the patriarchal bias of his thought. See William Bluhm, *Theories of the Political System* (Englewood Cliffs, N.J.: Prentice-Hall, 1965); Maurice Cranston and Richard Peters, *Hobbes & Rousseau* (New York: Doubleday Anchor, 1972); Andrew Hacker, *Political Theory: Philosophy, Ideology, Science* (Don Mills, Ont., Canada: Macmillan, 1961); John Plamenetz, *Man & Society*, vol. 1, *Machiavelli Through Rousseau* (New York: McGraw-Hill, 1963); George Sabine, *A History of Political Theory* (New York: Holt, Rinehart and Winston, 1937); Leo Strauss and Joseph Cropsey, *History of Political Philosophy* (New York: Rand McNally, 1969). Some exceptions to this treatment are Marshall Berman, *The Politics of Authenticity* (New York: Atheneum, 1970); Ron Christenson, "The Political Theory of Male Chauvinism: J. J. Rousseau's Paradigm," *Midwest Quarterly* 13 (1972); Eva Figes, *Patriarchal Attitudes* (Greenwich, Conn.: Fawcett, 1970); Kate Millett, *Sexual Politics* (New York: Doubleday, 1970); Susan Moller Okin, *Women in Western Political Thought* (Princeton: Princeton University Press, 1979); Judith Shklar, *Men and Citizens: A Study of Rousseau's Social Theory* (London: Cambridge University Press, 1969); and Victor Wexler, " 'Made for Man's Delight': Rousseau as Antifeminist," *American Historical Review* 81 (April 1976).

2. William Blanchard, *Rousseau and the Spirit in Revolt* (Ann Arbor: University of Michigan Press, 1967), p. 110. Also see Jean Jacques Rousseau, "Letter to M. d'Alembert on the Theatre" in *Politics and the Arts*, ed. Allan Bloom (Ithaca: Cornell University Press, 1960).

3. Jean Jacques Rousseau, *Emile* (London: J. M. Dent and Sons, 1911), p. 437.

4. Jean Jacques Rousseau, *La Nouvelle Heloise, Julie, or the New Eloise* (University Park: Pennsylvania State University Press, 1968).

5. Robert Forster and Orest Ranum, eds., *Rural Society in France* (Baltimore: Johns Hopkins University Press, 1977), p. 50.

6. Olwen Hufton, "Women and the Family Economy in Eighteenth-Century France," *French Historical Studies* 9, no. 1 (Spring 1975): 1. For further discussion of this economic period, see Elinor Barber, *The Bourgeoisie in Eighteenth-Century France* (Princeton:

Princeton University Press, 1955); and Henri Sée, *Economic and Social Conditions in France During the Eighteenth Century* (New York: Crofts, 1935).

7. Hufton, *French Historical Studies*, p. 2.

8. Ibid., p. 11.

9. Ibid.

10. Barber, *Bourgeoisie in Eighteenth-Century France*, p. 20.

11. Eileen Power, *Medieval Women*, ed. M. M. Postan (New York: Cambridge University Press, 1975), p. 9.

12. J. J. Rousseau, "The Social Contract," in *The Social Contract and Discourses*, ed. G. D. H. Cole (New York: Dutton, 1950), p. 4.

13. Ibid., p. 5.

14. Rousseau, "A Discourse on Political Economy," in Cole, *The Social Contract and Discourses*, p. 285.

15. Ibid., p. 288.

16. For a fuller discussion of the differentiation between the state and the family in bourgeois society, see Karl Marx, "On the Jewish Question," in *Writings of the Young Marx on Philosophy and Society*, ed. Loyd Easton and Kurt Guddat (New York: Anchor, 1967).

17. Rousseau, "A Discourse on Political Economy," p. 285.

18. Ibid., p. 286.

19. Ibid., p. 287.

20. Rousseau, *Emile*, p. 326.

21. Wexler, "Made for Man's Delight," p. 282.

22. For a discussion of the particular process of psychic (unconscious) transmission and socialization that is learned at the level of individual experience but expresses dominant sociocultural relations, see Nancy Chodorow, "Feminism and Difference: Gender, Relation, and Difference in Psychoanalytic Perspective," *Socialist Review* 46, vol. 9, no. 4 (July–August, 1979): 51–71; idem, *The Reproduction of Mothering, Psychoanalysis and the Sociology of Gender* (Berkeley: University of California Press, 1978); Dorothy Dinnerstein, *The Mermaid and the Minotaur, Sexual Arrangements and Human Malaise* (New York: Harper Colophon, 1977); Jane Flax, "The Conflict Between Nurturance and Autonomy in Mother-Daughter Relationships and within Feminism," *Feminist Studies* 4, no. 4 (June 1978): 171–89; and Michael Foucault, *The History of Sexuality* (New York: Pantheon, 1978).

23. Blanchard, *Spirit in Revolt*, p. 249.

24. J. J. Rousseau, *The Confessions of Jean Jacques Rousseau* (New York: Brentano's, 1928), 2:812.

25. J. J. Rousseau, *The Confessions of Jean Jacques Rousseau*, ed. J. M. Cohen (London: Penguin, 1953), p. 188.

26. Ibid., p. 303.

27. Ibid., p. 25.

28. Ibid., p. 26.

29. Ibid., p. 27.

30. Rousseau, *Emile*, p. 323 (italics mine).

31. Rousseau, "A Discourse on the Origin of Inequality," in Cole, *The Social Contract and Discourses*, p. 228.

32. Ibid.

33. Rousseau, *Emile*, p. 370.

34. Ibid., p. 208.

35. Ibid., p. 372.

36. Ibid., p. 328.

37. Rousseau, *La Nouvelle Heloise, Julie, or the New Eloise*, p. 32.

38. Ibid., p. 393.

39. Ibid.

40. Rousseau, "Letter to M. d'Alembert on the Theatre," p. 87.

41. Rousseau, *La Nouvelle Heloise*, p. 37.

42. Rousseau, *Emile*, p. 359.

43. Ibid., p. 408.

44. Shklar, *Men and Citizens*, p. 138.

45. Rousseau, *La Nouvelle Heloise*, p. 223.

46. Ibid., 261.

47. Ibid.

48. Rousseau, *Emile*, p. 289.

49. Ibid.

50. Ibid.

51. Rousseau, *La Nouvelle Heloise*, p. 301.

52. Rousseau, *Emile*, p. 357.

53. Barber, *Bourgeoisie in Eighteenth-Century France*, p. 20.

54. Ibid., p. 79.

55. Rousseau, *Emile*, p. 330.

56. Ibid.

57. Rousseau, "Letter to M. d'Alembert on the Theatre," p. 89.

58. Ibid. For a detailed discussion of women in classical antiquity, see Sarah Pomeroy, *Goddesses, Whores, Wives and Slaves, Women in Classical Antiquity* (New York: Schocken, 1975).

59. Rousseau, "Letter to M. d'Alembert on the Theatre," p. 88.

60. Rousseau, "A Discourse on the Moral Effects of the Arts and Sciences," in Cole, *The Social Contract and Discourses*, p. 156.

61. Rousseau, "A Discourse on the Origin of Inequality," p. 206.

62. J. J. Rousseau, "Considerations on the Government of Poland," in *Political Writings*, ed. F. M. Watkins (London: Nelson and Sons, 1953), p. 171.

63. Rousseau, "Letter to M. d'Alembert on the Theatre," p. 100.

64. Ibid., pp. 82–83.

65. Rousseau, *La Nouvelle Heloise*, p. 276.

66. See Berman, *Politics of Authenticity*, for a discussion of the question of authenticity in Rousseau.

67. Rousseau, *Emile*, p. 16.

68. Ibid., p. 324 (italics mine).

69. Ibid., p. 5, n. 1.

70. Ibid., p. 13.

71. Hufton, "Women and Family Economy," p. 12.

72. Rousseau, *Emile*, p. 11.

73. Shklar, *Men and Citizens*, p. 24.

74. Rousseau, *Emile*, p. 43. See Phillippe Aries, *Centuries of Childhood; A Social History of Family Life* (New York: Knopf, 1962), for a discussion of the new conception of childhood that emerges with the eighteenth-century ideology of motherhood. Isaac Kramnick, in "Children's Literature and Bourgeois Ideology: Observations on Culture and Industrial Capitalism in the Later Eighteenth Century," *English Politics and Culture from Puritanism to Enlightenment,* ed. Perez Zagorin (Berkeley: University of California Press, forthcoming), discusses the literature which develops in this period specifically for children.

75. Ibid., p. 44.

76. Ibid., p. 325.

77. Rousseau, "The Social Contract," p. 10.

78. Rousseau, "Considerations on the Government of Poland," p. 186.

79. Ibid., p. 183.

80. Rousseau, "A Discourse on the Origin of Inequality," p. 280.

81. Rousseau, *La Nouvelle Heloise*, p. 210.

82. Rousseau, *Emile*, p. 158.

83. The discussion here does not preclude Rousseau's classicism. His concerns with usefulness, freedom, and individualism are partially rooted in his classical visions of Sparta and Athens, but I argue they become reformulated in light of the bourgeois market. See Shklar, *Men and Citizens*.

84. Rousseau, *Emile*, p. 170.

85. Ibid.

86. Ibid., p. 158.

87. Ibid., p. 160.

88. Ibid.

89. Ibid., p. 304.

90. Rousseau, *La Nouvelle Heloise*, p. 208.

91. Ibid., p. 139.

92. Ibid., p. 142.

93. Ibid., p. 189.

94. Rousseau, *Emile*, p. 314.

95. Ibid., p. 161.

96. Rousseau, "The Social Contract," p. 50.

97. Louis Althusser, *Politics and History* (London: New Left Books, 1972), p. 159.

98. Rousseau, *Emile*, p. 62.

99. J. J. Rousseau, "Constitutional Project for Corsica," in Watkins, *Political Writings*, p. 317.

100. Ibid.

101. Rousseau, "A Discourse on the Origin of Inequality," p. 252.

102. Ibid., p. 233.

103. Rousseau, "A Discourse on Political Economy," p. 306.

104. Ibid.

105. Ibid., p. 324.

106. Ibid., p. 328.

107. Ibid., p. 329.

108. Rousseau, *Emile*, p. 24.

109. Rousseau, "Considerations on the Government of Poland," p. 225.

110. Rousseau, "Constitutional Project for Corsica," p. 311.

111. Ibid., p. 290.

112. Rousseau, "Considerations on the Government of Poland," p. 230.

113. Ibid.

114. Ibid., p. 226.

115. Rousseau, in Cohen, *The Confessions of Jean Jacques Rousseau*, p. 44.

116. For a more developed discussion of the use of money in the bourgeois market, see Karl Marx, *Capital*, vol. 1, ed. Frederick Engels (New York: International Publishers, 1967); and *The Grundrisse*, trans. Martin Nicolaus (London: New Left Review, 1973).

117. Rousseau, in Brentano's *The Confessions of Jean Jacques Rousseau* 1:54.

118. Barber, *Bourgeoisie in Eighteenth-Century France*, p. 41.

119. Rousseau, "Constitutional Project for Corsica," p. 289 (italics mine).

120. Rousseau, "The Social Contract," p. 105.

121. Ibid., p. 7.

122. Ibid., p. 55.

123. Ibid., p. 19.

124. Ibid., p. 14.

125. Ibid.

126. Ibid., p. 26.

127. Rousseau, *Emile*, p. 334.

128. J. J. Rousseau, "Discourse on the Origin and Foundations of Inequality Among Men," in *The First and Second Discourses*, ed. Roger Masters (New York: St. Martin's, 1964), p. 137.

129. Ibid., p. 140.

130. Ibid., p. 142.

131. Ibid., p. 147 (italics mine).

132. Ibid.

133. Ibid., p. 141.

134. Ibid., p. 101.

135. Ibid., p. 139.

136. J. J. Rousseau, *Emile, Julie and Other Writings* (New York: Barrons, 1964), p. 230.

137. Although the general will and the social contract recognize the connection and obligation which exist between individuals, they do so from the vantage point of the radical autonomy of the individual.

138. Rousseau, *Emile, Julie and Other Writings*, p. 92.

139. Ibid., p. 218.

140. Ibid.

5

Mary Wollstonecraft:
The Feminist Embrace and
Criticism of Liberalism

Mary Wollstonecraft[1] (1759–97) continues the critique of aristocratic rule that Locke and Rousseau began, but this time on behalf of women. Locke assumed that women would continue to be limited by their sexual status, whereas Rousseau articulated in specific terms why this should be so. Wollstonecraft, as we shall see, questions the male bias of their conceptions of rationality and citizenship and, instead, seeks to open this world of industrious, useful, active persons to women by extending equality of opportunity to them. "Let not men in the pride of power, use the same arguments that tyrannic kings and venal ministers have used, and fallaciously assert that woman ought to be subjected because she has always been so."[2] Wollstonecraft, although included in eighteenth-century radical circles in England, stood apart from the male radicals in that she specifically wished to open up the new freedoms of bourgeois society to women. Their "dissenting" voices, on the whole, did not extend to this realm.[3]

I want to explore how Wollstonecraft's support of the new bourgeois order and the adoption of its liberal political values helps highlight woman's oppression for her and lay the basis for her feminist political philosophy. Because she applauds the liberal values of economic independence, individual achievement and usefulness, and because as a woman she is unable to achieve these, she is committed to extending the newly won rights of the middle-class man to the middle-class woman.[4] Wollstonecraft represents, as Margaret George has noted in *One Woman's Situation*, "a remarkable and open account of female response to the exhortation and promises of liberal individualism, of one woman's demand for equal opportunity for self-creation."[5]

This liberal model of the rational, self-determining individual, which Wollstonecraft adopts from Locke, is the progressive core that initiates her feminist claim that woman (as an individual) is a rational being. This vision stands in stark contrast with the prevailing religious views of women. It openly contradicts Rousseau's model of woman discussed in the previous chapter. As such, Wollstonecraft must stand outside the confines of existing patriarchal theory to make her feminist claims. Yet Wollstonecraft's radical claims on behalf of women are in the end limited by the liberal individualist constructs of eighteenth-century thought. As we shall see, liberalism, as an ideology, is only able to define an area of public life in which woman would theoretically have unlimited opportunity without providing her access to it.

In order to fully understand Wollstonecraft's political priorities and to assess the relationship she posits between liberalism and feminism, her liberal challenge to aristocratic and male rule must be explored. In this discussion, I clarify Wollstonecraft's conception of the new middle-class woman and this woman's relationship to marriage and motherhood. I then assess the limits of the liberal theory of rationality and independence in relation to Wollstonecraft's understanding of the patriarchal underpinnings of bourgeois society. This is a difficult issue to resolve in Wollstonecraft's writing because she is contradictory in her treatment of what she terms the sexual caste[6] nature of society. I argue that Wollstonecraft's writing contains two different *and* contradictory models of citizenship and political participation for women. Her first model of participation for women is defined by an equality in the public sphere *like* men's. The second model defines woman's participation as a rational wife and mother. Actually, both visions are contradicted by her occasional insights regarding the necessity for women's economic independence.

Although Wollstonecraft develops a conception of "rational" motherhood that sounds very similar to Rousseau's, it is motivated by significantly different concerns. Wollstonecraft articulates this vision for women in her attempt to argue against their economic dependence and uneducated existence. Although she argues against both conditions, she ultimately lays claim only to one: woman's right to an education. Liberal ideology provides her with the necessary tools to claim woman's potential for rationality but not to dismantle the patriarchal relations that necessitate her sexual and economic dependence.

The Liberal Assault Against Aristocratic and Male Right

In much the same way Locke and Rousseau do, Wollstonecraft celebrates the importance of individual freedom and equality of opportunity. She uses the idea of liberal individualism to criticize the privilege of rank inherent in station, unrelated to individual merit. The aristocrat owes nothing to *himself* for his privilege. Wollstonecraft asks on what basis *he* claims *his* privilege: ". . . is it by knowledge, by industry, by patience, by self-denial, or by virtue of any kind?" [7] Deference to rank is not based on reason but on blind faith and reverence for birth. This rule of hereditary property and honor is the enemy of progress for Wollstonecraft.[8] In her *A Vindication of the Rights of Men*, she criticizes Burke for his love of antiquity: ". . . rank throws a graceful veil over vices that degrade humanity. . . ." [9] Inequality of rank stifles progress in that it ignores the rational capacities of the individual. "Inequality of rank must ever impede the growth of virtue, by vitiating the mind that submits or domineers." [10] There can be true happiness and virtue only among equals. Given this, people should be able to remake the laws of society according to their reason because the "original contract" is not perfect and should be reconstructed for each "epoch of civilization." [11] Wollstonecraft, like Locke before her, argues for the importance of the political contract between equal individuals.

In *A Vindication of the Rights of Woman* she argues that only by there being more opportunities for equality in society will it progress in virtue, and she now extends the necessity of this equality to women. Wollstonecraft applies these demands of the bourgeois revolution of reason, personal independence, and individual freedom to women on the same basis that they were extended to men. Men have obeyed kings, and it has not meant that they are inferior as men. Women obey men, and it does not mean that they are their inferiors as women. "The *divine right* of husbands, like the divine rights of kings, may, it is to be hoped, in this enlightened age, be contested without danger. . . ." [12] The law of reason itself requires the end of divine-right rule *and* the rule of men, for Wollstonecraft. She has taken Locke and Rousseau's vision of the rational and autonomous *man* and extended it to woman. "A king is always a king—and a woman always a woman: his authority and her sex ever stand between them and rational converse." [13] Woman should only submit to reason and never to a man simply because of his (ascribed) rank as man.[14] The fact that woman's submission to man exists is no justification for it, according to Wollstonecraft. Citizen rights, based on the law of reason, destroy the privilege of rank, and it is used to destroy woman's submission to man, on these same terms.

> Men have submitted to superior strength to enjoy with impunity the pleasure of the moment—women have only done the same, and therefore till it is proved that the courtier, who servilely resigns the birthright of a man, is not a moral agent, it cannot be demonstrated that woman is essentially inferior to man because she has always been subjugated.[15]

In the same way that Wollstonecraft understood that rule by rank no longer fit the political needs of bourgeois society and liberal ideology, she believed that the *basis* of this rule between men and women—the ascribed sexual inferiority of women—had to be challenged and denied. Only when women are ruled by reason will they be able to share in the equality of opportunities in society. Using the liberal theory of rationality that encompasses the self-determined individual, Wollstonecraft challenges the male bias of its definition.[16]

A sound politics for Wollstonecraft will include woman in the rational citizenry. It will not exclude her by assigning her an ascribed position of dependence due to her sex. If woman must defer to man because of his sexual station, rather than because of any particular individual ability or achievement, woman is debased by the vulgarities of an outmoded relation. Woman remains excluded from the new liberal citizen rights and the advance in human freedom they connote. "Love, in their bosoms taking place of every nobler passion, their sole ambition is to be fair, to raise emotion instead of inspiring respect; and this ignoble desire, like the servility in absolute monarchies, destroys all strength of character."[17]

Not only are the relations of submission between man and woman parallel to those of hierarchical relations of rank in feudal society, but the outmoded characteristics of the aristocracy are the ones society chooses to reproduce in its women. Wollstonecraft, while commenting on Adam Smith's description of the aristocracy in his *Theory of Moral Sentiments,* says his description of the rich could easily be the description of the female sex.[18] The aristocracy were not to be strong. They were to be patient and docile, good-humored and not intellectual. The same is true of women. "Women, commonly called Ladies, are not to be contradicted in company, are not allowed to exert any manual strength; and from them the negative virtues only are expected, when any virtues are expected, patience, docility, good-humour, and flexibility; virtues incompatible with any vigorous exertion of intellect."[19]

The picture of the ideal woman in bourgeois society is based on the anachronistic model of the aristocratic woman. Wollstonecraft believes and argues that just as bourgeois society requires the recognition of the male citizen whose privilege is based on his individual merit and usefulness, it also needs a woman representative of these values. Woman, like man, needs to be active, alert, virtuous, independent, and free. Instead, woman in bourgeois society is defined by the outmoded model of the aristocracy. "In short, women in general, as well as the rich of both sexes, have acquired all the follies and vices of civilization, and missed the useful fruit."[20] The accepted model of woman pictures her as necessarily ignorant and frivolous. "Women are everywhere in this deplorable state; for, in order to preserve their innocence, as ignorance is courteously termed, truth is hidden from them, and they are made to assume an artificial character before their faculties have acquired any strength."[21]

According to Wollstonecraft, the idealization of woman as weak and frail is debilitating to the progress of society because it keeps women passive and ignorant. She believes that women are degraded by the trivial attention they are paid by men, who believe they are superior to women anyway. "It is not condescension to bow to an inferior."[22] Women's charms are used to protect themselves in their submission to men. This female etiquette reflects women's artificial, not their true nature: ". . . but what a different aspect it assumes when it is the submissive demeanour of dependence, the support of weakness that loves, because it wants protection; and is forbearing, because it must silently endure injuries; smiling under the lash at which it dare not snarl."[23]

Wollstonecraft wants to replace this outdated picture of woman as dependent and submissive with the model of the autonomous, independent, rational self. In short, she wants to claim the ideology of liberal individualism for women.

Woman, Rationality, and Bourgeois Society

Given this view of individualism, woman must cultivate her reason. This will develop in her an independent character: ". . . bow to the authority of reason, instead of being the *modest* slaves of opinion."[24] Using Locke's argument that the rational man no longer needs the arbitrary rule of kings, Wollstonecraft argues that the rational woman no longer needs the arbitrary rule of men.

"Ignorance is a frail base for virtue."[25] Wollstonecraft wants to redefine woman's capacity for virtue in terms of her capacity for reason. To do this, women will have to be educated to their real capacities: ". . . I may be allowed to infer that reason is absolutely necessary to enable a woman to perform any duty properly and I must again repeat, that sensibility is not reason."[26] As she states in *Thoughts on the Education of Daughters*, "I wish them to be taught to think. . . ."[27] In order for this to happen, Wollstonecraft pleads in her *A Vindication of the Rights of Woman* for woman's education. But her meaning of education is not limited to the notion of formal education. She readily understands that people are educated to a large degree "by the opinions and manners of the society they live in."[28] Therefore, a change in education necessitates a change in society itself. Education in its broadest meaning will involve a "revolution in female manners."[29]

Women must acquire strength of body and mind. They must see through the language of femininity and understand that it requires an outmoded life for them. If women choose to be virtuous, they will have to base their life in reasoned activity. In this sense, Wollstonecraft agrees with Rousseau's vision that "in fact, it is a farce to call any being virtuous whose virtues do not result from the exercise of its own reason."[30] She specifically extends this view of virtue to women, while Rousseau applies it only to men. By extending this vision to women,

Wollstonecraft is directly at odds with Rousseau's vision of woman and the liberal partriarchal conception of citizen. Rousseau directs women to their artificial sensibilities and believes they were born to "feel" rather than think. He negates the very independence Wollstonecraft so desperately wishes to cultivate in woman. He wishes woman to be dependent and submissive. Wollstonecraft refers to Rousseau's conception of woman: ". . . that she should be governed by fear to exercise her *natural* cunning and made a coquettish slave in order to render her a more alluring object of desire, a sweeter companion to man, whenever he chooses to relax himself."[31]

Because Rousseau believes woman is the one with sexual passion and has a greater facility to excite desire,[32] she must be taught restraint and the ability to submit to the will of others.[33] Wollstonecraft rejects this notion because it counters the development of woman's individuality and independence. Nevertheless, Wollstonecraft embraces Rousseau's commitments to independence and freedom and parts with him only on his exclusion of women from this life of independence. In a letter written to her sister Everina, she discusses Rousseau's works in positive terms, although she had not read Book V—which presents his conception of women's education—at the time she wrote this letter. "I am now reading Rousseau's *Emile*, and love his paradoxes."[34] Rousseau and Wollstonecraft share the ideal of the freely independent individual, but as a feminist, she challenges the patriarchal view that woman cannot be a part of this ideal. The question remains as to how much Wollstonecraft understood the constraints of this patriarchal view.

It is the rational woman who can be independent, and Wollstonecraft means an economic and emotional independence from men. She also means an independence represented by the liberal individualist conception of the rational self. Right use of reason makes us independent.[35] It is this conception of freedom that defines Wollstonecraft's yearnings. "I long for a little peace and *independence!* Every obligation we receive from our fellow creatures is a new shackle, takes from our native freedom, and debases the mind, makes us mere earthworms—I am not fond of grovelling."[36]

She is plagued in her own life by the struggle for economic and emotional independence with limited options open to her to earn a living. This is complicated for her as well by her two sisters, Eliza and Everina, who remained dependent on her for most of their lives. Her conception of desired freedom reflects this. She defines it as a freedom from the dependence of others on you. This is translated for the condition of most women as meaning *freedom from* dependence on another. It is the classic notion of liberal individualism, but this time it is used to challenge woman's dependence on men. If woman was only specifically allowed to develop her skills, rather than her beauty, she would be able to create this independence: ". . . but were it not for mistaken notions of beauty, women would acquire sufficient means to enable them to earn their own subsistence, the true definition of independence. . . ."[37]

Although Wollstonecraft is not consistent in her demand for woman's economic independence, it is a repeated insight in her writing. This quality of woman's independence is necessitated by the new bourgeois marketplace; Wollstonecraft wants women to be able to take care of themselves.[38] "Independence I have long considered as the grand blessing of life, the basis of every virtue—and independence I will ever secure by contracting my wants, though I were to live on a barren heath."[39] Woman must actively partake in "the race of life" if she is to be a useful member of society. She needs the freedom that will accord her this; she must earn her own subsistence and become independent of men for this to happen.

In the above discussion, woman's independence from man is defined in the same way as one man must be independent of another man. There is no sense of how woman must be independent of man, in a way different from the way he is independent of other men: ". . . in the same manner I mean, to prevent misconstruction, as one man is independent of another."[40] There is no recognition of the specific relations that exist between men and women other than the economic dependence of the market. Women need to be free and independent of men in the same way men are independent of one another. This liberal conception of independent selves seems to be sex neutral. Wollstonecraft knows that it is not, and at the same time often acts as if it were. In other words, she extends the ideology of liberal individualism to women (because she knows women are excluded from it) and at the same time argues that women need independence from men, just as men need independence for themselves. This is a paradigm case of the problem Wollstonecraft is unable to resolve. She extends the view of independence to women, but does not recognize that in order to extend this view in a meaningful way, she must account for the fact that men and women have different starting places in the "race of life." Of course, Wollstonecraft knows this. It is what she is writing about. But she is unable to deal in the sexually specific way her own understanding demands; to develop a theory of individual independence for women that involves a different conception than what is involved in one *man* being free of another.

Even though Wollstonecraft is unable to successfully develop such a theory, I think that this is where her commitments are. A look at the changing nature of women's lives in eighteenth-century England explains why she was so concerned with finding a place for the somewhat displaced married middle-class woman. What was happening to this woman? Who was she? How was it that this woman, of this new economic class, could define a life of usefulness and independence for herself?

Woman, Work, and Economic Class in Eighteenth-Century England

Wollstonecraft's concern to find a useful place for the married middle-class woman in eighteenth-century England was not a reaction based solely on the patriarchal ideology of the time found in the literature, advice manuals, and religious doctrines. She was also reacting to the changing nature of work in women's lives. Eighteenth-century England can be characterized by the continued redefinition and separation of the home and the market and the home and the activity of wage labor.[41] Industrial capitalism, to the extent it existed, was restructuring the married woman's life in all economic classes. She had been a part of the productive life of society in domestic industry and now was increasingly becoming an economic dependent. The work that had been in the home and had been woman's was gradually being removed from the home and taken from her. The distinction between public and private life was being more fully delineated in relationship to this separation. As we saw in the chapter on Locke, as early as the seventeenth century, there were clear consequences for women resulting from the capitalist market: ". . . the wife of the prosperous capitalist tended to become idle, the wife of the skilled journeyman lost her economic independence and became his unpaid domestic servant, while the wives of the wage earners were driven into the sweated industries of that period."[42]

These consequences escalated in the eighteenth century. Although England was predominantly rural throughout this century, and domestic and family industry continued, married women were losing their place within the work system wherever domestic industry was under assault. Wives of wealthy farmers, who had taken an active part in the managing of their households, were beginning to hand these responsibilities over to servants. On the other hand, wives of tenant farmers, who had lost their land due to the enclosure acts, lost their base for productive work, which they once had in their homes.[43] This is further complicated by the fact that domestic industry was slowly disappearing as a source of work for them also.

Ivy Pinchbeck argues further that although marriage for many women had once meant a business partnership in agriculture and domestic industry, it no longer did.[44] Unless women became wage earners, they became economically dependent on their husbands. And even those married women who did work as day laborers in agriculture to "supplement" the wages of their husbands, because they could no longer do this by working at home, found it harder and harder to find work by the end of the eighteenth century. By the end of the nineteenth century, women had almost ceased to be employed as wage earners in agriculture.[45] As men's wages rose and the use of machinery was introduced further, women's labor continued to be dispensed with. "With the improvement in the pecuniary position of the male labourer and these changes in agriculture, women day labourers as a class disappeared."[46] These same changes in work affected women servants in husbandry: women workers who worked outdoors in agriculture weeding, feeding stock, pulling horses at the plough.[47] This work came to a close for women before the end of the nineteenth century.

The seventeenth and eighteenth centuries represent the enormous shifting of woman from her role in domestic industry and agriculture to what Wollstonecraft saw as a nonproductive role in the capitalist economy. Woman's nonproductive role has two different meanings for her. It can mean that women are economically dependent, and it can also mean that they are no longer "useful." The problem for Wollstonecraft is that she often confuses these two meanings by collapsing them into one. Then she wrongly assumes that woman's personal independence will flow from her usefulness[48] as a mother. This confusion is troublesome, as we shall see, because, in fact, as patriarchy takes on its particular bourgeois coloration, women become controlled more as economic dependents in marriage and motherhood. The view of the married woman as idle ignores women who are involved in the wage-labor sphere as workers, just as it does not point to the important new work of domestic home life as work. This domestic work had not existed, as such, before. It was not possible for women to involve themselves in the work of the home and family until it became differentiated from the rest of work. "Now that the home was no longer a workshop, many women were able, for the first time in the history of the industrial classes, to devote their energies to the business of home making and the care of their children, who stood to benefit greatly by the changed home conditions."[49] But this new work is not recognized as such by the patriarchal ideology, which presents married women as idle. Instead, the married woman is presented as a nonworking dependent.

Wollstonecraft is reacting to the process, described above, which is creating the enforced idleness of women who had previously been integrally involved in the productive economic activity of society. These women are defined in terms of their lack of economic independence and are disproportionately the women of the middle ranks. They are the women who would have been the wives of wealthy farmers. They had been the women of domestic industry. They were also the Elizabethan gentlewomen. As Alice Clark notes: "How rapidly the active, hardy life of the Elizabethan gentlewoman was being transformed into the idleness and dependence which has characterized the lady of a later age. . . ." [50]

These women of the "middle ranks" are the women Wollstonecraft says she is particularly concerned with. In the eighteenth century, they are the wives of the trading classes. They are the wives and daughters of new money rather than titled families. They are the women who have become economically dependent on their husbands. Although Wollstonecraft is usually interpreted as a theorist of the middle-class woman, and although she herself writes of the women of the middle ranks, her analysis of the economic dependence of woman on man has applicability for the entire sexual class of women. She occasionally alludes to this herself.

The economic and social position of most women declined in the seventeenth and eighteenth centuries. This reality affected working-class *and* middle-class women. Married women of both classes were losing their earlier productive position in domestic, home industry. The point here is that Wollstonecraft's arguments about the economic independence of women have broader implications for women as a sexual class than even she supposes. The condition of a poor tenant farmer's wife [51] and a middle-class woman are alike in that they are both losing a particular position as women in the eighteenth century and different in the way economic class cuts through this similarity. This difference can be seen most starkly between the married middle-class woman and the unmarried working-class woman.

Almost anticipating Victorian ideology, Wollstonecraft fears the developing notion of the middle-class woman as idle and decorative. Wollstonecraft's feminism originates here with her demand that the new woman of bourgeois society shall be "useful." It is her fear of the middle-class woman's dependence—economic, emotional, sexual—in all its complexity that lays the basis for her feminist theory.

According to Miriam Brody Kramnick, *A Vindication of the Rights of Woman* serves to "provide for the rehabilitation of the socially useless middle-class woman." [52] Wollstonecraft is concerned with the middle-class woman because she is in the most natural state, or can be. The "ladies" of the aristocracy, on the other hand, are defined by the artificiality of their station. "They live only to amuse themselves. . . ." [53] Although the woman of the middle class is currently directed toward her artificial senses and is groomed in sensibilities rather than reason, there is nothing inherent in her station that requires this. She can be directed toward her "abilities" as are men in the middle ranks: ". . . the middle rank contains the most virtue and abilities. . . ." [54] And one's ability is what counts for the middle class. Women and men alike can be a part of the independence the middle class enjoys. But at present, woman is reared away from developing individual abilities and is relegated to a noncreative, nonproductive existence.

> Men have thus, in one station, at least an opportunity of exerting themselves with dignity, and of rising by the exertions which really improve a rational creature; but the whole female sex are, till their character is formed, in the same condition as the rich; for they are born, if I now speak of a state of civilization, with certain sexual privileges, and whilst they are gratuitously granted them, few will ever think of works superogation, to obtain the esteem of a small number of superior people.[55]

Women need the same opportunities as men to develop their rational and deliberative capacities, and then their "talents can thrive" in the middle class. Therefore, when Wollstonecraft demands that woman be understood as a rational creature, she is at the same time arguing for woman's place as a productive, useful member of the middle class. She is challenging the male bias of the bourgeois revolution as much as she is applauding its commitment to independence and rationality. What she does not understand is that the middle-class woman, defined as economically dependent, encompasses a much larger group than the male middle class and is a group defined not only by the relations of bourgeois society but by the relations of patriarchy as well.

The Middle-Class Woman as Mother

Wollstonecraft's concern with defining a useful role for the new middle-class married woman pushes her to reconceptualize the relationship between the liberal values of independence and rationality and motherhood itself. Unlike Rousseau, she wishes to extend these values to women in their activity as mothers, rather than differentiate between them as incompatible. Although women are responsible for childrearing, they are least fit for it, in her mind, due to their present temperament and sensibility. They have not been allowed to develop the reasoning capacities necessary for motherhood in bourgeois society. One must be acquainted with a life of independence and self-assertion in order to rear one's child for it. "The management of the temper, the first, and most important branch of education, requires the sober steady eye of reason; a plan of conduct equally distant from tyranny and indulgence. . . ."[56]

Wollstonecraft's position is that if mothers are to rear their children adequately for the new society, they must take an active part in it. The dependent mother purported by Rousseau is as outdated as the aristocratic order is. "To be a good mother—a woman must have sense, and that independence of mind which few women possess who are taught to depend entirely on their husbands."[57] Woman's contribution will be to educate the new generation of children, and for this she must be educated herself: ". . . the ignorance that incapacitates them must be contrary to the order of things. And I contend that their minds can take in much more, and ought to do so, or they will never become sensible mothers."[58]

Wollstonecraft adopts the patriarchal definition of woman as the rearer of children but wishes to redefine it to reflect the new relations of bourgeois freedom and liberal individualism. In this sense, we no longer have the passive, submissive, dependent, ignorant mother, according to Wollstonecraft, but rather the active, independent, educated mother.

It is interesting that although she defines motherhood as middle-class woman's work and sees this as a central part of middle-class married women's lives, she never explicitly calls this the new work of women. Nor does she address the issue that, *as mothers*, married women are economically dependent on their husbands because there is no direct payment for this work. This would have been a challenge to patriarchy she was unable to make. In the early eighteenth century, the *idea* of motherhood as a vocation was brand new. It would take another century of living out this image before middle-class women understood the gap between it and political equality.

Wollstonecraft is aware of the emotional and economic dependence involved in marriage. Strongly critical of marriage, she did not marry until late in life. In her novel *Mary*, the heroine hopes for a world where there is no marriage: ". . . she thought she was hastening to that world *where there is neither marrying*, nor giving in marriage."[59] Wollstonecraft often describes the woman in marriage as a slave who puts up with abuse and disregard. "The common run of men have such an ignoble way of thinking, that, if they debauch their hearts, and prostitute their persons, following perhaps a gust of inebriation, they suppose the wife, slave rather, whom they maintain has no right to complain. . . ."[60] In a letter written in 1795 to an anonymous recipient, she speaks of being insulted by the thought that she would prostitute herself in marriage for a maintenance because of the poverty she suffered at the moment. In referring to her marriage to Godwin, she states: ". . . what I call an insult, is the bare supposition that I could for a moment think of *prostituting* my person for a maintenance. . . ."[61] In a letter to Jane Arden in 1782, she speaks of how quickly married life can become empty: "The joy, and all that is certainly over by this time, and all the raptures have subsided . . . and all the rest of the delights of matrimony are past and gone and have left no traces behind them, except disgust:—I hope I am mistaken, but this is the fate of most married pairs."[62]

The obedience required in marriage, along with the authority of the man, limits the capacities for rationality as well as independence in women. "Still, highly as I respect marriage, as the foundation of almost every social virtue, I cannot avoid feeling the most lively compassion for those unfortunate females who are broken off from society. . . ."[63] Marriage becomes legal prostitution for Wollstonecraft, because women look to men for their economic support.

In her novel *Maria*, marriage is described as an insufferable bondage,[64] and in a private correspondence, she refers to it as matrimonial despotism.[65] Wollstonecraft wanted to remove the relations of dependence of woman on man in both marriage and motherhood. She understood much of the dependence in marriage as economic and did not discuss how motherhood itself creates part of this dependence in marriage. Actually, the problem partially stems from Wollstonecraft's many meanings of the term *dependent*. Often she means that woman is dependent on man given her ascribed sexual status. It is Wollstonecraft's conception of woman's assignment to a sexual-caste, termed here a sexual-class, that allows her to challenge the male bias of the liberal society of which she was a part. But Wollstonecraft also demands woman's independence in order that she be a rational mother. The independence in this case is neither sexual nor economic. It is a liberal patriarchal version of independence.

Wollstonecraft is trying to define the bourgeois woman like the bourgeois man, but the starting point of woman is different from man because of the precapitalist system of patriarchy, which defines woman as a mother and excludes her from "the race of life." Wollstonecraft's adoption of liberal individualism helps her focus on women's exclusion but cannot help her understand how the sexual-class system structures the exclusion and opportunities of women differently than men.

> But I still insist, that not only the virtue but the knowledge of the two sexes should be the same in nature, if not in degree, and that women, considered not only as moral, but rational creatures, ought to endeavour to acquire human virtues (or perfections) by the *same* means as men. . . .[66]

As a result, she leaves monogamous marriage and dependent motherhood intact while defining their practice in particular bourgeois form. She has extended the bourgeois revolution to married women, especially the middle-class woman, in its patriarchal form by redefining motherhood as a rational purposive activity. Woman's sphere is still that of wife and mother, but Wollstonecraft has questioned the dependent relations that have defined it previously. She thinks she understands exactly what Rousseau did not: that woman defined as a dependent and emotional being stands counter to the new needs of bourgeois society, which necessitate a new conception of wife and mother. Although she is partially correct in that woman's role remained to be fully recognized by bourgeois society, she does not see how this patriarchal view of woman supports male bourgeois society. Her liberal individualist stance pushes her to her feminist claims, but it cannot help her understand why patriarchy continues to demand a dependence of woman, even in its bourgeois form. This dilemma is reflected in the theory of liberal feminism as well as in Wollstonecraft's personal life.

Liberalism vs. Radical Feminism

Wollstonecraft is so persuaded by the democratic qualities of the bourgeois revolution compared with the hierarchy of ascribed rank of the aristocracy that she uses the democratic promises of liberal society to criticize the false dependence created between rich and poor. She speaks in favor of the French Revolution on this basis: "The rich have for ages tyrannized over the poor teaching them how to act when possessed of power, and now must feel the consequence." [67] She speaks of the need of greater economic equality in her *A Vindication of the Rights of Men*: "Why cannot large estates be divided into small farms? These dwellings would indeed grace our land. Why are huge forests still allowed to stretch out with idle pomp and all the indolence of Eastern grandeur? Why does the brown waste meet the traveller's view, when men want work?" [68] She writes of the laboring poor as having no security or rest from their oppression: ". . . it is only the property of the rich that is secure; the man who lives by the sweat of his brow has no asylum from oppression. . . ." [69] The economic oppression of wage laborers disturbs Wollstonecraft and exemplifies woman's particular drudgery in this system.

> They are not *termed* slaves; yet a man may strike a man with impunity because he pays him wages; though these wages are so low that necessity must teach them to pilfer, whilst servility renders them false and boorish. Still the men stand up for the dignity of man, by oppressing the women. The most menial and even laborious offices are therefore left to these poor drudges. [70]

Wollstonecraft does not limit her criticism of wealth to that due to rank. She warns the Americans and the English that the tyranny of wealth can be worse than that of rank. "England and America owe their liberty to commerce, which created a new species of power to undermine the feudal system. But let them beware of the consequence; the tyranny of wealth is still more galling and debasing than that of rank." [71]

Because of this critical analysis of rank and privilege, it is hard to figure out Wollstonecraft's position on economic class and sexual class inequities. On the one hand, she seems to be committed to an egalitarian society, so much so that she believes schools should integrate rich and poor, boy and girl. "But nothing of this kind could occur in an elementary-day school where boys and girls, the rich and poor, should meet together." [72] At the same time, Wollstonecraft speaks of separating out those who seem destined for domestic and mechanical employment and trades. She also distinguishes between boys and girls for their "necessary" training.

> After the age of nine, girls and boys intended for domestic
> employments, or mechanical trades, ought to be removed to
> other schools, and receive instruction in some measure
> appropriated to the destination of each individual, the two
> sexes being still together in the morning; but in the afternoon
> the girls should attend a school where plain-work,
> mantua-making, millinery, etc., would be their employment. [73]

There does appear to be a ranking according to "talent" as well as sex alongside her commitments to equality. This becomes clearer as she discusses the necessity of destroying ranks while also discussing the necessity of nursemaids. It seems that there will still be a servant class, particularly in the domestic realm. As such, Wollstonecraft's feminism seems to offer little to the wage-laboring woman. One is left with the question whether the equality of opportunity she discusses applies only to the middle-class woman who can afford servants. She asks for the equality of women with men on the same terms that the demands were made for men against ascribed privilege. By adopting this position, however, she at the same time adopts the patriarchal structuring of liberalism that has been carried over from feudalism. Her acceptance of the separate spheres of male and female life, which defines the woman as mother in relation to the rearing of children within a new economy and which does not recognize the activity as economically rewarding and socially necessary, relegates woman to the very economic dependence she so feared and hated. The middle-class woman is still a sexual dependent in a society valuing independence. There is no way for Wollstonecraft to see this to the degree she is involved in the process of trying to extend this liberal individualist view of the world to women in the first place. Her liberal *feminist* position is at the same time both radical in its claims for women and yet patriarchal. As a feminist she stands in conflict with the status quo by demanding "rights" for women as a sexual class, although she never uses the term *sexual class* and only infrequently writes of women as a sexual caste. She also embraces (unknowingly, in a sense) the basic political structuring of the status quo via her theory of motherhood. [74]

The interesting point here is that Wollstonecraft's radical feminist demands for women as a sexual class are limited by the liberal individualism of eighteenth-century England and at the same time are indebted to it. Her concern with individual independence for women pushes her toward feminism. Yet this feminism is limited by Wollstonecraft's acceptance of the liberal patriarchal world view, which distinguishes and separates male and female life—public and private. As a result, she demands equality for women on the basis that the more rational and independent the mother, the better the citizen. "Would men but generously snap our chains and be content with rational fellowship instead of slavish obedience, they would find us more observant daughters, more affectionate sisters, more faithful wives, more reasonable mothers—in a word, better citizens."[75] What is lost here is Wollstonecraft's own understanding that woman's "miserable situation" derives from the fact that she is a woman—a member of a sexual class. Her liberal individualism overwhelms her insights into the reality of the sexual-class system. Women appear to float in the air by themselves as autonomous individuals rather than as a part of a sexual class.

Nevertheless, Wollstonecraft's radical feminist insights of woman as a sexual class should not be lost to the reader. They abound in her writing. She repeatedly discusses the domestic tyranny of women by their fathers, husbands, brothers, and sons. At one point, she writes that the only respite a woman has falls *between* the rule of her father and her husband: ". . . but there is a kind of interregnum between the reign of the father and husband, which is the only period of freedom and pleasure that the women enjoy."[76]

Wollstonecraft understands that all women share a like oppression, and in this sense are differentiated from men: ". . . I think the female world oppressed. . . ."[77] Women are degraded *as* a sex.[78] She believes that woman has always been a slave or a despot.[79] This is true of women of all classes: ". . . and women of all classes, naturally square their behavior to gratify the taste by which they obtain pleasure and power."[80] In her novel *Maria,* she states that woman's misery and oppression arise from the "partial laws" and customs of society.[81] In this novel, she describes the oppression of women in the varied forms of economic dependence, poverty, sexual abuse, madness, and the problems of abortion.

Her discussion of woman's subjugation recognizes its sexual-class character. "I speak of the improvement and emancipation of the whole sex, for I know that the behavior of a few women, who by accident, or following a strong bent of nature, have acquired a portion of knowledge superior to that of the rest of their sex has often been overbearing. . . ."[82] Woman's sexual-class position puts her in a different and unequal position to men. Men of genius, for Wollstonecraft, are of an economic class that women have never been allowed to enter. "I speak of bodies of men, and that men of genius and talents have started out of class, in which women have never yet been placed."[83] She clearly rejects the liberal individualist position that some women have been able to attain educations for themselves in this instance. These women are the exceptions to Wollstonecraft and not too much should be made of them. She is concerned with the case of most women: ". . . I shall not lay any great stress on the example of a few women who, from having received a masculine education, have acquired courage and resolution. . . ."[84]

Nothing less than a "revolution in female manners"[85] will restore women their lost dignity. As a woman and a mother, she laments the present sexual-class status of women.

> You know that as a female I am particularly attached to her—I feel more than a mother's fondness and anxiety, when I reflect on the dependent and oppressed state of her sex. I dread lest she should be forced to sacrifice her heart to her principles, or principles to her heart. With trembling hand I shall cultivate sensibility, and cherish delicacy of sentiment, lest whilst I lend fresh blushes to the rose, I sharpen the thorns that will wound the breast I would fain guard—I dread to unfold her mind, lest it should render her unfit for the world she is to inhabit—Hapless woman! What a fate is thine![86]

This sexual-class analysis leads Wollstonecraft to state that she pleads for her sex and not for herself.[87] And it is her commitment to the liberal notions of independence and rationality that highlight for her the "miserable situation of woman." Her feminist claims are excluded by the liberal theory of her day: woman's class oppression by men stands outside the bourgeois critique of the old aristocratic order. Liberal ideology recognizes individuals. It does not recognize economic and sexual classes as constituting the power relations of society.

Nevertheless, Wollstonecraft tries to blend her feminism and her liberalism, and what we see is an uneasy mix. In the end, independence becomes reduced to its liberal individualist formulation, and there is no particular quality of it that derives from woman's sexual-class oppression. Allow women to become rational, and they will become good mothers as well. They will also become good citizens: ". . . make women rational creatures, and free citizens, and they will quickly become good wives, and mothers; that is—if men do not neglect their duties of husbands and fathers."[88] Here Wollstonecraft slips into an acceptance of the precapitalist patriarchal remnants that equate the activities of the home with the activities of the state. Wollstonecraft argues that women will be good mothers as they are allowed to be good citizens. She assumes an *equality* between the realm of the family and the economy—between the mother and the citizen—and, as such, argues for an equality between men and women, which is actually negated by the growing differentiation of these two realms. The equality of opportunity she wishes to establish between men and women is limited by the *ascribed* status woman still has within the system of patriarchy. The problem here is that Wollstonecraft wants to end the exclusion of women, as a sexual class, from the newly won liberal rights of the individual, and yet she relegates woman to the ascribed sexual position of mother. She seeks a vision of woman as a rational being, while employing the division between sexual spheres that relegates woman to the emotional and passionate sphere of life. Her demand to "rationalize" motherhood involves a radical attack on feudal patriarchal ideology, but it also reestablishes motherhood as woman's sphere in particularly bourgeois form.

In analyzing these tensions in Wollstonecraft's work, it becomes clear that she personally understood sexual-class oppression even if her political analysis in *A Vindication of the Rights of Woman* does not address it as such. Within her private, personal life, she tried unsuccessfully to live the life of independence. She tried to commit suicide twice as a result of an intense and long love affair with Imlay, rejected the notion of marriage for herself until late in life, had a child out of wedlock by choice, supported her two sisters for most of their lives, and died in childbirth. Although she never allowed her marriage to Godwin to alter her sense of independence, her earlier tortuous love affair with Imlay denies the remotest notion of independence. She describes her desperate unhappiness to Imlay as she tells him she is going to commit suicide.

> I would encounter a thousand deaths, rather than a night like the last. Your treatment has thrown my mind into a state of chaos; yet I am serene. I go to find comfort, and my only fear is that my poor body will be insulted by an endeavour to recall my hated existence. But I shall plunge into the Thames where there is the least chance of my being snatched from the death I seek.[89]

She could as well be defiant and angry.

> You tell me that my letters torture you; I will not describe the effects yours have on me . . . certainly you are right; our minds are not congenial. I have lived in an ideal world, and fostered sentiments that you do not comprehend—or you would not treat me thus. I am not, I will not be, merely an object of compassion—a clog, however light, to teize you.[90]

Wollstonecraft suffered in her intimate life from the sexual-class system that defined her options and her subjugation. She seems to speak of her vulnerability as a woman most openly in her private letters and in her novels, which she hoped women would read. *A Vindication of the Rights of Woman* was written to men as much if not more so than to women, and here her political argument appears to be qualified by the liberal individualism of the time. She does not distinguish woman's oppression from man's but, rather, draws parallels between the system of woman's sexual subjugation and the dependence of men in aristocratic society and says women need to be independent of men in the same way men are independent of other men. We have lost the radical feminist sexual-class analysis of woman's oppression here. As a result, Wollstonecraft has redefined the aristocratic, patriarchal vision of woman and replaced it with a liberal patriarchal view: the rational, independent mother and wife. Her updating of the vision of woman in bourgeois society rehabilitates the married woman, especially the middle-class woman of eighteenth-century England, as a useful member of society. What Wollstonecraft remains unaware of is that this woman is not independent in any of the ways Wollstonecraft deems necessary. She has wrongly reduced her understanding of woman's sex-class oppression to the fact that women have been excluded from the newly gained rights of the bourgeois revolution. Therefore the question remains, How central is the sex-class nature of woman's oppression to her exclusion from public life and to the maintenance of bourgeois society and liberal ideology?

We get only glimmerings of an answer to this question from Wollstonecraft herself. She believed that women needed equality with men, not power over them. However, it is not clear whether Wollstonecraft thought men would still have power over women. "Indeed the word masculine is only a bugbear: there is little reason to fear that women will acquire too much courage or fortitude; for their apparent inferiority with respect to bodily strength, must render them, in some degree, dependent on men in the various relations of life. . . ."[91] Men and women are unequal only in terms of the law of nature. Woman is generally inferior in strength to the man.[92] But it is only this natural superiority of man that Wollstonecraft grants men. Nevertheless, one wonders what the contours of this natural superiority are. The attack on the economic class hierarchy of the aristocratic world does not seem to be carried over to the attack on the sexual hierarchy of patriarchy within the family. Instead, she argues for women's equality of opportunity within the context of the division of home life and political life that is proceeding forward in her century. She articulates the separate but equal doctrine in terms of the division of public and private life, home and work, male and female.

Given such a formulation, "opportunities" between men and women, not their starting points in the "race of life," are to be equal. Their spheres of activity and, hence, their starting points will actually be quite different. The patriarchal underpinnings of liberal society require this unequal differentiation between men and women. Liberal theory can, however, promise the equality of opportunities to these different spheres. We are therefore left with the question whether it is possible to create equality of opportunity between men and women (which is the liberal feminist formulation) without creating equality between men and women (which is the radical feminist formulation) that is neither liberal nor patriarchal in formulation, in that it destroys ascribed sexual status. Although Wollstonecraft poses this problem for us, she is unable to answer it.

NOTES

1. For biographical information, see Eleanor Flexner, *Mary Wollstonecraft* (New York: Coward, McCann and Geoghegan, 1972); Margaret George, *One Woman's Situation, A Study of Mary Wollstonecraft* (Urbana: University of Illinois Press, 1970); Edna Nixon, *Mary Wollstonecraft, Her Life and Times* (London: Dent and Sons, 1971); Claire Tomalin, *The Life and Death of Mary Wollstonecraft* (New York: Harcourt Brace Jovanovich, 1974); Ralph Wardle, *Mary Wollstonecraft, A Critical Biography* (Lincoln: University of Nebraska Press, 1951); and Mary Wollstonecraft, *A Vindication of the Rights of Woman,* ed. Miriam Brody Kramnick (London: Penguin, 1975).

2. Mary Wollstonecraft, *A Vindication of the Rights of Woman,* ed. Charles Hagelman Jr. (New York: Norton, 1967), p. 83.

3. Tomalin, *Life and Death of Wollstonecraft,* p. 103. Thomas Paine was one of the few dissenters who did address the question of women's equality. See Thomas Paine, "An Occasional Letter on the Female Sex," in *The Writings of Thomas Paine,* vol. 1, ed. Moncure D. Conway (New York: Putnam's, 1894).

4. Although eighteenth-century liberal thought had a middle-class bias that I do not wish to minimize as a problem for latter-day feminists, I want to alert the reader to the complicated and unanswered questions this middle-class bias raises for the study of Wollstonecraft in particular and feminism in general. Although we shall see that Wollstonecraft directs her concerns to the new middle-class woman, sometimes exclusively, one should keep in mind that this concern applies to a much wider audience in eighteenth-century England than she understood it did or is generally thought to be the case. As well, the

term "middle class" does not connote a position of privilege for women in Wollstonecraft's mind. Instead, it represents her concern with the married woman's loss of economic dependence. A majority of married women in both the middle and working classes were not wage laborers. Without denying the economic-class privilege that exists between middle- and working-class women, I think the question of their sexual position within the confines of these economic classes needs much greater study and careful reexamination.

5. George, *One Woman's Situation,* p. 6.

6. See Wollstonecraft, in Hagelman, ed., *Rights of Woman,* for a discussion of the sexual-caste nature of society. This is the term she uses, though seldomly, to apply to woman's "miserable situation" in her subjugation to men; women are degraded *as* a sex (p. 96). For the purposes of this chapter, sexual caste and sexual class are equatable.

7. Ibid., p. 102.

8. Mary Wollstonecraft, *A Vindication of the Rights of Men* (Gainesville, Fl.: Scholar's Fascimiles and Reprints, 1960), p. 12.

9. Ibid., p. 26.

10. Ibid., p. 110.

11. Mary Wollstonecraft, *An Historical and Moral View of the Origin and Progress of the French Revolution and the Effect It Has Produced in Europe,* vol. 1 (London: Johnson, 1979), p. 15.

12. Wollstonecraft, in Hagelman, ed., *Rights of Woman,* p. 78.

13. Ibid., p. 99.

14. Ibid., p. 72.

15. Ibid., p. 73.

16. The question remains whether the liberal theory of rationality can encompass woman as a fully equal and rational being with man, or whether this inclusion destroys the patriarchal foundation on which the liberal theory of rationality is based. In this case, real equality with men cannot be fully extended to women within liberal patriarchal society. However, the ideology of the equality of opportunity that takes as its starting point the patriarchal structuring of society can. In a parallel fashion, liberal ideology cannot encompass real egalitarian relations between individuals; it rather embraces the ideology of equality of opportunity in the "race of life." See Isaac Kramnick, "Religion and Radicalism, English Political Theory in the Age of Revolution," *Political Theory* 5, no. 4 (November 1977): 505–34, for an excellent discussion of the difference between real equality and equality of opportunity as an ideology.

17. Wollstonecraft, in Hagelman, ed., *Rights of Woman,* p. 72.

18. Ibid., p. 101.

19. Ibid.

20. Ibid., p. 104.

21. Ibid., p. 82.

22. Ibid., p. 100.

23. Ibid., p. 68.

24. Ibid., p. 92. Also see Wollstonecraft, *Rights of Men.*

25. Wollstonecraft, in Hagelman, ed., *Rights of Woman*, p. 108.

26. Ibid., p. 109.

27. Mary Wollstonecraft, *Thoughts on the Education of Daughters with Reflections on Female Conduct, in the More Important Duties of Life* (London: Johnson, 1787), p. 22. For related discussions of women's education see Mary Astell, *A Serious Proposal to the Ladies for the Advancement of Their True and Greatest Interest*, 1684, and Catherine Macauley, *Letters on Education*, 1790.

28. Wollstonecraft, in Hagelman, ed., *Rights of Woman*, p. 52.

29. Ibid., p. 266.

30. Ibid., p. 52.

31. Ibid., p. 58.

32. Ibid., p. 129.

33. Ibid., p. 134.

34. Ralph Wardle, ed., *Collected Letters of Mary Wollstonecraft* (Ithaca: Cornell University Press, 1979), p. 145.

35. Wollstonecraft, in Hagelman, ed., *Rights of Woman*, p. 184.

36. Wardle, *Collected Letters*, p. 159.

37. Wollstonecraft, in Hagelman, ed., *Rights of Woman*, p. 138.

38. Ibid., p. 107.

39. Ibid., p. 24.

40. Ibid., p. 247.

41. For a fuller discussion of this period, see Ivy Pinchbeck, *Women Workers and the Industrial Revolution, 1750–1850* (New York: Augustus Kelley, 1969); Lawrence Stone, *The Family, Sex and Marriage, In England 1500–1800* (New York: Harper & Row, 1977); E. P. Thompson, *The Making of the English Working Class* (New York: Pantheon, 1963); idem, "Eighteenth-Century English Society: Class Struggle Without Class?" *Social History* 3, no. 2 (May 1978): 133–65; and Louise Tilly and Joan Scott, *Women, Work and Family* (New York: Holt, Rinehart and Winston, 1978).

42. Alice Clark, *Working Life of Women in the Seventeenth Century* (New York: Kelley, 1968), p. 235.

43. Pinchbeck, *Women Workers, 1750–1850*, p. 28.

44. Ibid., p. 312.

45. Ibid., p. 110.

46. Ibid., p. 100.

47. Ibid., p. 16.

48. *Productive* (or *nonproductive*), when applied to women's activity, is of particular importance for our discussion of Wollstonecraft. Her

confusion about the changing nature of women's lives partially reflects the equation of useful work with productive labor for the market, which reflects the developing bourgeois market relations of this period. See Tilly and Scott, *Women, Work and Family*, p. 3. For a clarification of "productive Labor" in bourgeois society see Karl Marx, *Theories of Surplus Value*, part 1 (London: Lawrence and Wishart, 1969).

49. Pinchbeck, *Women Workers, 1750–1850*, p. 307.

50. Clark, *Women in the Seventeenth Century*, p. 38.

51. Thompson, *English Working Class*.

52. Wollstonecraft, in Kramnick, ed., *Rights of Woman*, p. 33.

53. Wollstonecraft, in Hagelman, ed., *Rights of Woman*, p. 33.

54. Ibid., p. 100.

55. Ibid.

56. Ibid., p. 115.

57. Ibid., p. 227.

58. Ibid., p. 280. Interestingly enough, this view continues to be rewired and continually revitalized. See chapters 8 and 9 of this volume.

59. Mary Wollstonecraft, *Mary and the Wrongs of Woman*, ed. Gary Kelly (London: Oxford University Press, 1976), p. 68.

60. Wardle, *Collected Letters*, p. 273.

61. Ibid., p. 237.

62. Ibid., p. 79.

63. Wollstonecraft, in Hagelman, ed., *Rights of Woman*, p. 119.

64. Mary Wollstonecraft, *Maria or the Wrongs of Woman* (New York: Norton, 1975), p. 137.

65. Wardle, *Collected Letters*, p. 392.

66. Wollstonecraft, in Hagelman, ed., *Rights of Woman*, p. 75.

67. Wollstonecraft, *Origin of the French Revolution*, p. 71.

68. Wollstonecraft, *Rights of Men*, p. 148.

69. Ibid., p. 24.

70. Mary Wollstonecraft, *Letters Written During a Short Residence in Sweden, Norway, and Denmark*, ed. Carol Poston (Lincoln: University of Nebraska Press, 1976), p. 26.

71. Ibid., p. 129.

72. Wollstonecraft, in Hagelman, ed., *Rights of Woman*, p. 25.

73. Ibid., p. 251.

74. Liberal ideology in this period is not in general a status quo theory. However, the patriarchal underpinnings of it remain so, and this is the dimension of it that Wollstonecraft seeks to correct.

75. Wollstonecraft, in Hagelman, ed., *Rights of Woman*, p. 224.

76. Wollstonecraft, *Letters Written in Sweden, Norway, and Denmark*, p. 160.

77. Wollstonecraft, in Hagelman, ed., *Rights of Woman*, p. 265.

78. Ibid., p. 96.

79. Ibid.

80. Ibid., p. 209.

81. Wollstonecraft, *Maria or the Wrongs of Woman*, p. 21.

82. Wollstonecraft, in Hagelman, ed., *Rights of Woman*, p. 261.

83. Ibid., p. 127.

84. Ibid.

85. Ibid., p. 84.

86. Wollstonecraft, *Letters Written in Sweden, Norway, and Denmark*, p. 55.

87. Wollstonecraft, in Hagelman, ed., *Rights of Woman*, p. 24.

88. Ibid., p. 264.

89. Wardle, *Collected Letters*, pp. 316–17.

90. Ibid., p. 310.

91. Wollstonecraft, in Hagelman, ed., *Rights of Woman*, p. 36.

92. Ibid., p. 32.

6

J. S. Mill and Harriet Taylor: Liberal Individualism, Socialism, and Feminism

This chapter presents the ideas of both John Stuart Mill and Harriet Taylor. Although there is much disagreement about the impact of Taylor's ideas on Mill,[1] no one denies that Mill and Taylor greatly affected each other's thinking. The writing discussed in this chapter, with the exceptions of "Considerations On Representative Government" and *On the Subjection of Women*, which were written after Taylor's death, is treated as their joint product. Because *On the Subjection of Women* contrasts significantly with "On the Enfranchisement of Women," which Mill and Taylor wrote together, I do not attribute the ideas in *On the Subjection of Women* to Taylor.[2]

J. S. Mill attests to the shared nature of his and Taylor's work:

> When two persons have their thoughts and speculations completely in common; when all subjects of intellectual or moral interest are discussed between them in daily life, and probed to much greater depths than are usually or conveniently sounded in writings intended for general readers; when they set out from the same principles, and arrive at their conclusions by processes pursued jointly, it is of little consequence in respect to the question of originality, which of them holds the pen; the one who contributes least to the composition may contribute most to the thought; the writings which result are the joint product of both, and it must often be impossible to disentangle their respective parts, and affirm that this belongs to one and that to the other.[3]

He credits Harriet Taylor with many of the revisions in the three different editions of *Principles of Political Economy*, especially the chapter on the "Probable Future of the Labouring Classes," which did not exist in the first draft.[4] Mill also states ". . . all my published writings were as much my wife's work as mine; her share in them constantly increasing as years advanced."[5]

The joint nature of their writing is particularly important for our study because Mill and Taylor's extraordinary relationship shaped the priorities of their writing. They met in 1830. Because Harriet Taylor was already married to John Taylor, her intimate friendship with Mill was a source of much criticism by even their close friends. The restrictiveness of Victorian morality made their relationship suspect. Their disgust with the ostracism they faced in their private lives because of their relationship can be recognized in Mill and Taylor's criticism of cultural conformity in *On Liberty*. In *On the Subjection of Women*, Mill discusses the problem of a brilliant woman trapped in patriarchal customs that deny her her individuality.

John Taylor died in 1849. Mill and Harriet Taylor married in 1851. They worked together on their joint revisions of *The Autobiography* and *On Liberty* between 1855 and 1858. Harriet Taylor died only seven years after their marriage. *On Liberty*, although written by Mill and Taylor in Taylor's lifetime, was not published until 1859. "Considerations On Representative Government" (1861) and *On the Subjection of Women* (1869), written after her death, include issues that Mill and Taylor discussed and studied throughout their lifetime together. It is nevertheless impossible to know what she would have thought of either manuscript in its final form.

The Problem of Individuality and Liberal Individualism

John Stuart Mill and Harriet Taylor explore socialism and feminism as possible remedies for the inadequacies of liberal democratic society. They wish to create a society that will better recognize individuality, personal freedom, and independence of thought. Their writing expresses their commitment to a conception of an individual's freedom that moves beyond liberalism and at the same time often reduces this image to the ideology of liberal individualism. By "liberal individualism," I mean the view of the individual pictured as atomized and disconnected from the social relations that actually affect his or her choices and options; by "individuality," I refer to the capacities of the individual conceptualized as part of a social structure that can either enhance or constrain his or her individual potential for human development. The first view promises equality of opportunity and freedom of choice and explains its absence in terms of the inadequacy or inability of the individual. The view of individuality tries to understand how the individual is not allowed to achieve the promises of liberal society given the structural constraints of society.[6]

I examine how Mill and Taylor's vision of liberalism, socialism, and feminism contains the beginnings of a theory of individuality and yet is constrained by the ideology of liberal individualism that ultimately applies only to middle-class men and an elite of middle-class women. Mill and Taylor accept a notion of individuality that assumes a potential for intellectual development in all human beings and recognizes that women, as a sexual class,[7] are denied this potential; but they also assume the ideology of liberal individualism, which excludes the working masses and married women in Victorian society from this possibility.

Underlying this tension in Mill and Taylor is the unresolved conflict that exists between the needs of the individual and the needs of the individual as a part of a group or social collectivity. This problem takes the particular form in Mill and Taylor of the tension between (1) the individual as a unit unto himself or herself needing protection from the tyranny of the community in order to develop his or her capacities, and (2) the view that the "masses" and women can develop into a responsible community if given the opportunities they need to act on their potential. Mill and Taylor do not accept the simplistic view of (patriarchal) liberal individualism that the working classes and/or women are what they are as merely a result of their own inadequacies. Yet Mill especially thinks that society needs to be protected from the inadequacies of the "masses," which in the end includes most men and women. One is left to ponder how one protects society from the masses and still gives them the opportunities they need to develop their potential. Given the problem of the masses, which is (not) incidentally made up of individuals, neither democracy (as it is at present practiced) or socialism (if it were to be instituted) is sufficient for Taylor and Mill. Neither system resolves the tension that exists for them between the individual and their social identity. It remains to be seen in the next several chapters how liberal feminism begins to redefine this dilemma.

By exploring how the tension between individuality and the ideology of liberal individualism underlies the analysis of *On Liberty, On Political Economy, On the Subjection of Women,* Mill's *Autobiography,* and "On the Enfranchisement of Women," we should better understand Mill and Taylor's discussion of socialism and liberal feminism. To the degree that Mill and Taylor embrace the relations of private property and the division between public and private life and its particular sexual division of labor, personal liberty becomes an exclusionary right for an elite of middle-class women. Mill and Taylor's discussion of liberal individualism, treated as an idea, in abstraction, disconnected from the patriarchal power relations of society, limits liberal feminism to the existing structural relations that divide the public and private worlds of home and work life. By doing so, they define their conception of woman's emancipation in terms of citizen rights, which limits their discussion to the ideology of liberal individualism, even though they recognize the exclusion of women as a group from public life. This recognition of women's "subjection" stands counter to a simplistic reading of liberal individualism, which recognizes only atomistic individuals.

The Problem of Liberal Individualism

Mill and Taylor's acceptance of the sovereignty of the individual leads them to explore the conflict between individual autonomy and the authority of the social community. Their conception of individuality presumes the separation of the individual from the social collectivity. Individual and social life are separable and distinct. Mill therefore asks, "What then is the rightful limit to the sovereignty of the individual over himself? Where does the authority of society begin?"[8] The individual appears in distinction to society. There is a difference of interests between the two realms: self and society. The different interests must be distinguished. "To individuality should belong the part of life in which it is chiefly the individual that is interested; to society, the part which chiefly interests society."[9] For Mill and Taylor, the essence of individuality appears transhistorical and as part of the nature of any individual within any society. They therefore speak of the problem of individual liberty in abstract terms.

The individual belongs to herself or himself. She or he is the proprietor of her or his own being. But there are limits to individual liberty when an individual's conduct affects the interests of another. "As soon as any part of a person's conduct affects prejudicially the interests of others, society has jurisdiction over it, and the question whether the general welfare will not be promoted by interfering with it becomes open to discussion."[10] Actions that affect others in some negative way can be curtailed; otherwise, the individual is sovereign. The distinction between self and other-regarding activity defines the contours of individual liberty. The individual is sovereign over that activity which affects only the self. Obviously, the lines drawn between individual and social activity are clear to Mill and Taylor. They view the individual as autonomous, atomistic, and distinct from the social relations of society. This separation posits the self and society, the individual and the masses, in conflict with one another.

Although the atomistic individual defines most of Mill and Taylor's writing, they do occasionally write of the interdependence between individuals. "No person is an entirely isolated being; it is impossible for a person to do anything seriously or permanently hurtful to himself without mischief reaching at least to his near connections, and often far beyond them."[11] Most of the time they envision individual and social life as antagonistic to each other. They fear the social collectivity because they think it enforces conformity. Therefore they hope to limit the impact of society on the individual instead of extending the collective experience to the individual.

But "individualism" for Mill and Taylor soon becomes a privilege for the few individuals who are able to achieve originality and/or education. "Genius can only breathe freely in an atmosphere of freedom." [12] The problem of individuality derives from the fact that ". . . mediocrity is the ascendent power among mankind." [13] The mediocrity of the masses tends to stifle the genius of the individual. "Originality is the one thing which unoriginal minds cannot feel the use of." [14] The individual must be freed from the common tendencies of the collective body; ". . . the individual was a power in himself. . . ." [15] This conception of liberal individualism fully celebrates the independent self. "The initiation of all wise or noble things comes and must come from individuals; generally at first from some one individual." [16]

Liberty for Mill and Taylor means the freedom *from* others, *from* social interference, *from* social mediocrity. It most often becomes the exclusionary right of those with original minds of genius stature. Intelligence and originality are viewed as individual attributes that develop best apart from common social interchange. Although the concern with individual genius is Mill and Taylor's priority throughout *On Liberty*, they acknowledge a very different view of the average individual and his or her need for education. This rare acknowledgment is an exception to the rest of their discussion of education. "Not that it is solely, or chiefly, to form great thinkers, that freedom of thinking is required. On the contrary, it is as much and even more indispensable to enable average human beings to attain the mental stature which they are capable of." [17]

Mill and Taylor want to protect the individual from society so that individual capacities can develop. What is not clear, however, is who exactly these masses are that the individual must be protected from. Most of the time "the masses" refer to the uneducated working class. But the discussion of the masses, by their own accounting, should include anyone who is a slave to custom. Given Mill and Taylor's fear of the mediocrity that uncritical acceptance of customary practices and ideas can create, they should fear the middle class, which is infected by this as much as, if not more than, the working class.

Because Mill and Taylor believe conscious choice distinguishes meaningful life activity from tyranny, they say, "He who does anything because it is the custom makes no choice." [18] They further state in *On Liberty*, "He who lets the world, or his own portion of it choose his plan of life for him has no need of any other faculty than the ape-like one of imitation. He who chooses his plan for himself employs all his faculties." [19] Nevertheless, when limits are put on the masses through the system of plural voting, it is the working class, not the middle class, that is affected. Although it is the tyranny of custom Mill and Taylor fear the most, Mill later reduces this issue to a question of education. He speaks in "Considerations On Representative Government" about the problem of the uneducated masses, rather than the conformist middle classes.

Mill and Taylor's treatment of the working class is complicated by their belief in the mediocrity of the majority. They believe that most individuals are only average in intelligence. "The general average of mankind are not only moderate in intellect, but also moderate in inclinations; they have no tastes or wishes strong enough to incline them to do anything unusual, and they consequently do not understand those who have, and class all such with the wild and intemperate whom they are accustomed to look down upon." [20] Although they sometimes say there is nothing inherent in human nature that makes this so, they more often assume mediocrity as a static characteristic of human existence. They therefore applaud the capacities of *the* individual at the same time that they fear the incapacities of the majority of individuals. The problem is that they applaud the individual and fear the collective body. In this view, the individual is something very different than the group; the group actually limits and distorts individual capacities. The problem with this view of liberal individualism derives from the fact that groups are actually made up of individuals. How, then, does one protect the individual *from* the group when these are not entirely separate identities?

Mill and Taylor vacillate between speaking about educating the masses to their potential and fearing that they are incapable of anything more than what they already are. Mill's compromise is a proposal for plural voting, which gives a greater number of votes to the educated individual, in the hope that everyone will eventually be ready to participate equally. As Mill states in "Considerations on Representative Government": "some mode of plural voting which may assign to education, as such, the degree of superior influence due to it, and sufficient as a counterpoise to the numerical weight of the least educated class." [21] Society must be guided by the intelligent; "universal teaching must precede universal enfranchisement." [22]

Mill and Taylor fear democracy and socialism because of the herdlike nature of the masses; they are viewed as an impediment to the exercise of true individualism. Liberal individualism, in this case, gives rights to the individual genius against rights to the masses. Because Mill and Taylor are concerned with setting up the appropriate conditions for individuals of genius and talent to flourish, they conceive of the majority of humankind in a passive way. In the end, society is organized around the needs of a few talented individuals. These talented few, who will include women, are defined by Mill as the intellectually gifted and "exceptionally adapted."

> But the utmost latitude ought to exist for the adaptation of general rules to individual suitabilities; and there ought to be nothing to prevent faculties *exceptionally adapted* to any other pursuit, from obeying their vocation notwithstanding marriage: due provision being made for supplying otherwise any falling-short which might become inevitable, in her full performance of the ordinary functions of mistress of a family.[23]

With this formulation, the majority of society as wage laborers and ordinary middle class are excluded, and the majority of women will be excluded as well.

Liberal Individualism and the Working Class

Mill and Taylor's concern with individualism and personal liberty reflects their concern with the constraints of society in general. They fear the effects of society on everyone, but they fear it the most for the working class. They reject political egalitarianism unless people have proved that they are prepared for it.[24] In Mill's discussion of parliamentary reform, he argues against egalitarianism; he insists that one person is not as good as another.[25] "A person who can read, but cannot write or calculate, is not as good as a person who can do both."[26] His schema of plural voting is based on this view.

> If every ordinary unskilled labourer had one vote, a skilled labourer, whose occupation requires an exercised mind and a knowledge of some of the laws of external nature, ought to have two. A foreman, or superintendent of labour, whose occupation requires something more of general culture, and some moral as well as intellectual qualities, should perhaps have three.[27]

Plural voting is his compromise between excluding the working class from enfranchisement, which renders it dependent on the other classes in society, and giving it equal votes with "the most highly educated person in the community."[28] Plural voting recognizes the superiority of knowledge at the same time as it allows for the (unequal) participation of the working class.

Mill believes that participation in voting will eventually elevate the working classes to a public conscience. Such political activity is "the first step out of the narrow bounds of individual and family selfishness."[29] He also thinks that the political participation of the working class will benefit society as long as this class does not have the political power to undermine the balanced rule of government by putting forth their own economic class interests.

The problem is that Mill does not believe the working class usually knows what its real interests are. He assumes a false consciousness on this class's part. The problem "is not what their interest is, but what they suppose it to be."[30] Mill presumes that the *real* interest of the working class is equivalent to the public interest, and that it is instead guided by private economic class interests. He especially fears that the working class does not understand that the security of private property is in the public interest and that it is therefore not to its advantage to weaken the relations of private property.[31]

Whereas Mill believes that the conditions of the working class deny it the understanding of its *real* interests, he otherwise believes that the general environment has educational impact on most individuals: ". . . men are shaped by daily work, by sharing in local government, by the responsibilities of ownership."[32] Because of this acceptance of environmental influence, Mill's belief that the daily life of the working class does not help to inform it of its real needs seems unfounded. Engels, writing in this same period, does not agree with Mill. Engels thinks the working class knows its true interest and the antagonistic interests of the bourgeoise. "The English working-man who can scarcely read and still less write, nevertheless knows very well where his own interest and that of the nation lies. He knows, too, what the special interest of the bourgeosie is, and what he has to expect of that bourgeoisie."[33] Mill views these special interests of the working class as its selfish, sinister, economic class interest; sinister interests conflict with the general good.[34]

Mill hopes to create a plurality of interests within government to limit the predominance of any particular economic class interest.

> If we consider as a class, politically speaking any number of persons who have the same sinister interest,—that is, whose direct and apparent interest points towards the same description of bad measures; the desirable object would be that no class, and no combination of classes likely to combine, should be able to exercise a preponderant influence in the government.[35]

In the hopes of limiting economic class legislation, he wishes to balance the different political forces and economic class interests in government. The interests of employer and employee have to be weighed against each other: ". . . manual labourers and their affinities on one side, employers of labour and their affinities on the other, should be, in the arrangement of the representative system, equally balanced, each influencing about an equal number of votes in Parliament. . . ."[36] Government, as such, operates to regulate economic class interests and protect "the educated from the class legislation of the uneducated; but it must stop short of enabling them to practice class legislation in their own account."[37] Mill assumes that governmental policy will be representative of a pluralist politics.

Although Mill maintains that the working class is unable to see beyond its particular interest, he assumes the ruling class will identify the public interest and act on it. One is left to wonder whether education alone divests the ruling class of its selfish interests. In the same view, one can only assume that Mill sees education as liberating individual capacities rather than enforcing an intellectual conformity. As such, education appears disconnected from the economic class interests and realities of society. His view of liberal individualism, which posits the individual isolated and disconnected from social relations, reflects this belief.

> I saw that though our character is formed by circumstances, our own desires can do much to shape those circumstances; and that what is really inspiriting and ennobling in the doctrine of free will, is the conviction that we have real power over the formation of our own character; that our will, by influencing some of our own circumstances, can modify our future habits or capabilities of willing.[38]

Given the liberal individualist view of social life, Mill, as well as Taylor, does not focus on the structural relations of private property to understand the problem of individuality for the working class. The wage/capital relation is not understood as extractive and exploitative. Instead, Mill and Taylor believe that capitalism can be made more equitable if the violations of private property relations are removed. They criticize the economic distribution within capitalism; but without recognizing the relations of production as inherently unequal, they are unable to see that capitalist production necessitates its own form of distribution. They rather view the laws of production as natural, while they understand that the laws of distribution are societally formed [39] and, hence, changeable.

As a result, the capitalist class relations of production remained unchallenged by Mill and Taylor. They were unable to extend their conception of individuality to a critique of the violations of the working class in the system of production. The economic class relations of capitalism were not seen as a violation of the principle of personal autonomy and individual liberty. "That principle is that the sole end for which mankind are warranted, individually or collectively, in interfering with the liberty of action of any of their number is self-protection."[40] One is left asking how the independence of self can be absolute or the individual be completely sovereign for the wage laborer who is dependent on his or her employer for wages. Mill and Taylor mystify this conflict between the wage laborer and the collective authority of the capitalist in their discussion of the tension between individual and collective authority. The conflict is misrepresented by Mill and Taylor as existing between the intellectually gifted, who can advance the progress of society, and the uninformed masses.

It is not the exploration for a new system of production that leads Mill and Taylor to socialism, but rather their theory of knowledge, which underlies their conception of individuality. Human knowledge requires the reconciling and combining of opposites.[41] Progress is dependent upon resolving these contradictory elements of human existence. The development of true individuality, and eventually democracy, hinges on creating the necessary circumstances to make the dialectic of ideas possible.

> Unless opinions favorable to democracy and to aristocracy, to property and to equality, to cooperation and to competition, to luxury and to abstinence, to sociality and individuality, to liberty and discipline, and all the other standing antagonisms of practical life are expressed with equal freedom and enforced and defended with equal talent and energy, there is no chance of both elements obtaining their due: one scale is sure to go up, and the other down.[42]

Both Mill and Taylor believe that the only way one knows what one thinks is by testing it through a variety of opinions as well as studying it from several vantage points and perspectives. It is necessary to hear "what can be said about it by persons of every variety of opinion, and studying all modes in which it can be looked at by every character of mind." [43] This is how true genius develops. This commitment to individuality and the plurality of ideas it necessitates lays the basis for Mill and Taylor's discussion of socialism. In this sense, it is as liberals that they entertain the question of socialism.

On Socialism

The Problem of Individuality and Social Collectivity
Mill studied Louis Blanc, Fourier, M. Considerant, and Owen, but he found the Saint-Simonian critique of liberalism the most persuasive.

> Their criticisms on the common doctrine of Liberalism seemed to me full of important truth; and it was partly by their writings that my eyes were opened to the very limited and temporary value of the old political economy, which assumes private property and inheritance as indefeasible facts, and freedom of production and exchange as the *dernier mot* of social improvement.[44]

Mill and Taylor agreed that a vision of socialism which operated as an ideal to guide necessary changes within capitalism was valuable. This conception of socialism, however, as an ideal, remained a vague notion in Mill and Taylor. It allowed them to identify as socialists, and at the same time to think it was impossible, given the selfishness of the masses, to create a socialist society. As Mill states in his *Autobiography:* "... we dreaded the ignorance and especially the selfishness and brutality of the mass: but our ideal of ultimate improvement went far beyond Democracy, and would class us decidedly under the general designation of Socialists."[45] Socialism became an abstracted ideal, used to guide reform: "... I felt that the proclamation of such an ideal of human society could not but tend to give a beneficial direction to the efforts of others to bring society, as at present constituted, nearer to some ideal standard."[46]

For Mill and Taylor, political reform was necessary to create greater individual liberty within capitalism. The question of individual liberty also remained a problem in socialism for Mill and Taylor; they wondered how the common ownership of raw materials would affect individual liberty.[47] They specifically considered whether a system based on private property *or* a system based in the common ownership of land and the instruments of production was more conducive to the greatest amount of human liberty. They ask, "... which of the two systems is consistent with the greatest amount of human liberty and spontaneity?"[48] Mill and Taylor's primary concern here is with freedom of opinion and thought, which they fear will be controlled by the "dictatorship of the proletariat." "The question is whether there would be any asylum left for individuality of character. ..."[49] They fear "a tame uniformity of thoughts, feelings and actions"[50] in socialism, although they recognize that this is already a "glaring evil of the existing state of society."[51]

There are times when Mill and Taylor recognize the way economic classes, by definition, curtail the individuality of the working classes. They speak of the way these individuals are demeaned by their work and the nature of their undifferentiated labor. In their estimation, communism and socialism will at least free laborers from this servitude. "The restraints of Communism would be freedom in comparison with the present condition of the majority of the human race."[52]

Socialism and communism, terms they use interchangeably, should relieve the working class from a life that enforces demeaning uniformity. Yet Mill and Taylor are hesitant about the conformity of ideas they associate with the practice of socialism. Neither system, in their minds, can provide both freedom of ideas and freedom from economic necessity. They applaud the possibility of pluralism in capitalism and the freedom from want in socialism. Unwilling to give up a vision of either, they vacillate between liberalism and socialism in the hope of constructing what they would term a real democracy.

> While we repudiated with the greatest energy that tyranny of society over the individual which most Socialistic systems are supposed to involve, we yet looked forward to a time when society will no longer be divided into the idle and the industrious; when the rule that they who do not work shall not eat, will be applied not to paupers only, but impartially to all; when the division of the produce of labor, instead of depending, as in so great a degree it now does, on the accident of birth, will be made by concert on an acknowledged principle of justice; and when it will no longer wither be, or be thought to be, impossible for human beings to exert themselves strenuously in procuring benefits which are not to be exclusively their own, but to be shared with the society they belong to.[53]

Mill and Taylor's acceptance of Malthusian population theory and their essential theory of private property seems to support a desire to reform capitalism rather than a desire to reform socialism. They agree with the socialist critique that too many workers earn too little, but they do not agree that wages will continue to decline. Nor do they see this problem as merely a problem of the competitive marketplace that holds wages down. They instead believe low wages reflect the problems of overpopulation[54] and that this problem will recur in socialism. This means that limitations must be placed on the system of distribution. No one should be allowed to become enormously rich, and no one should be forced to be extremely poor. Their vision encompasses a "well paid and affluent body of labourers; no enormous fortunes, except what were earned and accumulated during a single lifetime; but a much larger body of persons than at present, not only exempt from the coarser toils, but with sufficient leisure, both physical and mental, from mechanical details, to cultivate freely the graces of life."[55] More specifically, the worker must be allowed to obtain his or her fair share from labor, after the capitalist has been allowed his, "by distributing among all who share in the work, in the form of a percentage on their earnings, the whole or a fixed portion of the gains."[56] Because both worker and capitalist must first learn what is their rightful amount, the question of redistribution of goods is primarily an issue of education. Socialism, therefore, requires an equivalent change in the characters of the laboring classes *and* the capitalist class.[57]

Given this picture of the problem, capitalism can be reformed by a new system of distribution posited on the change of individual character through education. The public rather than the private good must predominate. Mill's conception of private property further elucidates this political analysis. Private property, in principle, reflects an equal exchange between partners who need each other. Workers merely need to learn and then understand this.

On Private Property

In *On Political Economy*, private property is defined as the individual right one has to his or her labor, produce, and faculties. It also includes the right to exchange them. "Nothing is implied in property, but the right of each to his (or her) own faculties, to what he can produce by them, and to whatever he can get for them in a fair market: together with his right to give this to any other person if he chooses, and the right of that other to receive and enjoy it." [58] The marketplace expresses the equality of opportunity one has to exchange his or her labor or produce. "The right of each to what he has produced, implies a right to what has been produced by others, if obtained by their free consent; since the producers must either have given it from good will or exchanged it for what they esteemed an equivalent. . . ." [59] The exchanges, according to Mill, are free and equal, in principle. Laborers are free to do as they please with their own labor and earnings. The worker and capitalist cooperate because they need each other. "Each is necessary to the other. The capitalists can do nothing without laborers, nor the laborers without capital. If the laborers compete for employment, the capitalists on their part compete for labor, to the full extent of the circulating capital of the country." [60]

Mill and Taylor understand that the institution of private property recognizes the rights of property among those who have not directly produced anything. But they think that this is fair to the extent that labor is only one of the necessities for the production of a commodity. The capitalist supplies the necessary machines and tools without which nothing could be made. They make what is now considered to be the classic liberal argument.

> The labor of manufacture is only one of the conditions which must combine for the production of the commodity. The labor cannot be carried on without materials and machinery, nor without a stock of necessaries. . . . If the labourers were possessed of them, they would not need to divide the produce with anyone; but while they have them not, an equivalent must be given to those who have. . . . [61]

They argue that even though the capital provided by the possessor was probably not created by his or her own labor, but rather the labor of some previous worker, this worker also probably transferred his or her

claims to the capitalist. Such a view assumes that private property relations reflect the equality of opportunity between individuals; private
property does not therefore restrict one's individuality and/or freedom.
Mill and Taylor do realize, however, that violations of individual rights
must be addressed within the present system of property. They believe
that legislation which favors the distribution of wealth rather than its
concentration and actively seeks to limit the inequalities arising from
the misuses of private property can create a much greater equality.
Then, "the principle of individual property would have been found to
have no necessary connection with the physical and social evil which
almost all socialist writers assume to be inseparable from it." [62]

According to Mill and Taylor, the principle of private property has
never had a fair hearing. The violators and violations that have accom-
panied private property have obscured its real nature. "They have made
property of things which never ought to be made property, and absolute property where only a qualified property ought to exist." [63] Unfair
impediments have been created, and as a result inequalities have been
fostered that have "prevented all from starting fair in the race." [64] As a
result, Mill and Taylor believe it is impossible to know whether individualism or socialism is the best form for human society. "We are too
ignorant either of what individual agency in its best form, or socialism
in its best form, can accomplish, to be qualified to decide which of the
two will be the ultimate form of human society." [65]

Mill and Taylor's discussion of private property helps one understand the tension between their conception of liberal individualism and
their notion of individuality. They most often adopt the ideology of
liberal individualism in that they work within an exclusionary framework which assumes an equality of opportunity where economic class
inequalities in actuality exist. Mill and Taylor view the individual as a
finite being, separate and apart from society, a property unto itself,
with the rights of control over itself. This notion of liberal individualism is structured tightly in relation to the values of the bourgeois
market; the individual *owning him/her*self. According to Mill and Taylor,
one is left to speculate whether private property must be maintained
within socialism to ensure this understanding of individualism and
whether the relations of private property are what ensure the autonomous, self-determining individual for them.

Although Mill and Taylor are unable to redefine a conception of
individuality within socialism that transcends the exclusivity of property relations and still recognizes individual autonomy, they have provided insights for a conception of individuality. They recognize the
need for intellectual diversity and the expression of unique per-
sonalities. Just because Mill and Taylor most of the time confuse the
conception of individuality with the ideology of liberalism, it does not

mean that one cannot distinguish between them and retain the important core for the purposes of developing a useful feminist theory and
practice.

Mill and Taylor begin to do this for us as they extend the ideology
of liberal individualism to women in their struggle for equal rights. We
shall see that to the extent Mill and Taylor accept the structural base of
society—the separation of public and family life—out of which the
ideology of liberal individualism is defined, a true individuality is not
open to most women. The legal-rights doctrine they adopt is premised
on this ideology of liberal individualism in that they wish to secure an
independent, autonomous identity for women as distinct individuals.
And yet, implicit in this desire is a recognition of woman as part of a
subjugated "social collectivity." Although Mill and Taylor adopt the
individualist ideology of liberal individualism for women, they do so
with a recognition that woman is a member of a sexual class. This
recognition of woman's social identity, as a member of a sexual class,
conflicts with the individualist structure of liberalism.

Liberal Individualism and Women

Whereas liberalism was no longer a radical ideology in the second
half of nineteenth-century England, liberal feminism certainly was. The
extension of the promise of liberal individualism to women had not yet
been accepted by English society. Citizen rights still excluded women
and did not recognize women as individuals in the legal-liberal sense of
the term. Taylor and Mill, therefore, argue to extend the established
freedoms of bourgeois society to women. Much like Wollstonecraft before them, they argue that women's freedom of choice must replace the
arbitrary rule of men. Taylor and Mill's replacement of aristocratic rule
with the equality of opportunity doctrine is also reminiscent of Locke's
First Treatise On Government. They directly apply the critique of the
arbitrary rule of kings to the arbitrary rule of husbands. "The power of
husbands had reached the stage which the power of kings had arrived
at, when opinion did not yet question the rightfulness of arbitrary
power, but in theory, and to a certain extent in practice, condemned the
selfish use of it." [66] They view the struggle by women for equality as
part of the whole movement toward citizen rights, which have only
recently been extended to men, and not even equally to them. "It is only
beginning to treat any men as citizens, except the rich and a favoured
portion of the middle class. Can we wonder that it has not yet done as
much for women?" [67]

Mill reiterates the importance of the equality of opportunity doctrine in *On the Subjection of Women* and argues that one's birth should
not determine one's station in life. "But if the principle is true, we
ought to act as if we believed it, and not to ordain that to be born a girl

instead of a boy, any more than to be born black instead of white, or a commoner instead of a nobleman, shall decide the person's position through all life. . . ." [68] Mill and Taylor also argue that equality of opportunity for women requires their full citizenship. Much to the delight of Elizabeth Cady Stanton and Susan B. Anthony, they state that the Declaration of Independence must apply to women as well as men. A true democracy must recognize the citizenship of all its members.

> We do not imagine that any American democrat will evade the force of these expressions by the dishonest or ignorant subterfuge that "men" in this memorable document, does not stand for human beings, but for one sex only . . . and that the governed, whose consent is affirmed to be the only source of just power, are meant for that half of mankind only who in relation to the other, have hitherto assumed the character of governors. [69]

Both Mill and Taylor call for the enfranchisement of women in England and the United States. Women's enfranchisement represents the struggle for woman's equality for them.

Mill fought for women's "rights" the entire time he was in Parliament. After becoming a member of the House of Commons in 1865, he fought for an amendment to the Reform Bill of 1867 to politically enfranchise women. He believed "that women were entitled to representation in Parliament on the same terms with men." [70] He made a motion to "strike out the words which were understood to limit the electoral franchise to males." [71] He argued that if manhood suffrage becomes the law, equality will not regulate political life; ". . . the voters would still have a class interest, as distinguished from women." [72] In his defense of woman's right to vote, he argued that she is not adequately represented as an individual through her husband's vote. He was critical of the idea that husbands, through the vote, serve in the capacity of protector for their wives. "I should like to have a return laid before this House of the numbers of women who are annually beaten to death, kicked to death, or trampled to death by their male protectors. . . ." [73]

In 1868 he fought unsuccessfully to amend the laws that gave husbands control over their wives' money and property. In this same year he supported the campaign of Charles Bradlaugh, the well-known birth-control advocate. These unpopular political stands contributed to his defeat in the next election. He nevertheless led a campaign in 1871 to try to repeal the Contagious Diseases Acts because of what he considered the insufferable indignities it levied against the wives and daughters of the poor.

The struggle for the greater opportunity for women that Mill and Taylor carried on must be examined against the backdrop of the Victorian society in which it took place. The separation of the home and the marketplace that we have followed throughout the seventeenth and eighteenth centuries was more firmly instituted in nineteenth-century England. The promise of women's equality with men stood in stark contrast with the accepted view of the married Victorian woman, separate from society, cloistered in her home.

Woman's Work at Home and in the Marketplace in the Victorian Age

The Victorian age spanned the last two-thirds of the nineteenth century. Because it was a period of economic prosperity,[74] the middle class and its values became more visible and established. Domestic life developed a particular identity and greater intricacy. It was an era that experienced the full effects of eighteenth-century invention: Hargreave's spinning jenny, Watt's steam engine, and Eli Whitney's cotton gin. The effects were felt within the home as more and more labor was transferred from the home to the factory. The second half of the century was marked by its own series of inventions: the steam turbine, the telephone, the gas automobile. The sewing machine, the use of gas and electricity for the kitchen, municipal water systems, and canning and refrigeration also developed in this period. Gas for lighting developed in the 1850s. The first department store opened in 1863; the first grocery store opened in the 1890s. New improvements in medical technology made childbearing and early childhood less dangerous. All these discoveries had a direct effect on domestic life, and the nature of women's work within the home as England became more industrial and urban.

The Victorian Married Woman: Ideology vs. Reality

By the second half of the nineteenth century, the division between work and home had become fully visible in the ideology defining married woman as a housewife. Victorian patriarchal ideology did not recognize domestic labor as work; woman was therefore seen as idle in the home—and as a housewife. The Victorian woman was a wife and mother first. Her life was defined in terms of this private sphere of domesticity. This image of the married woman not only relegated her to the home but represented her as idle within it. She supposedly represented the luxury of the new middle class by the fact that she did not work for wages outside the home. The prosperous husband could support his wife. The wife was supposed merely to represent the new wealth and privilege of *his* household. This picture of woman's confinement to the home was a reaction to the actual separation between home and work and the potential erosion of patriarchal power that this division held. At the same time, the ideology of this new personage, the housewife, characterized the division.

Mrs. Ellis, the author of several books of this period, *Women of England* (1839), *Daughters of England* (1843), and *Mothers of England* (1843), views middle-class women as the wives of men in manufacture, trade, or the professions, and as women who have the help of several servants.

> It was those women who belong to that great mass of the population of England which is connected with trade and manufacture, as well as the wives and daughters of professional men of limited incomes; or, in order to make the application more direct to that portion of it who are restricted to the services of from one to four domestics—who, on the one hand, enjoy the advantages of a liberal education, and, on the other, have no pretension to family rank.[75]

According to this definition, Duncan Crow estimates that up to one-quarter of the female population in England in the latter half of the nineteenth century fit this category. The middle-class woman's husband is a part of the urban population that does not work with its hands. She, as his wife, is said not to work at all. These women identify with the middle-class values of "entrepreneurial spirit, optimism, the belief in progress and rational decision-making."[76]

The view of the middle-class woman with multiple servants and as herself idle is only one view of the middle-class woman found in the advice manuals of this period. According to Patricia Branca,[77] the particular view that assumes the married middle-class woman's idleness is reflected in Mrs. Beeton's advice manuals. "Her main duties were supervising the servants, seeing that the children were properly attended to by the nurse, making and receiving calls from her friends, and attending or giving lavish dinner parties."[78] There is also a different view found in the household directions of Mrs. Warren's manuals, which describes the middle-class woman as preoccupied with household chores. "The average day of the mistress of the house was filled with housework, washing, cooking, crying children, quarrels with the maid, shopping and never-ending financial problems."[79]

According to Branca, the description of the idle woman applied to families living on at least £200 per year. The middle-class income in this period varied from £60 to £1,400 per year. An income of £300 per annum was representative of the upper middle class; £100 to £300 was the middle income range. Only one-fifth of the families made over £300, whereas more than two-thirds made between £100 and £300.[80] Because 42 percent of the middle class in 1867 earned from £100 to £300,

Branca argues that it is impossible for the majority of middle-class women to have had an average of three servants; the typical middle-class home could not afford a cook, a parlor maid, and a nurse or housemaid. The wages for three servants would be £56, which would mean that a middle-class family would be spending from more than 50 percent to slightly less than 20 percent of its income on servants.[81] Such luxury was possible only for the upper reaches of the middle class.

Middle-range middle-class women most often had the aid of one servant. But a woman with one servant could hardly be said to be idle. The amount of work in the *average* middle-class family was more than enough to keep two women busy. There was still cooking, serving, and cleaning to be done. The average home had three children, and the wife was responsible for them. The wife was also responsible for the household budget and for dealing with tradesmen. She was first learning her new role as a consumer, deciding as frugally as possible the necessary purchases of the home. She was also responsible for smoothing the way into the urban and commercial society for her family.[82]

One does not want to deny the privilege of middle-class women in relation to working-class women, particularly insofar as the former had their servants. Nevertheless, the issue here is whether the conception of the idle woman was a realistic depiction of the Victorian middle-class married woman. The married middle-class woman, who in overwhelming numbers did not work in the market, still appears to have labored within her home, along with her servant help. The small part of the upper middle class that did not are the exception to the rule in Victorian England, although the ideology of this period presents these women as the norm.

Although most married middle-class women labored in their own homes, few worked in the labor force. The few wage-earning jobs open to middle-class women were nursing, teaching, clerical, and sales jobs. These jobs were most often held by the unmarried middle-class woman. This is especially true of governesses, in which profession more middle-class women were employed than in any other field. In 1850 over 21,000 women were governesses; there were few married middle-class women in other areas of paid work.[83] "In 1851 67,000 or 0.73 percent of the total female population were teachers; and by 1881 this number had increased to 127,000 or 0.95 percent of the female population."[84] In 1861 only 279 women were employed as clerks; in 1891, 18,947 women were working in offices; and by 1901, 57,736 were.[85]

More married working-class women worked than did married middle-class women, but the greatest number of working-class women in this period were unmarried. Most women working in factories were unmarried and under twenty-six years of age. Anderson's study of the industrial town of Preston confirms this. In Preston, he found that only 23 percent of all wives with children worked in the labor force, and only 20 percent of those women had children under ten years of age. Of the 23 percent who received wages, only 15 percent performed their work outside their homes.[86] The number of married women in the labor force varies little according to place or industry. Margaret Hewitt finds that in 1851 ". . . in the main cotton districts slightly fewer than one in three (30.02%) of all married women of all social classes were employed. . . ."[87]

Married women workers of nineteenth-century England worked in lacemaking, strawplaiting, needlework, and hat making. Engels' description of nineteenth-century England focuses on working-class women in factories. They have little energy left for their children or household responsibilities. "A mother who has no time to trouble herself about her child, to perform the most ordinary loving services for it during its first year, who scarcely indeed sees it, can be no real mother to the child, must inevitably grow indifferent to it, treat it unlovingly like a stranger."[88]

Patriarchal Victorian ideology presents woman's idleness as though it were a description of reality, whereas it conflicts with the reality of married and unmarried, working-class and middle-class women's lives. In contrast with the patriarchal Victorian vision of woman exists the prevalent liberal-individualist values of the market. Mill and Taylor's concern with the subjugation of women is partially a product of this tension between the patriarchal vision of womanhood in Victorian society, her actual life, and the egalitarian ideology of citizenship in liberal society. If women were to become individuals in their own right, they would have to gain recognition as persons before the law. Women were not yet legal citizens. Married women could not own property. Women could not vote. Mill and Taylor's analysis follows accordingly. Their major political concern was to enfranchise women. The ideology of liberal individualism is extended to women through women's claim to citizen rights.

The Patriarchal Bias of Liberal Feminism

The equality of opportunity doctrine that supposedly exists for men is extended to women in On the Subjection of Women.[89] Equality before the law must therefore be extended to women because "no male human being is under any legal ban: neither law nor opinion superadd artificial obstacles to the natural ones."[90] In order that women will be able to share in the opportunities of society, the laws that are the main regulators of social life will have to be altered: ". . . the legal subordination of one sex to the other—is wrong in itself and now one of the chief hindrances to human improvement."[91] Woman's legal subordination and with it the legal slavery of marriage must be replaced by perfect equality.[92]

Although the problem of woman is defined as a legal one, Mill and Taylor are aware that the problem is also one of cultural subordination. Mill writes, "They are so far in a position different from all other subject classes, that their masters require something more from them than actual service. Men do not want solely the obedience of women, they want their sentiments."[93] Because women must be willing, not forced slaves, they are socialized and educated as young girls to accept their subordination. The legal system remains only part of this system of patriarchal control. The culture itself enforces woman's subordination.

Mill and Taylor in "On the Enfranchisement of Women" speak of the power of custom as part of the system of cultural control. "Custom hardens human beings to any kind of degradation, by deadening the part of their nature which would resist it."[94] Custom presents woman's subjugation as her honor, and women often misinterpret this degradation for privilege.

The economic dependence of woman on man stems from her cultural training that convinces her she needs a man to provide for her. Mill and Taylor, in letters written between themselves, speak of woman's economic independence as crucial to her sense of equality. The only dependence between man and woman should be that which grows out of affection: "a voluntary surrender, renewed and renewing at each instant by free and spontaneous choice."[95] Such a model requires that women control their own livelihood: ". . . women will never be what they should be, until women, as universally as men, have the power of gaining their own livelihood: until, therefore, every girl's parents have either provided her with independent means of subsistence, or given her an education qualifying her to provide those means for herself."[96] Mill and Taylor, while discussing the working-class family, state that these women would not be as susceptible to the abuses of their husbands if they had a right to keep the wages they labored for. "These excesses could not exist if women both earned, and had the right to possess, a part of the income of the family."[97]

They believe it is only fair that woman be given the equality of opportunity to partake in society like man. "But so long as competition is the general law of human life, it is tyranny to shut out one-half of the competitors."[98] As long as there is dependence in pecuniary circumstances, the perfect independence between man and woman cannot exist. Mill and Taylor therefore believe that woman's economic independence will eventually end the arbitrariness of marriage.

According to Mill, a change in education will help lay the basis for woman's economic independence. Woman first must be educated to think that she should not be economically dependent on her father or her husband. In this way, the cultural underpinnings of her economic dependence will be challenged. "The first and indispensable step, therefore, towards the enfranchisement of woman, is that she be so educated, as not to be dependent either on her father or her husband for subsistence. . . ." [99]

Both Mill and Taylor's belief in the equality of women with men stems from their view of woman's nature. Whatever inequalities exist, exist as a result of societal and cultural manipulation of woman's true self. Mill in *On the Subjection of Women* is explicit on the question of woman's nature. He does not believe that anyone knows what it is: ". . . I deny that anyone knows, or can know, the nature of the two sexes, as long as they have only been seen in their present relation to one another." [100] Woman's nature, according to his analysis, is merely an artificial creation of societal needs. "What is now called the nature of women is an eminently artificial thing—the result of forced repression in some directions, unnatural stimulation in others." [101] He therefore believes it is impossible to know what the true differences are between men and women when all one knows are those men and women who have grown up under present cultural pressures. "For however great and apparently ineradicable the moral and intellectual differences between men and women might be, the evidence of there being natural differences could only be negative." [102]

Nevertheless, when Mill defines the desirable division of labor between man and woman, husband and wife, in *On the Subjection of Women*, he adopts the patriarchal division of male and female sexual spheres. Mill's design of the desirable division of labor within the family generally envisions the man as the income earner and the woman as caring for the home. "When the support of the family depends, not on property, but on earnings, the common arrangement, by which the man earns the income and the wife superintends the domestic expenditure, seems to me *in general* the most suitable division of labor between the two persons." [103] Mill believes that for the majority of women, their role is to be a mother and supervisor of the home. Such a division of work should define the average household. "Like a man when he chooses a profession, so, when a woman marries, it may in general be understood that she makes choice of the management of a household, and the bringing up of a family, as the first call upon her exertions." [104] Even though Mill corresponded with Taylor about the need for woman's economic independence, he does not think this is really desirable. "It does not follow that a woman should *actually* support herself because she should be *capable* of doing so: in the natural course of events she will not." [105] The desirable allocation of work, according to Mill, is that men sustain the family economically while women adorn and beautify it.

> In a healthy state of things, the husband would be able by his single exertions to earn all that is necessary for both: and there would be no need that the wife should take part in the mere providing of what is required to *support* life: it will be for the happiness of both that her occupation should rather be to adorn and beautify it. [106]

The sexual division of labor between male and female domains extends to the labor market itself. When women work for wages, it should be work that is delicate and in the area of the fine arts "which require delicacy and taste rather than muscular exertion." [107]

Mill, in accepting the sexual division of labor between men and women, home and market, argues that these are equal domains. He believes the woman does more than her fair share in the joint existence of marriage.

> If in addition to the physical suffering of bearing children, and the whole responsibility of their care and education in early years, the wife undertakes the careful and economical application of the husband's earnings to the general comfort of the family; she takes not only her fair share but usually the larger share, of the bodily and mental exertion required by their joint existence. [108]

Mill recognizes the activity of women as childrearers and domestics within the home as work and as completely necessary and valuable to society. He perceives woman's role as a mother as unique and important in shaping the character of her children. "It is not by particular effects, but imperceptibly and unconsciously that she makes her own character pass into the child; that she makes the child love what she loves, venerate what she venerates and imitate as far as a child can her example." [109]

Mill never says why it should be exclusively women who rear children. Considering his own argument about the lack of an innate woman's nature, there does not seem to be a justification (or reason) for the sexual spheres he ascribes to. This argument also contrasts with his explicit rejection of the sexual sphere's doctrine in "On the Enfranchisement of Women." Mill and Taylor wrote: "We deny the right of any portion of the species to decide for another portion, or any individual for another individual, what is and what is not their 'proper sphere.' The proper sphere for all human beings is the largest and highest which they are able to attain to." [110] It would appear there is no reason for Mill's position except for the existing patriarchal culture and custom that sustains female childrearing, although this is viewed by him as an artificial creation. "I have said that it cannot now be known how much of the existing mental differences between men and women are natural, and how much artificial; whether there are any natural differences at all; or, supposing all artificial causes of difference to be withdrawn, what natural character would be revealed." [111]

He also states in *On the Subjection of Women* that it would be presumptuous for anyone to pretend to know what women are or are not, can or cannot be, by natural constitution. [112] Nevertheless, Mill prescribes the role of mother and wife for women and is critical of the social necessity of women working for wages. "In an otherwise just state of things, it is not, therefore I think, a desirable custom, that the wife should contribute by her labour to the income of the family." [113]

Mill and Taylor's rejection of a view of woman's nature and their criticism of the "separate spheres" doctrine is contradictory to Mill's preferred model of woman as mother, and father as income earner. Mill has removed whatever explanations can be used to justify this division in his rejection of a static conception of woman's nature. The contradiction between Mill and Taylor's critique of the oppressiveness of custom and Mill's acceptance of the patriarchal division of separate sexual spheres because it is custom reflects the cultural pervasiveness of woman's subjugation. The enforcement of woman's economic dependence on man by prescribing that woman's responsibilities are within the home, making her dependent on the wages of her husband and father, further contradicts the necessity of woman's economic independence discussed in the letters exchanged between Mill and Taylor.

Mill believed that because the home and children are woman's responsibility, she should not have to be doubly burdened by laboring for wages outside the home. "If she undertakes any additional portion, it seldom relieves her from this, but only prevents her from performing it properly. The care which she is herself disabled from taking of the children and the household, nobody else takes. . . ." [114] Although Mill tries to protect woman from carrying the double burdens of work inside and outside the home, he at the same time relegates woman to the position of an economic dependent, with all the burdens inherent to this role. Women remain limited to the patriarchal definition of motherhood, and their rights are limited by the needs of this system. One is left wondering how women experience the personal liberty Mill writes of when women are the economic dependents of their husbands. Or how they actualize their individuality when women do not experience the freedom to choose their "sphere" in life.

Mill criticizes the legal slavery of marriage without understanding that women's slavery in marriage is rooted in the confinement of woman to the private sphere of the family and the sexual division of labor within the family. Hence, Mill makes his argument for women's rights while positing a view for women that entails the existing patriarchal relations that make her an economic dependent. This reflects Mill's inadequate understanding of how woman's inequality exists within the patriarchal institutionalization of public and private life through her role as mother.

Mill does believe that individual women who want the opportunity to choose a life other than motherhood and marriage should have the freedom to do so. He nevertheless believes that most women will not make this choice. It is not necessary to force women into marriage by closing off other alternatives to them by restricting their other options. The legal barriers are unnecessary and unjust.[115] Because of Mill's opinion that ordinary men and women are slaves to custom, he believed legal barriers restricting women's opportunities were unnecessary; the majority of women will continue to choose marriage.

Mill pleads in defense of the extraordinary woman. Those few exceptional women who will choose another life should have the liberty to do so. Most women will be conventional and follow patriarchal custom. In discussing the necessities of marriage, he questions whether the "average" human nature doesn't need the constraints of marriage. "But will the morality which suits the highest natures, in this matter, be also best for all inferior natures?"[116] For women as for men, he differentiates between the highest natures of individuals and the common person. Mill assumes most women will choose married life without recognizing the continued economic and cultural necessity of such a choice. Women will still be defined as economic dependents. Marriage will still be defined culturally as a necessity for motherhood. Motherhood will remain a cultural definition of womanhood, even after women vote or hold property. The exclusiveness of Mill's argument emerges: change the laws to enable gifted women who wish to experience alternatives to be able to do so. But most women will remain within the home. Individual choice and development remain a possibility for only a few women. The promise of individuality becomes an exclusionary patriarchal individualism.

In the same way Mill spoke of liberal individualism while positing the dependence of the economic class structure, he speaks of personal liberty for women in *On the Subjection of Women* while positing their dependence within separate sexual spheres. His understanding of the political inequality within the family is in terms of property and legal rights. He does not recognize the sexual division of labor as a reflector and instigator of woman's larger economic and sexual inequality existent outside the law. Although we do not know Taylor's thoughts in regard to *On the Subjection of Women*, we can only assume from her earlier writing that she would have differed with Mill. It remains an unwritten mystery as to how she would have resolved the tension between her liberal individualism and her feminist insights.

Neither Mill nor Taylor recognized the political relationship between patriarchy and the sexual division of labor within their liberal feminist political framework, which pictured the individual as atomized and disconnected from the patriarchal social structure that defines women's lives. They themselves were not limited to this view in that they made demands on behalf of women as a subjugated group that required a critique of the liberal individualist position. They did not merely blame individual women for their condition. But this understanding of women as a sexual class is not developed by Mill in his later writing, as it will be by Stanton in the next chapter.

Mill and Taylor's recognition of the importance of motherhood in women's lives required that they move beyond their liberal-legal view of equality because equality before the law does not address women's inequality due to their exclusion from public life as mothers. Once one recognizes not only the legal but the extralegal[117] patriarchal privileges men enjoy through the sexual division of labor, it becomes clearer how the vote recognizes woman as a citizen within the patriarchal relations of sexual and economic class society. If Mill and Taylor had recognized this, they would have had to recognize the political implication of woman defined as mother and wife for *both* the ordinary and exceptional woman. They would have had to understand that such a division of labor creates the "ordinary" woman and virtually makes impossible the development of the exceptional woman.

In the same way that Mill and Taylor do not free most men to become intellectuals, they do not free most women either. The difference is that women are kept from this option not only because of the capitalist-class relations of society but because of the patriarchal sexual division of society defining their lives. Mill's commitment to the *exceptional* woman via the work done by the rest of the common women as mothers of society reflects a misunderstanding of the relations of power of society. There is no way that any single "exceptional" woman can become completely free of the patriarchal structural relations of society. She remains defined in relationship to this structure even when, as an "exception," she tries to defy it. This is the consequence of the structural reality of power rather than a reflection of liberal individualist options.

Although Mill and Taylor are responsible for presenting some of the most radical liberal feminist ideas that existed in England in their lifetime, inherent in their liberal feminism is a disturbing inadequacy. At the heart of this limitation is the violation of working-class men's and working- and middle-class women's freedom. If the liberal feminism of today is to remain progressive in its demands, it needs to realize that feminism must challenge the patriarchal bias of liberalism by challenging the patriarchal reality of public and private life. Although Mill and Taylor seem to have begun this challenge in their criticism of separate sexual spheres, this understanding becomes reduced to the ideology of liberal individualism via the acceptance of patriarchal sexual spheres.

Mill and Taylor's contribution to feminist theory is in extending and developing the ideology of individualism *for women*. As an ideology, it asserts the subversive claims of woman's independence, autonomy, and selfhood, even if these do not apply in practice given the social constraints. The conception of liberal individualism Mill and Taylor work from has ideological import in presenting a promise of equality to women. Feminism is left with the interesting question of how a conception of individuality that recognizes intellectual diversity and sexual equality can distinguish itself from the ideology of liberal individualism. Mill and Taylor only begin to pose this problem in their criticism of liberalism and socialism. Until one moves beyond liberalism, one cannot begin to uncover the promise of sexual egalitarianism in the idea of individuality.

NOTES

1. For a full discussion of this issue, see Gertrude Himmelfarb, *On Liberty and Liberalism, The Case of John Stuart Mill* (New York: Knopf, 1974); Josephine Kamm, *John Stuart Mill in Love* (London: Gordon and Cremonesi, 1977); and Alice Rossi, ed., *Essays on Sex Equality* (Chicago: University of Chicago Press, 1970).

2. For the purposes of this chapter, I assume the joint authorship of "On the Enfranchisement of Women," in *Female Liberation*, ed. Roberta Salper (New York: Knopf, 1972), as I do for the other writings discussed here. I make this judgment while recognizing that the problem of Mill and Taylor's joint collaboration cannot be resolved in these pages. Therefore, I treat all their writing on socialism and women written while Taylor was alive as co-authored, even though these manuscripts are attributed to Mill. There is no satisfactory way to resolve the question of primary authorship between Mill and Taylor, particularly for the manuscript "On the Enfranchisement of Women." The question of sole authorship is even more difficult. Everything Mill wrote while Taylor was alive, on women or socialism, was completely discussed with her. The same can be said of Taylor's writing and her relationship to Mill. It is inconceivable that they did not discuss "Enfranchisement of Women" at great length with each other. Mill and Taylor acknowledge this collaboration in their correspondences. Although Salper in

Female Liberation and Rossi in *Essays on Sex Equality* attribute the article to Harriet Taylor, and although there is convincing documentation that "Enfranchisement" contains insights that Mill's *On the Subjection of Women* (Greenwich, Conn.: Fawcett, 1971) does not contain, the proof of sole authorship of this manuscript stands beyond the limits of the analysis here. For further detailed discussion of the joint nature of the writing of "Enfranchisement," see Himmelfarb's *On Liberty and Liberalism,* pp. 183–86. After all this has been said, it is important to note that little hinges on the proof of sole authorship of this article for the analysis of this chapter. No matter if one thinks Taylor wrote "Enfranchisement" by herself or Mill wrote it or it was a shared product, the important contradictions exist regardless. This is especially true for Mill's works written after Taylor's death. The contradictions in Mill's writing do not exist merely between "Enfranchisement" and *On the Subjection of Women,* they are internal to the latter manuscript.

3. John Stuart Mill, *Autobiography of John Stuart Mill* (New York: Columbia University Press, 1924), p. 171.

4. Ibid., p. 17. Acknowledgments such as these have led analysts of Mill to argue that it was primarily Taylor who had the strong socialist commitment. Himmelfarb unconvincingly argues in *On Liberty and Liberalism* that it was the socialist commitments of Taylor that created the contradictory nature of Mill's treatment of liberalism.

5. Ibid., p. 171.

6. For an interesting discussion of this distinction, see Rosalind Petchesky, "Reproductive Freedom: Beyond a 'Woman's Right to Choose,' " *Signs* (Summer 1980, forthcoming).

7. Taylor identifies woman as a member of a sexual "caste," separate and distinct from man, in "On the Enfranchisement of Women," in Salper. Her conception of "sexual caste" parallels my conception of "sexual class." I have chosen to discuss Mill and Taylor's understanding of woman's subjugation in terms of sexual class (rather than caste) because their own analysis denies the "determined," and "static," condition of caste relations. Although Mill and Taylor's understanding of sexual-class oppression is left underdeveloped, their implicit recognition of woman as sexual class is essential to their demand for women's equality of opportunity with men.

8. John Stuart Mill, *On Liberty* (Indianapolis: Bobbs-Merrill, 1956), p. 91.

9. Ibid., p. 94.

10. Ibid., p. 92. This notion of liberty, premised on the clear separation of self and other, also reflects the distinct separation of individual thought and action. See *On Liberty.*

11. Ibid., p. 97.

12. Ibid., p. 79.

13. Ibid., p. 80.

14. Ibid., p. 79

15. Ibid., p. 80.

16. Ibid., p. 81.

17. Ibid., pp. 41–42.

18. Ibid., p. 71.

19. Ibid.

20. Ibid., p. 84.

21. John Stuart Mill, "Considerations On Representative Government," in *John Stuart Mill, Three Essays,* ed. Richard Wollheim (New York: Oxford University Press, 1975), p. 287.

22. Ibid., p. 278.

23. Mill, *Subjection of Women,* p. 68 (italics mine).

24. John Stuart Mill, "Thoughts on Parliamentary Reform" in *Essays on Politics and Culture,* ed. Gertrude Himmelfarb (New York: Doubleday, 1962), p. 339.

25. Ibid.

26. Ibid., p. 340

27. Ibid., p. 341.

28. Ibid., p. 340.

29. Ibid., p. 338.

30. Mill, "Representative Government," p. 240.

31. Ibid., p. 289.

32. Francis W. Garforth, ed., *John Stuart Mill on Education* (New York: Teachers College Press, 1971), p. 15.

33. Frederick Engels, *The Condition of the Working Class in England* (Moscow: Progress Publishers, 1973), p. 152.

34. Mill, "Representative Government," p. 237.

35. Ibid., p. 245.

36. Ibid., p. 246.

37. Ibid., p. 286.

38. Mill, *Autobiography,* p. 119.

39. See Graeme Duncan, *Marx and Mill: Two Views of Social Conflict and Social Harmony* (New York: Cambridge University Press, 1973), for a full elaboration of this point.

40. Mill, *On Liberty,* p. 13.

41. Ibid., p. 58. Mill and Taylor's belief that one must always rethink and reexamine ideas in the hope that one moves closer to the truth appears to have directed their own intellectual examination of socialism.

42. Ibid.

43. Ibid., p. 25. This has become the classic liberal argument for the importance of freedom of speech. For a critique of this position, see Herbert Marcuse, "Repressive Tolerance," in *A Critique of Pure Toler-*

ance, ed. by B. Moore, R. P. Wolff, and H. Marcuse (Boston: Beacon, 1969).

44. Mill, *Autobiography,* p. 117. Mill was especially persuaded by St. Simon's eagerness to create the "perfect equality" between men and women.

45. Ibid., p. 162.

46. Ibid., p. 117.

47. John Stuart Mill, "From the Autobiography," in *Socialism,* ed. W. D. P. Bliss (New York: Humboldt, 1890), p. 9.

48. John Stuart Mill, "From the Political Economy, Book II, Chapter I," in Bliss, *Socialism,* p. 25.

49. Ibid., p. 26.

50. Ibid.

51. Ibid.

52. Ibid.

53. Mill, *Autobiography,* p. 162.

54. John Stuart Mill, "From the Fortnightly Review, March 1879," in Bliss, *Socialism,* p. 95.

55. J. S. Mill, "From the Political Economy, Book V, Chapter VI," in Bliss, *Socialism,* p. 95.

56. Mill, "From the Fortnightly Review, April 1879," in Bliss, *Socialism,* p. 120.

57. Mill, *Autobiography,* p. 163.

58. J. S. Mill, "From the Political Economy, Book II, Chapter II," in Bliss, *Socialism,* p. 38.

59. Ibid., p. 36.

60. Ibid.

61. Ibid., p. 35.

62. Mill, "From the Political Economy, Book II, Chapter I," p. 24.

63. Ibid., p. 23.

64. Ibid.

65. Ibid., p. 25.

66. Harriet Taylor Mill, "On the Enfranchisement of Women," p. 45.

67. Ibid., p. 39.

68. Mill, *Subjection of Women,* p. 34.

69. J. S. Mill, "From Dissertations and Discussions, vol. III," in Bliss, *Socialism,* p. 186.

70. Mill, *Autobiography,* p. 198.

71. Ibid., p. 21.

72. Mill, "On Parliamentary Reform," in Himmelfarb, *On Liberty and Liberalism,* p. 352.

73. Kamm, *Mill in Love,* p. 160.

74. For a general discussion of this period, see Arthur Allen, *Vic-*

torian England, 1850–1900 (London: Rockliff, 1956); Duncan Crow, *The Victorian Woman* (New York: Stein and Day, 1971); R. J. Evans, *The Victorian Age, 1815–1914* (London: Edward Arnold, 1968); Marion Lochhead, *The Victorian Household* (London: John Murray, 1964); and Barbara Rees, *The Victorian Lady* (London: Gordon and Cremonesi, 1977).

75. Crow, *The Victorian Woman*, p. 48.

76. Ibid., p. 17.

77. Patricia Branca, *Silent Sisterhood, Middle-Class Women in the Victorian Home* (London: Croom Helm, 1975).

78. Ibid., p. 16.

79. Ibid.

80. Ibid., pp. 40–41. According to Branca, merchants, manufacturers, shipbuilders, and lawyers most often made over £300 in a given year; whereas clerks, educators, and clergy earned below this. In comparison, highly skilled members of the working class earned between £50 and £73.

81. Ibid., p. 54. According to Rees, *The Victorian Lady*, Mrs. Beeton suggested five servants for families with incomes of about £1000 a year: a cook, upper housemaid, a nursemaid, under housemaid and a man (p. 63). Lochhead, *Victorian Household*, states that only in homes with incomes over £5000 does one find multiple servants (p. 30).

82. See Ann Oakley, *Woman's Work: The Housewife, Past and Present* (New York: Vintage, 1974).

83. Wanda Neff, *Victorian Working Women* (London: Frank Cass, 1966), p. 153. Also see Margaret Hewitt, *Wives and Mothers in Victorian Industry* (London: Rockliff, 1958); and Lee Holcombe, *Victorian Ladies at Work, Middle-Class Working Women in England and Wales, 1850–1914* (Hamden, Conn.: Archon, 1973).

84. Rees, *The Victorian Lady*, p. 98.

85. Ibid., p. 106.

86. Michael Anderson, *Family Structure in Nineteenth-Century Lancashire* (London: Cambridge University Press, 1971).

87. Hewitt, *Mothers in Victorian Industry*, p. 29,

88. Engels, *The Working Class in England*, p. 182. For a discussion of the economic class aspects of women's work, see Sally Alexander, "Women's Work in Nineteenth-Century London; A Study of the Years 1820–50," in *The Rights and Wrongs of Women*, ed. Juliet Mitchell and Ann Oakley (New York: Penguin, 1976); J. M. Goldstrom, ed., *The Working Classes in the Victorian Age* (London: Gregg International, 1973); Karl Marx, *Capital*, vol. 1 (New York: International Publishers, 1967); Neil McKendrick, "Home Demand and Economic Growth: A New View of the Role of Women and Children in the Industrial Revolution," in *Historical Perspectives: Studies in English Thought and Society in Honor of*

J. H. Plumb, ed. Neil McKendrick (London: Europa, 1974); Sheila Rowbotham, *Hidden from History* (London: Pluto, 1976); and Neil Smelser, *Social Change in the Industrial Revolution: An Application of Theory to the British Cotton Industry* (Chicago: University of Chicago Press, 1969).

89. Mill, *Subjection of Women*, p. 35.

90. Ibid.

91. Ibid., p. 15.

92. Ibid., p. 103.

93. Ibid., p. 30.

94. Harriet Taylor Mill, "Enfranchisement of Women," p. 51.

95. Friedrich A. Hayek, *John Stuart Mill and Harriet Taylor, Their Friendship and Subsequent Marriage* (London: Routledge and Kegan Paul, 1951), p. 64.

96. Ibid., p. 68.

97. Harriet Taylor Mill, "Enfranchisement of Women," p. 42, note 2.

98. Ibid., p. 43.

99. Hayek, *Mill and Taylor*, p. 65.

100. Mill, *Subjection of Women*, p. 37.

101. Ibid., p. 38.

102. Ibid., p. 39.

103. Ibid., p. 67 (italics mine).

104. Ibid., p. 68.

105. Hayek, *Mill and Taylor*, p. 65.

106. Ibid.

107. Ibid., p. 68.

108. Mill, *Subjection of Women*, p. 67.

109. Ibid.

110. Harriet Taylor Mill, "Enfranchisement of Women," p. 39. One might argue that if "Enfranchisement" was solely written by Taylor rather than Mill, the problem does not hold. But it does because Mill himself rejects the notion of a woman's nature in *Subjection of Women*

111. Mill, *Subjection of Women*, p. 89.

112. Ibid., pp. 89–90.

113. Ibid., p. 67.

114. Ibid.

115. Ibid., p. 45.

116. Hayek, *Mill and Taylor*, p. 60.

117. Although my meaning here applies to the sexual structuring of society, see Rosa Luxemburg, "Social Reform or Revolution," in *Selected Political Writings, Rosa Luxemburg*, ed. Dick Howard (New York: Monthly Review Press, 1971), for a discussion of the extralegal paradigm of economic class power.

7

Elizabeth Cady Stanton: Radical Feminist Analysis and Liberal Feminist Strategy

Elizabeth Cady Stanton (1815–1902) continues the feminist struggle started by Wollstonecraft, John Stuart Mill, and Harriet Taylor, but as part of an American women's movement.[1] Along with Lucretia Mott, Stanton called for the first Seneca Falls women's rights convention in 1848. In 1853 Susan B. Anthony left the ranks of temperance and abolitionism to help her begin building an independent women's movement.

Stanton has often been called the philosopher of nineteenth-century feminism, but there has been little examination of the theory she expounded.[2] In this chapter I examine her theory of liberal feminism, as well as the political strategy she adopted. It is my purpose to define the radical feminist as well as the liberal influences that construct her theory. Her radical feminist understanding of woman's oppression, the recognition of women as part of a sexual class, is found in her discussions of marriage, motherhood, and divorce. In these writings, she begins to question the division of public and private life as male and female spheres. However, the liberal and republican influences in Stanton's thought cannot help her in this feminist endeavor because they seek to protect the relationship between the state and the family as a sexual division. Liberalism and republicanism reproduce the patriarchal division between public and private life as male and female, respectively, by emphasizing the important role of the (male) citizen in public life. Stanton's analysis of the family and marriage allows her to recognize a relationship between these sexual spheres, but their separation in liberal and republican thought[3] causes confusion in her presentation.

I argue that the demand for the vote for women reflects Stanton's liberal, republican, and radical feminist commitments. However, it was her understanding of woman as an oppressed sexual class that underlay the demand for the vote *for women*. I also argue that Stanton's theory of liberal individualism underpins her feminist analysis. I specifically want to draw attention to the possibility of distinguishing, in Stanton's thought, between the idea of the independent individual, which is so crucial to feminist theory, and the liberal ideology of emancipation, meaning the formal rights given the individual within the state. Stanton's feminism owes its origins to her view of liberal individualism, although this theory instigates, rather than completes, her radical feminist analysis of women's oppression within the system of patriarchy. A study of Stanton's theoretical work allows us to understand the contribution of liberalism to the development of the radical feminist position and its limitations.

It is often not possible to separate Stanton's liberalism from her feminism. She defines her feminism in liberal terms, and sometimes the analytic distinctions become fused in practice. But there are also times when her feminism transcends its liberal limits. It is my concern to distinguish the two systems and uncover the tension between them in order to see which of her feminist insights have been lost to liberal political strategy.

The New Femininity vs. Liberal Ideology

At the same time that liberal ideology, with its emphasis on personal freedom and social equality, began to take hold in America and sparked a vision of female emancipation among such women as Stanton, another ideology advocating what was called the "new femininity" stressing woman's submissiveness and economic dependence was gaining an even wider audience. The growing split between woman's role in the home and her role in the wider economy gave rise to this ideology, which sought to confine women, not to extend their sphere. Woman's developing role as mother, homemaker, and economic dependent was new to nineteenth-century America.

We need to recall our earlier discussion about industrial capitalism's impact on the family.[4] By the mid-eighteenth century, the market had begun to change women's lives significantly. The emergence of new bourgeois relations led to the abolition of social rank,[5] just as it had done earlier in Europe. The ideology of liberal individualism and equality of opportunity became part of the spirit of the times. Much the same as it had happened in England, domestic manufacture was moving to the factories, and married women of both the working and middle classes were increasingly defined in relation to the home.[6] The supposed idleness of the home is now taken by contemporaries to define the woman herself. According to Gordon and

Buhle: "The older traditions of feminine usefulness, strength, and duty were cast aside for moral and decorative functions, and subjugation to domesticity became the most revered feminine virtue."[7]

The ideology that reflected the transition to industrialism redefined the new priorities of women's work. According to Mary Ryan, "the manual labor of the wife now centered around personal services to the sole male breadwinner."[8] By the second half of the nineteenth century, the home had become "the woman's sphere." Woman could best aid society from the home, as wife and mother. This redefined picture of woman's role corresponded to a real change in her position within the family. Married women, in fact, became caretakers and nurturers of husbands and children. Domestic life took on a reality and dimension that it had not had before; it became a world unto itself.

> The family concentrated itself and turned inward, privacy became important, the education of children assumed major proportions, and women acquired a great many new duties and responsibilities. This process, which began with the middle class, was completed in the nineteenth century when all classes developed at least a formal commitment to bourgeois standards of familialism.[9]

Married women's lives were more fully circumscribed than ever because of their economic displacement.[10] As economic opportunities opened up for men, women, especially married women, became economically more dependent. This contrast highlighted woman's political and social inequality, especially in a period in which ascribed social hierarchy was under attack in the push for universal *man*hood suffrage. Equality of economic opportunity undermined status inequality for men. But options for the married woman were shrinking. Housework and child care were not paid labor. Men became less involved in domestic life. Women were relegated to the private realm at the very moment status and power were equated with positions in the public world.[11] The ideology of the new femininity endorsed this process. It assigned woman a lower status because of her sex. She was not supposed to "achieve" the status of citizen.

Sex and Race

Stanton held this ideology of the "new femininity" up to the critique of liberal individualism and found it wanting in much the same way she extended the ideology of liberal individualism to the question of the enfranchisement of blacks. One cannot write of Stanton's sexual politics without addressing her position on the enfranchisement of blacks because the two issues were entwined for her. She believed that the exclusion of women and blacks from citizenship, on the basis of their ascribed status by race and/or sex, was a violation of the liberal promise of equality of opportunity as a universal goal. The exclusion of blacks and women from citizen rights involved the same question for her: the right of an individual to an independent and self-fulfilling life. Stanton as well as Susan B. Anthony and Sarah Grimke were sensitized to their own sexual oppression through their earlier antislavery involvement. Most active feminists of their period had been abolitionists first.

Only when Stanton felt that the abolitionist struggle did not recognize the question of women's rights as of equal import with their own struggle did she disassociate herself from it. When the world Anti-Slavery Convention of 1840 in London refused to seat the women in the American delegation,[12] Lucretia Mott and Elizabeth Cady Stanton, the decision was made to begin a women's rights movement. The feminist movement began to build its autonomous base in reaction to the sexism of the abolitionist movement, although the actual split between abolitionists and feminists did not come until 1866–67.[13] The critical issue that brought the split centered around the vote for the black *man*. Stanton wrote to Susan B. Anthony in 1865 that she feared that black men would be enfranchised without women: ". . . but I fear one and all will favor enfranchising the negro without us. Woman's cause is in deep water. With the league disbanded, there is pressing need of our Woman's Rights Convention. Come back and help. There will be a room for you. I seem to stand alone."[14] Stanton also wrote to Martha Wright in 1865 arguing that, as feminists, they must insist on women's right to the vote along with the right of black men. They should not defer to the "negro's hour."

> We have fairly boosted the negro, over our own heads, and now we had better begin to remember that self-preservation is the first law of nature. Some say, "Be still, wait, this is the negro's hour." But I believe this is the hour for everybody to do the best thing for reconstruction. A vote based on intelligence and education for black and white, man and woman—that is what we need.[15]

Stanton saw no sense in distinguishing among the various categories of disenfranchised citizens. All the disenfranchised suffered alike. She therefore questioned enfranchisement for the black man that excluded the black woman. In a letter to Wendell Phillipps in 1865, she wrote:

> You say, "this is the negro's hour." I will not insist that there are women of that race, but ask, Is there not danger that he, once entrenched in all his inalienable rights, may be an added power to hold us at bay? Why should the African prove more

just and generous than his Saxon compeers? Again, if the two millions of Southern black women are not to be secured in their rights of person, property, wages, and children, then their emancipation is but another form of slavery.[16]

She could not defer to "the negro's hour" because she believed black men would rule black women if women were not enfranchised at the same time. This formulation reveals her early understanding of patriarchy: that white and black men share a sexual partnership as males, which on the basis of the historical record, Stanton did not trust.

It is her espousal of the notions of self-sovereignty and independence that makes Stanton both an abolitionist and a feminist. It is a commitment to the liberal conception of the independent and autonomous self that connects the political struggles for racial and sexual emancipation. For Stanton, the logic of liberal theory demands equality of opportunity for black and white, man and woman. Liberalism as an ideology recognizes individuals and their particular rights. Stanton wished to force the liberal democratic state to make good on its individualist promise.

Her radical feminist position, however, would not allow her to defer the question of women's rights to abolitionist demands. Her liberal political strategy of enfranchisement could not help her overcome the state's pitting of sex interests against race interests. Nor could it address how the state *used* the patriarchal stance of many abolitionists to fight women's enfranchisement. Neither analysis, radical feminist or liberal individualist, could fully help Stanton develop a strategy that could aid her in achieving political victory.

Women's "Rights" Against "The Aristocracy of Sex"

Stanton wanted to give women the possibility of achieving something for themselves. Individual freedom, personal independence, and the equality of opportunity, which were in practice privileges only open to men, would have to be opened to women if they were to remain valid as political ideals for her. She pointed out that in the Preamble to the Constitution these rights were extended to people in general, not merely to men.

> This is declared to be a government "of the people." All power it is said, centers in the people. Our state constitutions also open with the words, "We the People." Does any one pretend to say that men alone constitute races and peoples? When we say parents, do we not mean mothers as well as fathers? When we say children, do we not mean girls as well as boys? When we say people, do we not mean women as well as men? [17]

The ideology of liberal democracy requires that freedom and equality apply to "all" persons equally. The very basis of individual rights is that everyone supposedly shares them alike. Stanton takes the language of the Constitution seriously and demands that women be able to enjoy personal independence. Her demand, however, requires freeing women from their present subservient, dependent status by destroying the arbitrary rule by men. "When we place in the hands of one class of citizens the right to make, interpret and execute the law for another class wholly unrepresented in the government, we have made an order of nobility." [18] White males are the nobility in America, according to Stanton: ". . . they are the privileged order, who have legislated as unjustly for women and negroes as have the nobles of England for their disfranchised classes." [19]   As long as women are denied representation in government, government will remain an oligarchy of males rather than a republic of the people.[20] "I detest the words royalty and nobility and all the ideas and institutions based on them." [21] The "rule of men" resonates with the outworn dogma of divine-right rule. "Hence, he takes upon himself the responsibility of directing and controlling the powers of woman, under that all-sufficient excuse of tyranny, 'divine right.' " [22] Just as men used the liberal idea of individual sovereignty to dislodge the power of the king, Stanton, like Wollstonecraft before her, now extends this notion along with natural-rights doctrine to dislodge the power of men.

According to natural-rights doctrine, women should have the individual right to self-determination. Natural rights are a component part of individuals and cannot be taken from them. Stanton therefore argues that women bring their rights into the world with them: ". . . every individual comes into this world with rights that are not transferable. He does not bring them like a pack on his back, that may be stolen from him, but they are a component part of himself, the laws which insure his growth and development." [23] Because Stanton believes "her rights were born with her" and apply universally,[24] she cannot accept "the man-made constitution the man-interpretation thereof, the man-amendment submitted by a convention of aristocrats" [25] that denies her these rights. The right to govern one's own destiny is woman's at birth and cannot rightfully be denied her. In a phrase again reminiscent of Wollstonecraft, Stanton describes the rule of men as the "aristocracy of sex." [26] In her eyes it is the most harmful form of rule, for it is based on force rather than reason. "Of all kinds of aristocracy, that of sex is the most odious and unnatural; invading, as it does, our homes, desecrating our family altars, dividing those whom God has joined together, exalting the son above the mother who bore him, and subjugating, everywhere moral power to brute force." [27]

Stanton takes the liberal ideas of nineteenth-century America in much the same way Wollstonecraft took eighteenth-century English liberalism and applies them to women because she believes that women should share in the newborn liberties of their time.

> In gathering up the threads of history in the last century, and weaving its facts and philosophy together, one can trace the *liberal social ideas,* growing out of the political and religious revolutions in France, Germany, Italy and America; and their tendency *to substitute for the divine right of kings, priests, and orders of nobility, the higher and broader one of individual conscience and judgment,* in all matters pertaining to this life and that which is to come. It is not surprising that in so marked a transition period from the old to the new, as seen in the eighteenth century, *that women, trained to think and write and speak, should have discovered that they, too, had some share in the new-born liberties suddenly announced to the world.* [28]

This position against the anachronistic rule of men led Stanton to fight against the Fifteenth Amendment to the Constitution, which would enfranchise black men but not women. As such, the Fifteenth Amendment, in Stanton's view, would establish the aristocracy of sex, once again.

> A government, based on the principle of caste and class, cannot stand. The aristocratic idea, in any form, is opposed to the genius of our free institutions, to our own declaration of rights, and to the civilization of the age. All artificial distinctions, whether of family, blood, wealth, color, or sex, are equally oppressive to the subject classes and equally destructive to national life and prosperity. [29]

Women's exclusion from citizenship contradicts the universal promise of equality of opportunity. Stanton asks, "While all men, everywhere, are rejoicing in new-found liberties, shall woman alone be denied the rights, privileges, and immunities of citizenship?" [30]

This concern with citizenship inspired the "Declaration of Sentiments and Resolutions," drawn up at Seneca Falls in 1848. The feminists present at this first meeting took the liberal theory of individual freedom, personal independence, and social equality and finally applied it to themselves. They wrote: "We hold these truths to be self-evident: that all men and women are created equal. . . ." [31] Women citizens of the United States were therefore entitled to all the rights of citizenship. As late as 1902, Stanton was still fighting this battle. She writes of this in her letter to Theodore Roosevelt in which she complains of the tyranny of "taxation without representation." "In the beginning of our nation, the fathers declared that no just government can be founded without the consent of the governed, and that "taxation without representation is tyranny." Both of these grand declarations are denied in the present position of woman, who constitutes one half of the people."[32] Stanton wanted women to have an equal chance with men in the "race of life." To create equality of opportunity with men, women had to be recognized as citizens.

Liberal Individualism and Feminism

Stanton believed that personal merit and not artificial inheritance or family position should decide one's place in life. An individual should work hard to make his or her mark on the world. One's particular individuality will be expressed by one's performance. "Nothing adds such dignity to character as the recognition of one's self-sovereignty; the right to an equal place, everywhere conceded—a place earned by personal merit, not an artificial attainment by inheritance, wealth, family and position."[33] To attain such results, one needs certain personal qualities. Speaking of her father in an 1898 entry in her diary, she writes of the importance of a person's self-assertion and drive: "It is those with push who have the rougher time, and it is generally these last that get the so-called honors of life. . . . When such men or women attain success, it is *due to pure personal merit*. But he would have attained still higher honors if he had been more self-asserting."[34]

Woman is instead reared for obedience and self-sacrifice to others rather than taught how to assert her own needs. Her situation of subordination denies her the opportunities for individual achievement that are rightly hers.

> To every step of progress which she has made from slavery to the partial freedom she now enjoys, the church and the State alike have made the most cruel opposition, and yet, under all circumstances she has shown her love of individual freedom, her desire for self-government, while her achievements in practical affairs and her courage in the great emergencies of life have vindicated her capacity to exercise this right. . . .[35]

Men's notion of womanliness requires women's deference and submissiveness. "It is to have a manner which pleases him—quiet, deferential, submissive, approaching him as a subject does a master. He wants no self-assertion on our part."[36] The situation is appalling to Stanton. She agrees with Mill; men cannot be virtuous unless women are their equals. "Men will be wise and virtuous just in proportion as women are self-reliant and able to meet them on the highest planes of thought and of action."[37] In contrast to Rousseau, Stanton argues that individual independence and freedom for men requires that their partners be self-sufficient persons. The question remains whether either Stanton or Rousseau is correct. For although in Stanton's mind men can be independent and free alongside the emancipated woman, the question whether liberal feminist citizen rights will emancipate women is left unresolved.

The demands of the women's rights movement emphasize the importance of individual merit. "The right of suffrage is simply the right to govern one's self." [38] The notion of woman's individuality also led some feminists, like Lucy Stone, to demand the right to keep her own name in marriage. Such a demand recognizes women's independence from men. "A woman's dignity is equally involved in a life long name to mark her individuality. We cannot overestimate the demoralizing effect on woman herself, to say nothing of society at large, for her to consent thus to merge her existence so wholly in that of another." [39] This concept of individuality also led Stanton to advise fathers to educate their daughters to "self support, if they were to become happy and independent." [40] They should not have to live at "the bounty of another." [41] The concern with woman's individuality presupposed Stanton's commitment to woman's freedom from the aristocracy of males and her equality with men. The resolution passed at the woman suffrage convention of 1885 stated that ". . . man was made in the image of God, male and female, and given dominion over the earth." [42]

The above discussion elaborates the progressive import of the theory of liberal individualism for feminism. It is used to establish woman's rightful independence from men. This theory, however, makes for difficulties in Stanton's feminist thinking in much the same way it did for Taylor and Mill. They confused woman's individuality and, hence, independence from men with the ideology of liberal individualism, the atomized individual, conceptualized as separate and apart from social life. Stanton articulates this conception of liberal individualism most clearly in her address "Solitude of Self," delivered at the National Woman Suffrage Association in 1892. [43]

In this address she stresses woman's isolation and separation from others, men and women alike. In the end, when the crises of life hit one, the woman stands alone. Stanton therefore believes that women must learn to count on themselves, because ultimately this is all they have. Women must be self-reliant and self-sufficient because they are entities unto themselves.

> The isolation of every human soul and the necessity of self-dependency must give each individual the right to choose his own surroundings. The strongest reason for giving woman all the opportunities for higher education, for the full development of her faculties, her forces of mind and body; for

> giving her the most enlarged freedom of thought and action . . .
> is the solitude and personal responsibility of her own
> individual life.[44]

Stanton argues the isolation of each human soul[45] in order to establish
what belongs to woman as an individual with a clear set of necessary
rights. Woman is "an imaginary Robinson Crusoe with her woman
Friday on a solitary island."[46]

The problem arises when one tries to sort through the meaning of
woman as an independent self-contained individual. Much of the time
Stanton uses the conception of liberal individualism to establish
woman's independence from men. This is what she means when she
criticizes the women in *Anna Karenina*, who are disappointed and un-
happy; "and well they may be, as they are made to look to men, and not
to themselves for their chief joy."[47]

Individualism posits the importance of self-sovereignty and independence as a universal claim and therefore can be used to justify
women's independence from men. When the ideology of liberal individualism is used in this way, it lays the basis for feminism. When I
argue that a conception of the individual as a person with autonomy is
the starting point of feminism, this is what I mean. It lays the base for
recognizing women's economic, sexual, and political independence
from men. Feminism uses the individualist stance against men because
men inhibit women's self and collective development; it need not extend this vision to premise women's isolation from one another. In
other words, the liberal conception of an individual with rights and of
woman's independence from men are important contributions to
feminist theory. These points must be distinguished from the ideology
of liberal individualism that posits the isolated, competitive individual.

This brings us to the problem with Stanton's usage of the ideology
of liberal individualism. Although she sometimes encourages this vision in her view of woman's separateness and distinctness from all
others, she also is aware that in order for women to develop their
capacities as individuals, they need connection to other women. My
point is that Stanton often confuses the issue that women must be
understood as independent from men with a view of atomized woman.
And Stanton's theory of sex class, as we shall shortly see, rejects the
atomized view of woman and instead recognizes woman as part of a
social collectivity. For her, understanding woman's oppression requires
a recognition of the social *and* individual nature of a woman's existence.
Being a woman is not merely an individual experience because woman
is always defined *in relation to* her sexual class. Stanton's radical
feminist vision allows her to use the ideology of liberal individualism
for women. This claim, however, recognizes both the rights women

have as individuals within the ideology of liberal individualism and their exclusion from these rights as part of a sexual class that recognizes women as a social collectivity. She therefore understood that women would not gain their rights without a social movement. This runs counter to her tendency to deal with women as "atomized individuals."

Stanton as a Radical Feminist

When one reads the letters written between Stanton and Susan B. Anthony about the feminist struggle they were engaged in, it is clear that they believed they were engaged in revolution. "We are in the midst of a social revolution, greater than any political or religious revolution that the world has ever seen, because it goes deep down to the very foundation of society."[48] It was a moral revolution that Stanton knew could not be brought about in a day or even a year.[49] She was aware that many of the reforms she was fighting for were insufficient. They even appeared superficial in terms of what she understood needed to be changed. She writes: "But above all this I am so full of dreams of the true associative life that all the reforms of the day beside that seem to be superficial and fragmentary."[50]

Stanton and Anthony named their newspaper the *Revolution*. Stanton stood firm against criticism that the name for the newspaper was too radical, curtly replying to her critics that maybe they would be more pleased with a title like the "Rosebud." Stanton writes to Anthony:

> There could not be a better name than *Revolution*. The establishing of woman on her rightful throne is the greatest revolution the world has ever known or ever will know. To bring it about is no child's play. You and I have not forgotten the conflict of the last 20 years. . . . A journal called the *Rosebud* might answer for those who come with kid gloves . . . but for us . . . there is no name like the *Revolution*.[51]

Stanton spoke of revolution, and signed her letters to her father "your affectionate and radical daughter," yet she was not a political revolutionary. Although much of her political analysis would seem to support revolutionary activity, she focused on the transformation of liberal law. She saw it as a necessary, though not a sufficient, step in women's struggle for emancipation. Because a significant contrast exists between Stanton's radical feminist analysis of women's oppression and her liberal political strategy demanding citizen rights and legal reform, we need to better understand both facets in order to understand the lost potential within liberal feminism. We can begin to do this by examining Stanton's radical feminist analysis of woman's oppression in the family, in marriage, and in motherhood.

Woman as a Sex Class

Stanton sees woman's subjugation as a reflection of man's power over woman. Woman is forced to be who she is. There is nothing natural about her subordination. "It has taken the whole power of the civil and canon law to hold woman in the subordinate position which it is said she willingly accepts." [52] She parallels the position of woman and man with that of slave and slaveholder. She therefore opposes men being elected to the office of president of the woman's suffrage association. "I would never vote for a man to any office in our societies, not, however, because I am 'down on' men *per se*. Think of an association of black men officered by slaveholders." [53]

All history reflects the sexual class struggle between man and woman for Stanton. The struggle is reflected in the laws, which are made by men and for men.

> All history shows that one class never did legislate with justice for another, and all philosophy shows they never can, as the relations of class grow out of either natural or artificial advantages which one has over the other and which it will maintain if possible. *It is folly to say that women are not a class, so long as there is any difference in the code of laws for men and women, any discrimination in the customs of society, giving advantages to men over women. . . .* [54]

Woman has been the great sufferer in history for so long that most people cannot [55] conceive of a future without her subjugation. "Aristotle could not conceive of any form of government without slavery. Modern writers on social science cannot imagine any kind of civil or domestic government without the subjection of woman." [56]

According to Stanton, woman's degradation stems from men's ideas of their sexual rights over women. "Our religion, laws, customs, are all founded on the belief that woman was made for man." [57] Men's rights to women's bodies are age old. The feudal law known as Marchetta, or Marquette, which forced a newly married woman to have intercourse with the feudal lord from one to three days after her marriage,[58] is an example of this male sexual privilege. "Women were taught by Church and State alike, that the Feudal lord or Seigneur had a right to them, not only as against themselves, but as against any claim of husband or father." [59]

On Marriage

Stanton criticizes the inequalities between men and women in marriage from the vantage point of the liberal individual rights men enjoy as citizens. Woman's individual sovereignty and personal independence must be recognized within both the home and the state.

"This same law of equality that has revolutionized the State and the Church is now knocking at the doors of our homes, and sooner or later there too it must do its work." [60] This is why men fight against woman's equality in the state and the church. They fear that once women are recognized as equal in the public realm of the state, women will demand equality within marriage and the home. She writes in agreement with John Stuart Mill that "the generality of the male sex cannot yet tolerate the idea of living with an *equal* at the fireside, and here is the secret of the opposition to woman's equality in the state and the church; men are not ready to recognize it in the home." [61]

According to Stanton, the marriage relation merely embodies the unequal power relations existing between the sexes. The marriage contract itself shows that these relations are ones of domination and subordination. "If the contract be equal, whence comes the terms 'marital power,' 'marital rights,' 'obedience and restraint,' 'dominion and control,' 'power and protection,' etc. etc. . . ." [62] The marriage contract also reflects the fact that men and women have a different (and unequal) *relation to* marriage. The man gives up nothing and the woman gives up everything.

> The contract of marriage is by no means equal. . . . In entering this compact, the man gives up nothing that he before possessed, he is a man still; while the legal existence of the woman is suspended during marriage, and hence forth, she is known but in and through the husband. She is nameless, purseless, childless—though a woman, an heiress, and a mother. [63]

As long as marriage remains the sole object in women's lives [64] and is only one among many choices for men, women will remain dependent on marriage in a way men are not. As long as this continues, alongside the impossibility of divorce, Stanton advises women not to marry. "Verily, under such circumstances, it is better, as the apostle says, not to marry." [65]

Women have no individual sovereignty in marriage. They are forced to live their lives through another. There is no personal freedom for a woman in the role of wife. "Personal freedom is the first right to be proclaimed, and that does not and cannot now belong to the relation of wife, to the mistress of the isolated home, to the financial dependent." [66] Wifehood and motherhood occupy too much of a woman's life when, in fact, they should be incidental relations that expand her horizons. [67] Women should share the responsibilities of the home with the man rather than be relegated to this "sphere" by herself. "It would be nearer the truth to say the difference indicates different duties in the same sphere, seeing that man and woman were evidently made for each other and have shown equal capacity in the ordinary range of human duties."[68]

Stanton tries to dismantle the notion of separate sexual spheres for men and women. She asks why women should accept the sphere assigned them by men when men make such serious mistakes about their own lives anyway.[69] "There is no such thing as a sphere for sex."[70] Only the individual herself can say what her sphere should be. "If God has assigned a sphere to man, one to woman, we claim the right ourselves to judge of His design in reference to us, and we accord to man the same privilege."[71] Stanton uses Lucretia Mott as an example to prove her point. Mott is both a wonderful orator and a perfect domestic and mother: ". . . who shall tell us that this divinely inspired woman is out of her sphere in her public endeavors to rouse this wicked nation to a sense of its awful guilt, to its great sins of war, slavery, injustice to woman, and to the labouring poor."[72]

Stanton also criticizes marriage as an institution of legalized prostitution. She states that no man suffers as a woman does in marriage, because the woman gives up control of her own body. "A man in marriage gives up no right; but a woman, every right, even the most sacred of all—the right of her own person."[73] Lucy Stone urged her to argue for the wife's right to her own body.[74] Before this could be argued in any sustained form, Stanton would have to first uncover the inequities existent in the marriage system that were cloaked in a language of mutual agreement. In reality, the emphasis on love in marriage covers up a particular form of slavery.

> They live the lives, these married couples, generally of mutual spies and tyrants over each other, and it is the most subtle form of slavery ever instituted because it is seemingly so fair, based as it is on mutual agreement and not incompatible with the full concession of the equality of the parties to this mutual treaty of self-stultification.[75]

Stanton also believes that woman is made into a drudge of the household in marriage. Woman's labor is stolen from her; she becomes an unpaid domestic. This rings particularly true for the married woman of the nineteenth century.

> The influence the Catholic Church has had on religious free thought, that monarchies have had on political free thought, that serfdom has had upon free labor, have all been cumulative in the family upon woman. . . . Taught that the fruits of her industry belonged to others, she has seen man enter into every avocation most suitable to her while she, the uncomplaining drudge of the household, condemned to the severest labor, has

been systematically robbed of her earnings, which have gone to build up her master's power, and she has found herself in the condition of the slave, deprived of the results of her own labor.[76]

"Woman has been the great unpaid laborer of the world . . ."[77] in the home, and when she works in other employments she is not paid according to the value of her work, but instead, according to her sex.[78] Stanton uncovers the dependence of women in marriage in economic and sexual terms. Woman's role as a wife requires this dependence; the sexual class dependence that stands in stark contrast to the personal independence required by liberal individualism.

Stanton's discussion of woman as a part of a sexual class underlines her criticism of marriage: woman lacks power as a woman. There are sexual, economic, and legal components to woman's dependence on her husband. Stanton in the end focuses on the legal component of woman's oppression within marriage. She argues that because women give up their legal existence in marriage, they become nameless, purseless, and childless.[79] The husband and wife become one person legally—the husband. The man has custody of his wife's person. He is guardian of their children, owner of her property, and has rights to her industry.[80] Hence, the married woman has no legal status, and propertied single women are taxed without representation. If this is the problem, the solution in Stanton's mind was passage of the Married Woman's Property Act (1836–48). This would allow married women to continue to control their own property. The legislation reads:

> The real and personal property of any female who may hereafter marry, and which she shall own at the time of her marriage, and the rents, issues and profits thereof, shall not be subject to the disposal of her husband nor be liable for his debts and shall continue her sole and separate property as if she were a single female.[81]

Beyond the Married Woman's Property Act, Stanton fought for changes in the divorce laws.

In the end, she argues that the problems in marriage can be dealt with by a change in the laws defining it. "Again, I ask, is it possible to discuss all the laws of a relation, and not touch the relation itself!"[82] For Stanton, the law can regulate equality. Changes in the sphere of the law bring changes to the sexual and economic spheres. Hence, Stanton's belief that if one changes all the legal relations of the marriage contract, the relation itself must change. But this, of course, assumes that all the relations of marriage are embodied within the law. The point here is that the purpose of law in liberal and patriarchal society is to define certain relations of power outside the law. This mystifies these relations on two levels. First, it makes it seem as though the power does not exist. Second, if the relation of power does not exist within the law, but liberal analysis focuses on the law, one is trying to change the wrong thing. For instance, how does one try to restructure patriarchy through changing the law when there is no law that states that women shall be the mothers or the secondary wage earners? The question remains how the liberal-legal analysis will encompass the economic dependence of woman on her husband when there are no laws directly regarding woman as the unpaid laborer of the household. The control of woman's sexuality within marriage is also not completely embodied (directly) within the law. The patriarchal relations of marriage remain cloaked by an emphasis on liberal law, as we shall see in the final chapter.

On Motherhood

One might not be immediately aware of Stanton's criticisms of motherhood by merely studying her suggestions for the legal reform of marriage and divorce. Even though Stanton sees woman's inequality tied to motherhood, this discussion never takes a central place in her legal reform strategy. A partial reason for this is the idea, raised earlier, that many of Stanton's radical feminist commitments could not be addressed by her liberal-legal political strategy. Most constraints on women in terms of the rearing of children were not embodied in the law, which applied to the public realm of social activity. Although Stanton did not accept the divorce of private and public life (as female and male spheres), she often adopted a politics that did. As such, it was difficult to directly address issues she herself was committed to.

Stanton, as a mother of seven children, could be highly critical of the organization of the isolated home from firsthand experience. Her work in her family and the responsibility for her children made it difficult for her to partake in activities and meetings outside the home. She was not free to partake fully in the feminist movement until after her own children had grown up. Susan B. Anthony, her beloved friend and colleague, often came to help Elizabeth with her domestic chores when all seemed hopeless. Stanton's husband, Henry, traveled a good deal in his abolitionist work and appears to have taken no responsibility for the care of the home or the children. Of course, if he had, he would have been a rare man indeed.

Stanton often writes to Anthony that she will be unable to attend conventions or meetings because of her competing responsibilities in the household. "I have so much care with all these boys on my hands. But I will write a letter. How much I do long to be free from housekeeping and children, so as to have some time to read, and think, and write. But it may be well for me to understand all the trials of woman's lot, that

I may more eloquently proclaim them when the time comes."[83] She complains to Anthony that she does not have the time to search for the books she needs to write her speeches, and even when she does, she cannot find an hour of uninterrupted time in which to write: ". . . I seldom have one hour undisturbed in which to sit down and write . . . unlike men . . . when they wish to write a document, shut themselves up for days with their thoughts and their books. . . ."[84]

There are times when Stanton longs for the pressures on her time to subside. In such moments, she writes to Susan B. Anthony and pleads with her not to ask her to make any trips or attend any conventions while she is still nursing her new baby. "I am determined to make no effort to do anything beyond my imperative home duties until I can bring about the following conditions; first, Relieve myself of housekeeping altogether; second, Secure some capable teacher for my children; third, See my present baby on her feet."[85] Anthony usually cooperates, although she sometimes pushes her friend to continue her suffrage work regardless: ". . . 'I beg you, with one baby on your knee and another at your feet, and four boys whistling, buzzing, hallooing, 'Ma,' 'Ma,' set yourself about the work.' "[86]

Stanton's feminist criticism of motherhood is not a denial of its importance and value. Although she is critical of the arrangements of the isolated home, the difficulties of motherhood that arise from this, and longs for some peace and quiet from her children, she thinks motherhood is one of the most important activities of women. Her criticism is that motherhood at present defines and limits woman and relegates her to a separate sphere. But in and of itself, motherhood is important and necessary to reproduce the next generation. She therefore criticizes the practice of motherhood while noting its importance in women's lives. "There is no such sacredness and responsibility in any human relation as in that of the mother. . . . To this end we must learn how to live and how to marry, how to educate ourselves and children for the reproduction not only of the mortal but immortal part of our natures."[87]

Stanton even believes that women's potential for motherhood should make them sacred. "One would think that potential motherhood should make woman as a class as sacred as the priesthood."[88] Woman's capacity for motherhood is a source of added power for women; bearing children is something men cannot do.

> There would be more sense in insisting on man's limitations because he can not be a mother, than on woman's because she can be. Surely maternity is an added power and development of some of the most tender sentiments of the human heart and not a "limitation." Yes, and it fits her for much of the world's work;

a large share of human legislation would be better done by her because of this deep experience.[89]

Stanton notes, however, that instead of recognizing the value of women as mothers, woman is usually dismissed from other privileges because she is a mother. Men always dwell on how maternity disqualifies women for civil and political rights. They take the unique capabilities of woman and turn them against her. Stanton begins to uncover the mystification of this reality within patriarchal ideology. She believes that women have a unique capacity to bear children and that men twist this to disqualify women from equality with men.

Stanton's discussion of marriage and motherhood is radical feminist in that she speaks to the unequal power relations of the sex-class system. She questions the dependent relations created between men and women as women are relegated to a separate sexual sphere. By doing so, Stanton begins to lay the foundation for attacking the patriarchal division of public and private life. She wants to ready women for participation in public life, rather than have them be exclusively directed toward the private duties of the family. Similar to Wollstonecraft, she writes about the narrowness of mind created by isolated family life: "Women have been sedulously trained to regard this as their crowning glory which best fits them for family life. Hence the vast majority of women are deficient in patriotism, they are but little for public interests; they are generally absorbed in a narrow, personal and family selfishness."[90]

However, the division between public (citizen) and private (family) remains within the liberal feminist political strategy to gain the franchise for women, even if these realms are no longer to be sexually defined. In this liberal feminist vision, woman defined as a mother (private sphere) can *also* be a citizen. Instead of being relegated to the private world of the family, woman is to participate as *both* a mother and a citizen. Stanton's understanding of how motherhood and woman's domesticity *exclude* her from public (male) life appears to be forgotten here.

The Enfranchisement of Women as Liberal Feminist Strategy

The radical feminist understanding of male sexual power stands outside the liberal theory of power and politics, defined as governmental activity. The sex-class theory of power actually contradicts the liberal differentiation of state and family rule. Liberal ideology, as we have seen, is in fact based in the differentiation of political and family life. Radical feminist theory presumes their collaboration in the oppression of women. From this feminist base, Stanton demands the political enfranchisement of women. As Ellen Dubois has stated, "It was a particularly feminist demand, because it exposed and challenged the assumption of male authority over women."[91] Stanton sidesteps woman's place in the home and argues for her place in the public world. By doing so, Dubois argues that Stanton rejects the (patriarchal) notion that women's place is in the home.[92]

My analysis has sought to explicate more fully the roots of Stanton's feminism in her analysis of the sexual-class status of women. Although citizen rights are individualist in nature, they are made by Stanton on behalf of women as a social and sexual class. By doing so, Stanton recognizes the political identity of women as part of a sex class. The claim for their individual rights is made on behalf of their social identity as women.

Although I agree with Dubois that women's demand for the franchise was a feminist one, I also think it was significantly liberal and republican in origin. The liberal feminist problem stems from this fact: the political understanding behind women's claim for the vote was primarily feminist, and the adoption of a legal political strategy for citizenship rights is basically liberal. The contradiction derives from the patriarchal base of liberalism and republican theory and the antipatriarchal priorities of feminism. Another way of stating this is that although Stanton wished to break down the division between public and private life, nineteenth-century liberal politics was premised on this division. I argue that American feminism lost out as a result of this contradictory mix.

Stanton's republican roots help her focus on the importance of citizen activity for women. Republican theory defines the virtuous being as one who takes part in the public duties of society. The concept republican stems from the term *res publica,* meaning "things public." The concept of a republic signifies the importance of the public realm over the concerns of private households. One becomes virtuous by contributing to the public sphere. Interestingly enough, the word virtue stems from *vir,* meaning "man."[93]

Of course, Stanton's purpose is to challenge the view that only men are capable of citizenry and, hence, that only men are capable of virtue. She rejects the ancient Greek and modern American view that public life should be open to men only. Stanton argues that no government should be called republican "in which one-half the people are forever deprived of all participation in its affairs."[94] The right to participation in government, of each and every citizen, is the key to a republic. Until women gain their citizen rights, liberal democracy is made a mockery of. "The basic idea of a republic is the right of self-government, the right of every citizen to choose his own representatives and to have a voice in the laws under which he lives. As this right can be secured only by the exercise of the suffrage, the ballot in the hand of every qualified citizen constitutes the true political status of the people in a republic." [95] The enfranchisement of women will equalize the opportunities between them and men in the republic. "The right of suffrage in a republic means education, development, self-reliance, independence, courage in the hour of danger." [96]

The liberal theory of politics is very much tied to the republican view of public life. The liberal ideology of the state—that the state represents the differing interests of society; that as such, it protects one's individuality and one's property; that it is the arena where decisions are made which affect and decide policy—focuses on the centrality of governmental politics and its separation from private life. Because politics is defined in relation to the governmental realm, political participation is defined as voting. Stanton wants women to be able to function as a part of this world. "To refuse political equality is to rob the ostracized of all self-respect, of credit in the marketplace, of recompense in the world of work, of a voice in choosing those who make and administer the law. . . ." [97]

She therefore fought for woman's suffrage along with the other rights that would allow women to become active, participating citizens. The National Woman's Rights Convention, 1858, states these as "their right to suffrage—their right of property—their right to the wages they earn—their right to their children and their homes—their sacred right to personal liberty—to a trial by a jury of their peers. . . ." [98] These rights are a mix of the liberal rights of the new society, such as property and the suffrage, and rights that address the patriarchal base of women's oppression more directly, like the right of women to their children and to their bodies. [99]

The problem is that the liberal state can grant equality of opportunity to women in the legal sense without creating the equality of conditions for them to participate. For there to be an equality of conditions, woman's sexual, economic, and racial equality have to be established. I have already argued that legal equality cannot in and of itself establish this. But Stanton sidesteps this issue and instead argues for woman's right to operate in *both* the public and private spheres. "Why should representative American women be incapable of discharging similar public and private duties at the same time in an equally commendable manner?" [100]

Stanton is not always clear in her treatment of the relationship between public and private life. She answered those who fought the idea of women voting because women would have to face the "vulgarities of public life" [101] at the polls, that women already face these abuses by drunkard husbands in the "privacy" of the home. In this instance, Stanton, in effect, argues that the separation of these two worlds does not hold in actual fact. But she also believed that the family suffered from the separate "sexual spheres" doctrine. To the degree men are schooled for the commercial life, they ignore their children; and to the degree women are prepared only for the family, they are unable to educate their children to be responsible members of the state.

> In a busy commercial life, fathers have but little time to guard their children against the temptations of life, or to prepare them for its struggles, and the mother educated to believe that she has not rights or duties in public affairs, can give no lessons on political morality from her standpoint. Hence, the home is in a condition of half orphanage for the want of fathers, and the State suffers for need of wise mothers.[102]

It is with this view to breaking down the separation between the family and public life, and between women and men, that Stanton, along with the feminist movement, demands the ballot. Woman's exclusion is based solely on the nature of her sex. This is no longer acceptable, given liberal "rights" theory.

> Women are the only class of citizens still wholly unrepresented in the government, and yet we possess every requisite qualification for voters in the United States. Women possess property, and education; we take out naturalization—papers and passports and register ships. . . . We are neither idiots, lunatics, nor criminals, and according to our state constitution lack but one qualification for voters, namely, sex, which is an insurmountable qualification, and therefore equivalent to a bill of attainder against one-half the people. . . .[103]

The National Woman Suffrage Association was formed to introduce an amendment to the federal constitution to ensure women's right to the vote. The Nineteenth Amendment stated women's right to the vote and disqualified sex as a basis for determining the right to the franchise. "The right of suffrage in the United States shall be based on citizenship, and shall be regulated by Congress, and all citizens of the U.S., whether native or naturalized, shall enjoy this right equally, without any distinction or discrimination whatever founded on sex."[104] Stanton thought that once women were put on par with men as citizens, they would be able to more easily continue the struggle for their equality. She knew the vote was only a first step. Woman's equality, expressed through the franchise, even if only an ideological cloaking of women's real economic dependence and sexual servitude, contradicted the patriarchal ideology of woman's inferiority. Stanton was forcing the liberal state, on the tenets of liberal individualism itself, to openly contradict patriarchal ideology's notion of woman's inequality.

At the same time Stanton fights for woman's recognition by the state, she knows the state oppresses women. There are moments when she understands that the problem is not merely the exclusion of women from participation in the state but actual oppression by it. She speaks of "the hard iron rule we feel alike in the church, the state, and the home." [105] She writes of the fourfold bondage of woman as including the state. "To emancipate woman from the fourfold bondage she has so long suffered in the state, the church, the home and the world of work, harder battles than we have yet fought are still before us." [106]

Stanton even discusses the self-interest of all classes in their own rule and the fact that rulers within the state fear woman's emancipation because they know women are superior to them. Men only fear that they will no longer be able to control women.

> The narrow self-interest of all classes is opposed to the sovereignty of woman. The rulers in the State are not willing to share their power with a class equal if not superior to themselves, over which they could never hope for absolute control, and whose methods of government might in many respects differ from their own. The anointed leaders in the Church are equally hostile to freedom for a sex for wise purposes to have been subordinated by divine decree. The capitalist in the world of work holds the key to the trades and professions, and undermines the power of labor unions in their struggle for shorter hours and fairer wages, by substituting the cheap labor of a disenfranchised class, that cannot organize its forces, thus making wife and sister rivals of husband and brother in the industries, to the detriment of both classes . . . where then, can we rest the lever with which to lift one-half of humanity from these depths of degradation but on that columbiad of our political life—the ballot. . . . [107]

The patriarchal state and the capitalist class appear to be separate entities in the above discussion, although both manipulate women. Stanton speaks of the degradations of capitalism for the laboring poor. She asks: ". . . is it right that a large majority of the race should suffer all their days the cruel hardships of poverty that a small minority may enjoy all life's blessings and benefits?" [108] Women, like the laboring classes, are denied the fruits of their labor. "The great motive for making a man a slave was to get his labor or its result for nothing." [109] Women have been denied the product of their labor by denying them the right to property and the right to inheritance.

> Property is a delicate test of the condition of a nation. It is a singular fact of history that the rights of property have

everywhere been recognized before the rights of persons. . . .
The enslavement of woman has been much increased from the
denial of the rights of property to her, not merely to the fruits of
her own labor, but to the right of inheritance.[110]

At the same time that capitalism degrades the worker and pits sister
against brother, man against wife, it denies both men and women the
fruits of their labor. The corruptness of politics, however, reflects more
than the needs of the capitalist class. It reflects the patriarchal "family of
men" sharing the same interests. "The family of men are amazingly like
one another; Republicans and Democrats, saints and sinners, all act
alike and talk each in his turn the same cant."[111]

Given Stanton's critical analysis of the patriarchal state, capitalist-
class relations, marriage, and the family, it is not surprising that she
believed that gaining the vote for women was only the beginning of the
long struggle toward true independence. The franchise would only lay
the basis for woman's equality of opportunity with men in the public
sphere. "But the battle is not wholly fought until we stand equal in the
church, the world of work, and have an equal code of morals for both
sexes."[112] Underlying this battle would be Stanton's attempt to change
the way people think about women. She herself states the importance of
this activity: ". . . when men and women think about a new question,
the first step in progress is taken."[113]

One needs to recognize the different theoretical strains within Stanton's feminist theory. Her sexual-class analysis of woman's oppression
is not easily encompassed in the liberal feminist political strategy of the
nineteenth-century American women's movement. Yet the roots of
American feminism are found here, in Stanton's radical feminist criticism of marriage, the isolation of the family, and the oppressiveness of
the patriarchal state. They are also to be found in the liberal demand for
self-sovereignty, economic independence, and individuality, which
can be distinguished from the ideology of liberal individualism that
merely recognizes woman as a citizen with voting rights. However else
one's feminism comes to be defined, its starting point is the notion of
the separateness, distinctness, and independence of woman from man.
This notion is as liberal as it is feminist.

NOTES

1. Stanton's writing was done in close collaboration with Susan
B. Anthony and other women in the feminist movement. She wrote as a

leader of a social movement, not in isolation or divorced from political activity. See the biographies, Alma Lutz, *Created Equal, A Biography of Elizabeth Cady Stanton, 1815–1902* (New York: John Day, 1940); Mary Ann Oakley, *Elizabeth Cady Stanton* (New York: Feminist Press, 1972); and the autobiography, Elizabeth Cady Stanton, *Eighty Years and More, Reminiscences 1815–1897* (New York: Schocken, 1971).

2. One of the major exceptions to this lack of theoretical analysis of Stanton's work is the writing of historian Ellen Dubois. The discussion provided in this chapter is very much indebted to Dubois' pioneering research and study of Stanton and the feminist movement of which she was a part. Although I present a somewhat different interpretation of Stanton than Dubois does, her excellent and groundbreaking work is used throughout my analysis. See Ellen Dubois, *Feminism and Suffrage, The Emergence of an Independent Women's Movement in America, 1848– 1869* (Ithaca: Cornell University Press, 1978); and her soon to be published *Stanton-Anthony Reader* (New York: Schocken, 1980). Also see her "The Nineteenth Century Woman Suffrage Movement and the Analysis of Women's Oppression," in *Capitalist Patriarchy and the Case for Socialist Feminism,* ed. Zillah Eisenstein (New York: Monthly Review Press, 1978); "The Radicalism of the Woman Suffrage Movement," *Feminist Studies* 3, no. 1–2 (Fall 1975); and "On Labor and Free Love: Two Unpublished Speeches of Elizabeth Cady Stanton," *Signs* 1, no. 1 (Autumn 1975): 257–69. For a somewhat different yet interesting discussion of Stanton's work, see Gerda Lerner, *The Female Experience: An American Documentary* (Indianapolis: Bobbs-Merrill, 1977).

3. For a full discussion of republican theory, see J. G. A. Pocock, *The Machiavellian Moment, Florentine Political Thought and the Atlantic Republican Tradition* (Princeton: Princeton University Press, 1975).

4. For a discussion of this process in nineteenth-century America, see Mary Ryan, *Womanhood in America, From Colonial Times to the Present* (New York: New Viewpoints, 1975); and Nancy Cott, *The Bonds of Womanhood, "Woman's Sphere" in New England, 1780–1835* (New Haven: Yale University Press, 1977). For a discussion of cultural and religious changes in this period, see Ann Douglas, *The Feminization of American Culture* (New York: Knopf, 1977). Harriot Stanton Blatch, Elizabeth C. Stanton's daughter, writes of this transformation of woman's labor in Harriot Stanton Blatch and Alma Lutz, eds., *Challenging Years, The Memoirs of Harriot Stanton Blatch* (New York: Putnam's, 1940). She states that "within the span of a generation the economic world was transformed from a system of individual workers on hand loom and spinning wheel to interdependent employees tending steam-driven machines, housed in factories, and women passed out of the realm of individual work in their own cottages, away from the farm and manor house. . . . They passed out of this to the centralized,

specialized workshop or mill and became 'hands' under the director-ship of men. Working women passed from a woman's world to a man's world" (p. 297).

5. Previously, American society was organized around graded rank, not equality, "which viewed the whole of society as an intricate series of ranks, a profusion of finely graded positions of authority and subordination, which neither male nor female could circumvent. No individual, of either sex, could presume to be one among equals in the seventeenth-century community." Ryan, *Womanhood*, p. 40.

6. Cott, *The Bonds of Womanhood*, pp. 35–42.

7. Ann Gordon and Mari Jo Buhle, "Sex and Class in Colonial and Nineteenth Century America," in *Liberating Women's History*, ed. Berenice Carroll (Urbana: University of Illinois Press, 1976), p. 284.

8. Ryan, *Womanhood*, p. 156.

9. William O'Neill, ed., *The Woman Movement, Feminism in the United States and England* (Chicago: Quadrangle, 1969), p. 17.-

10. In mid-nineteenth-century America, less than one-fifth of the labor force was employed in the manufacturing sector; more than half were still farmers. Nevertheless, the home had already ceased to be the major focus of the economy. See Ryan, *Womanhood*.

11. Daniel Scott Smith, "Family Limitation, Sexual Control, and Domestic Feminism," in *Clio's Consciousness Raised*, ed. by Mary Hartman and Lois Banner (New York: Harper & Row, 1974), instead argues "that over the course of the nineteenth century the average woman experienced a great increase in power and autonomy *within* the family" (p. 119). He discusses the Victorian period as a period of domestic feminism, defined as "sexual control of the husband by the wife" (p. 123).

12. Eleanor Flexner, *Century of Struggle, The Woman's Rights Movement in the United States* (Cambridge, Mass.: Harvard University Press, 1975), p. 71.

13. Dubois, "On Labor and Free Love," p. 258.

14. Theodore Stanton and Harriot Stanton Blatch, eds., *Elizabeth Cady Stanton* (New York: Arno and The New York Times, 1969), 2:105.

15. Ibid., p. 109.

16. Ibid., p. 110.

17. Elizabeth Cady Stanton, Susan B. Anthony, and Matilda Jos-lyn Gage, eds., *History of Woman Suffrage* (New York: Source Book Press, 1970), 3:81.

18. Ibid.

19. Stanton, Anthony, and Gage, *History of Woman Suffrage*, 2:273.

20. Susan B. Anthony and Ida Husted Harper, *History of Woman Suffrage* (New York: Source Book Press, 1970), 4:42.

21. Stanton and Blatch, *Elizabeth Cady Stanton*, 2:237.

22. Stanton, Anthony, and Gage, *History of Woman Suffrage* (New York: Fowler and Wells, 1881), 1:26.

23. Ibid., p. 679.

24. Stanton and Blatch, *Elizabeth Cady Stanton*, 2:164.

25. Ibid.

26. Ibid., p. 130.

27. Elizabeth Cady Stanton, "Address to the National Woman Suffrage Convention," in *The Concise History of Woman Suffrage*, ed. by Mari Jo and Paul Buhle (Chicago: University of Illinois Press, 1978), p. 252.

28. Stanton, Anthony, and Gage, *History of Suffrage*, 1:50 (italics mine).

29. Stanton, "Address to Woman Suffrage Convention," p. 251.

30. Ibid., p. 30.

31. "Declaration of Sentiments and Resolutions, Seneca Falls," in *Feminism: The Essential Historical Writings*, ed. Miriam Schneir (New York: Vintage, 1972), p. 77.

32. Stanton and Blatch, *Elizabeth Cady Stanton*, 2:368.

33. Elizabeth Cady Stanton, " 'Solitude of Self' Address before the U.S. Senate Committee on Woman Suffrage, February 20, 1892," in Buhle and Buhle, *History of Woman Suffrage*, p. 327.

34. Stanton and Blatch, *Elizabeth Cady Stanton*, 2:335 (italics mine).

35. Anthony and Harper, *History of Suffrage*, 4:41.

36. Elizabeth Cady Stanton, "Womanliness," in Schneir, *Essential Writings*, p. 155.

37. Elizabeth Cady Stanton, *The Woman's Bible, Parts I and II* (New York: Arno, 1972), p. 57.

38. Anthony and Harper, *History of Suffrage*, 4:41.

39. Stanton, Anthony, and Gage, *History of Suffrage*, 1:80.

40. Paulina Davis, comp. *A history of the national woman's rights movement, for twenty years, with the proceedings of the decade meeting held at Apollo Hall, October 20, 1870, from 1850 to 1870* (New York: Journeymen Printers', 1871), p. 63.

41. Ibid.

42. Stanton and Blatch, *Elizabeth Cady Stanton*, 2:223.

43. Stanton was seventy-seven years old at the time of this address. One can argue that this address reflects the fact that she was an aging woman, and was concerned with the situation of older women. Ellen Dubois thinks that this speech also reflects the political isolation of Stanton after she had been pushed out of her leadership role in the feminist movement. My point is that it is particularly in such moments that one's view of life is stated most straightforwardly. I therefore think

one gains a real insight into Stanton's view of "liberal individualism" from this speech. Stanton writes in Blatch and Stanton, *Elizabeth Cady Stanton,* of this speech, that ". . . I am much inclined myself to think it is the best thing I have ever written at least in my declining years" (2:281–82).

44. Stanton, "Solitude of Self," p. 326.

45. Ibid., p. 325.

46. Ibid.

47. Stanton and Blatch, *Elizabeth Cady Stanton,* 2:237.

48. Davis, *History of woman's rights,* p. 60.

49. Stanton and Blatch, *Elizabeth Cady Stanton,* 2:67.

50. Ibid., p. 51.

51. Ibid., p. 124.

52. Anthony and Harper, *History of Suffrage,* 4:41.

53. Stanton and Blatch, *Elizabeth Cady Stanton,* 2:253.

54. Anthony and Harper, *History of Suffrage,* 4:42 (italics mine).

55. Stanton and Blatch, *Elizabeth Cady Stanton,* 2:171.

56. Ibid., p. 145.

57. Ibid., p. 82.

58. Stanton, Anthony, and Gage, *History of Suffrage,* 1:762.

59. Ibid.

60. Davis, *History of woman's rights,* p. 62.

61. Ibid., p. 60. Stanton thought Mill understood the situation of women better than any man before him. She wrote in Blatch and Stanton, *Elizabeth Cady Stanton,* "To my mind, no thinker has so calmly, truthfully, and logically revealed the causes and hidden depths of woman's degradation. . . . it is the first response from any man to show that he is capable of seeing and feeling . . . degrees of woman's wrongs" (2:122).

62. Stanton, *Eighty Years and More,* p. 222.

63. Ibid., p. 221.

64. Elizabeth C. Stanton, "Debates on Marriage and Divorce, 1860," in Buhle and Buhle, *History of Woman Suffrage,* p. 175.

65. Davis, *History of woman's rights,* p. 76.

66. Stanton and Blatch, *Elizabeth Cady Stanton,* 2:70.

67. Stanton, Anthony, and Gage, *History of Suffrage,* 1:22.

68. Ibid., p. 18.

69. Stanton and Blatch, *Elizabeth Cady Stanton,* 2:19.

70. Ibid.

71. Ibid.

72. Ibid., p. 20.

73. Ibid., p. 70.

74. Ibid., p. 68.

75. Dubois, "On Labor and Free Love," p. 266.

76. Stanton, Anthony, and Gage, *History of Suffrage*, 1:28.

77. Ibid.

78. Harriot Stanton Blatch wrote at greater length than her mother did on the economic value of women's domestic work. She agreed with Charlotte Perkins Gilman that women's work as mothers remained unpaid labor to keep women economically dependent on men. In Blatch and Lutz, *Challenging Years*, Blatch recommended a motherhood endowment (p. 333). She corresponded with Theodore Roosevelt about the idea of a motherhood pension, which, according to Blatch, he appears to have greeted with some enthusiasm (p. 332). Also see Charlotte Perkins Gilman, *Women and Economics* (New York: Harper & Row, 1966); and idem, *The Home: Its Work and Influence* (Urbana: University of Illinois Press, 1972).

79. Elizabeth C. Stanton, "Address to the New York State Legislature, 1854," in Schneir, *Essential Writings*, p. 113.

80. Stanton, Anthony, and Gage, *History of Suffrage*, 1:261.

81. "Married Woman's Property Act, New York, 1848," in Schneir, *Essential Writings*, p. 73.

82. Stanton, *Eighty Years and More*, p. 225.

83. Stanton and Blatch, *Elizabeth Cady Stanton*, 2:41–42.

84. Ibid., p. 55.

85. Ibid., pp. 51–52.

86. Ibid., p. 64.

87. Davis, *History of woman's rights*, p. 82.

88. Stanton, *The Woman's Bible, Part I*, p. 102.

89. Anthony and Harper, *History of Suffrage*, 4:58.

90. Elizabeth C. Stanton, " 'Patriotism and Chastity' from *The Westminster Review*, January 1981," in O'Neill, *The Woman Movement*, p. 126.

91. Dubois, *Feminism and Suffrage*, p. 46. For other interpretations of the nineteenth-century feminist movement, see Barbara Berg, *The Remembered Gate: Origins of American Feminism, The Woman and the City 1800–1860* (New York: Oxford University Press, 1978); Flexner, *Century of Struggle*; Alan Grimes, *The Puritan Ethic and Woman Suffrage* (New York: Oxford University Press, 1967); Aileen Kraditor, *The Ideas of the Woman Suffrage Movement, 1890–1920* (New York: Columbia University Press, 1965); William O'Neill, *Everyone Was Brave, A History of Feminism in America* (Chicago: Quadrangle, 1969); and Ross Evans Paulson, *Women's Suffrage and Prohibition: A Comparative Study of Equality and Social Control* (Illinois: Scott, Foresman, 1973).

92. Dubois, *Feminism and Suffrage*, p. 46.

93. Pocock, *The Machiavellian Moment*, p. 37. By focusing on these particular strains within Stanton's thought, I do not mean to deny the importance of other forces like the Protestant Reformation in changing

the way women thought about themselves. See Stanton's *The Woman's Bible;* and Ann Douglas, *The Feminization of American Culture.*

94. Stanton, Anthony, and Gage, *History of Woman Suffrage,* 3:81.

95. Anthony and Harper, *History of Suffrage,* 4:41.

96. Ibid.

97. Stanton, "Solitude of Self," p. 326.

98. Stanton, Anthony, and Gage, *History of Suffrage,* 1:675.

99. The rights to property and suffrage were more concerned with the rights of the middle-class woman than the working-class woman in this period. However, the other concerns mentioned here—rights to their children, rights to their own bodies, and especially rights to the wages they earned—affected working-class women as well.

100. Stanton, *The Woman's Bible, Part I,* p. 78.

101. Stanton, Anthony, and Gage, *History of Suffrage,* 1:682.

102. Stanton, *The Woman's Bible, Part I,* p. 137.

103. Stanton, Anthony, and Gage, *History of Suffrage,* 3:85.

104. Ibid., p. 83.

105. Stanton, "Address to Woman Suffrage Convention," p. 253.

106. Anthony and Harper, *History of Suffrage,* 4:114.

107. Stanton, Anthony, and Gage, *History of Suffrage,* 3:vi.

108. Dubois, "On Labor and Free Love," p. 261.

109. Ibid.

110. Stanton, Anthony, and Gage, *History of Suffrage,* 1:770.

111. Stanton and Blatch, *Elizabeth Cady Stanton,* 2:101.

112. Ibid., p. 338.

113. Ibid., p. 20.

PART

III

THE CONTEM-
PORARY PRACTICE OF
LIBERAL
FEMINISM

This section begins with a discussion of the second wave of the liberal feminist movement. From the late nineteenth century to the enfranchisement of women in America in 1920 to Friedan's *Feminine Mystique* in 1963, liberal feminism lost much of its radical content. First, liberal citizen rights were extended to women. But more important is the loss of the radical feminist insights about patriarchy alluded to by Wollstonecraft, Mill, Taylor, and Stanton.

This non-radical period of liberal feminism must be distinguished from the liberal feminist politics of the 1970s, which began to revitalize radical feminist analysis. A political under-standing that goes beyond liberal (self-help) individualism and the naive belief that one rewrites the laws to remake women's lives has once again emerged within the politics of the National Organization for Women. The politics of liberal feminists like Elizabeth Holtzman, Bella Abzug, Eleanor Smeal, Pat Schroeder, and Patsy Mink move beyond Friedan's liberal individualist feminism. They have yet to develop a political analysis and theory that encompass their feminist understand-ing.

In order to fully understand the import of liberal feminism today, I first explicate, in Chapter 8, Friedan's liberal feminist position. Then, in Chapter 9, I discuss the particular structural changes in women's lives that heighten the potential for their awareness of the contradictions between the promises of liberalism and the limitations of patriarchy. Finally, in Chapter 10, I examine the priorities of the capitalist patriarchal state that are to contain and deradicalize this feminist consciousness.

8

Friedan's Liberal "Feminist Mystique" and the Changing Politics of NOW

Betty Friedan's book *The Feminine Mystique* (1963) and the founding of the National Organization for Women (NOW) (1966) mark the collaboration between the state and liberal feminism for the 1960s. Women of the New Left, black and white women of the civil rights movement, radical feminists, specifically the group Redstockings, were all important forces in shaping the women's movement of the 1960s and '70s.[1] However, it is Friedan's liberal feminist analysis that took hold of the majority of women, both inside and outside the movement. I argue in the next several chapters that part of the reason for this is because the state has come to accept this expression of feminism as the least threatening form and, therefore, has given the liberal part of the movement the most publicity and public recognition. Part of the way it has done this is by distorting the politics of radical, socialist, and lesbian feminists in such a way as to cut them off from the majority of women. These groups are presented in the media as antifamily and antimotherhood and, in the end, are seen as antiwoman by other women.[2]

Friedan has played a particularly important role in this process by accepting the state's version of radical feminism as antifamily. Her most recent involvement in the one-day conference "The Future of the Family," sponsored by NOW's Legal Defense and Educational Fund, which sought workable new concepts of the family, reflects her latest conception of feminist accommodation to the state. Friedan believes that society can accommodate the switch to equality between men and women. We are left asking the question: given the historical record, on what basis does Friedan believe that an equality which is in the interests of women can be legislated by a capitalist patriarchal state?

It is an oversimplification of liberal feminism to say that it is merely

177

a reflection of the manipulation of women by the state. The hold that liberal feminism has on women reflects women's consciousness in a society that presents the ideology of liberalism as its world view. Therefore, the concern here is to examine why Friedan and the liberal feminist position she represents had such force in the 1960s and, to a lesser extent, in the 1970s. Although critics of Friedan's work argue that it applies to the white middle-class woman alone, I believe it can appeal to any woman who identifies with middle-class values and the liberal ideas of equality of opportunity and independence. One does not have to be white or middle class to aspire to these values, and therefore the ideas of liberal feminism are accepted by more women than is commonly thought. The political appeal of Friedan's writing lies in this fact; her analysis addresses the liberal individualist consciousness of a majority of American women.

Betty Friedan's discussion of the "feminine mystique" focused on the entrapment of women by patriarchal culture. She criticized the "mystique" for crippling women's individual potential by prescribing their role as mothers and wives. Women do not know who they are as independent individuals. They only know who they are supposed to be according to the cultural definition of femininity. If the "feminine mystique," which celebrates women's femininity at the expense of everything else,[3] is the problem, the solution to the problem is to free women from its hold on them. Friedan therefore wants to free women from the destructive dependence patriarchal culture breeds.

We need to examine how Friedan intends to create this psychological independence in women. Instead of developing the skeletal outlines of Wollstonecraft's analysis of woman's "miserable situation" as a sexual caste and Stanton's criticism of the "aristocracy of men," she argues against a theory of woman's oppression rooted in a sex-class system. I want to argue that she lacks an understanding of her own radical feminist position as a result. Although Wollstonecraft and Stanton are unsuccessful in integrating their radical feminist analysis into their political strategy, Friedan says she has no such theory and instead implicitly accepts and uncritically uses the ideology of liberal individualism for a theory of woman's oppression. Friedan's dismissal of the sex-class theory of power *erodes the radical dimension of liberal feminism that existed in Wollstonecraft's and Stanton's writing*. Instead of criticizing liberalism from this radical feminist vantage point, Friedan is forced to contain her feminism with liberalism. Her feminist demands become what she thinks is politically feasible, and as such, she accommodates the patriarchal state. She tries to smooth over the tensions between the liberal state and feminists rather than uncover them.

Because Friedan has no consciousness of liberalism as a *specific* political ideology, she remains unaware of many of its patriarchal biases. She therefore employs liberal-rights theory on behalf of feminism with little cognizance that liberalism cannot bring about the equality of women with men. She adopts the liberal values of independence, equality of opportunity, and liberal individualism (discussed throughout the first half of this book) as the predominant and accepted values of society to define her feminism. These values have no particular identity and history for her. They are accepted as the norm rather than as a specific ideology. She therefore believes that she has no particular politics or political theory. She identifies herself as a pragmatist. Until Friedan sees liberalism itself as a distinct set of political ideas and recognizes the importance of a structural analysis of patriarchy, she cannot understand the contradictory nature of liberalism as patriarchal and feminism as sexually egalitarian.

Although Friedan by her own admission rejects the sex-class theory of women's oppression and appears to fully accept the individualism of liberal ideology, her writing reflects a much more confused state of affairs. As a result, Friedan's politics is contradictory in its very nature. *She accepts a liberal individualist analysis of woman's problem alongside an implicit understanding of the social nature of woman's common condition, an implicit notion of woman's sex-class identity alongside the explicit rejection of a sex-class theory of power, and a liberal-individualist theory of power alongside the implicit conception of sex-class power.* These two views—the ideology of liberal individualism and the social reality of sex-class oppression—cannot be fully contained within the same politics successfully.

Feminist Politics and a Liberal Theory of Power

Reminiscent of Stanton, Friedan calls the women's movement of the 1960s and '70s the second American Revolution[4] because women are once again applying the ideas of political participation and self-determination to themselves. They are demanding woman's inalienable human right to the opportunities that will allow her to achieve equality. The demands apply to *all* women because they are all human beings with these inalienable rights: ". . . we are a revolution for all, not for an exceptional few."[5] According to Friedan, it is "the *right* of every woman in America to become all she is capable of becoming—on her own and/or in partnership with a man."[6]

If woman is to achieve equality with man, she must have political power to do so. She therefore must become directly involved in the political process. "We will do it by getting into city hall ourselves, or by getting into Congress ourselves. . . ."[7] This is the way Friedan believes that women will be able to affect the platforms of both political parties and, hence, to affect society in general. This political activity is the "nitty-gritty" of self-determination for women.[8] This view is reflected in the platform of The National Women's Political Caucus, which calls for women's active participation in politics; politics being the activity of political parties within government. Once women have their own voice in the political decisions affecting their lives,[9] they will have achieved full equality with men. This means bringing "women into the mainstream of American society,"[10] which becomes the purpose of feminist activity for Friedan and for NOW in 1966.

Friedan accepts the liberal view of politics as involving activity within the governmental realm and in the party process. In order for women to affect their chances for equality of opportunity, they must enter the public/governmental arena and fight for legislation that will create and then protect their freedom. Women, as an interest group, must represent their own interests. Woman's problem is one of exclusion and nonrepresentation within the mainstream, not oppression by it.

But Friedan herself states that she does not think women will wield power any better than men. "Women can't evade its realities in any system."[11] Why then she believes that women need to take a greater part in the political system is unclear. She takes the liberal theory of politics as given and tries to gain a better place for women within it. She does not ask women to look at alternatives to power outside the governmental arena. As a matter of fact, Friedan rejects any discussion of political change that she believes is not "feasible." She argues that we must deal with the foreseeable future in practical terms [12] and not get lost in ideological debates. Friedan states openly that she is uncomfortable with the new feminist ideology and its demands.[13] The "rhetoric" in the movement seems like a dead end to her. She advises women in the movement to stay away from the radical feminist analysis of man-hating, sexual shock tactics and sex-class warfare. She also wishes to stay away from questions of capitalism and socialism.[14] She believes that feminism in and of itself is radical and will bring about radical changes in society.[15] It therefore does not need an ideology; feminism is sufficient unto itself. "I saw that in the end equality for women confronts the whole system—every system—and implies changes in them all cutting across the conventional lines of right and left."[16]

Although the demand for the equality of women with men is a revolutionary demand in and of itself, Friedan's feminism articulates this demand in liberal equality of opportunity terms. Her feminism does not cut across conventional political lines; it accepts them. Her emphasis on the political party process is itself indicative of a larger ideology. She assumes the liberal view that the important political and social decisions are made within government,[17] narrowly defined. This view does not understand *how* the governmental realm is connected to the power relations of patriarchy and capitalism, nor that many decisions which affect our lives are not made through the governmental party process.[18] Nor does Friedan see how equating the governmental realm with politics and power obscures the relations between women's lives and their sexual oppression in the system of patriarchy.

The definition of politics as government activity makes it impossible for her to view the structural relations of women's lives—the family, the sexual division of labor, sex-class oppression—as part of the political life of a society. The liberal equation of politics with the public sphere excludes an understanding of the relationship between politics and the private realm of sex-class relations. The liberal equation between public power and politics excludes the family from political analysis. This liberal conception of power implicitly excludes daily life activity from political analysis. Given this narrow view of political life, women are said to need power to make decisions within the public, governmental realm in order to control their lives. Equality within the family or the so-called private spheres of sex stands outside this liberal framework.

It is important to note that many women who by the late 1970s adopted the liberal feminist political strategy of Friedan no longer accepted the liberal definition of power and politics as an adequate explanation of their own oppression. Wollstonecraft and Stanton actually never did. Friedan did and still does. By not recognizing the sexual-class oppression of women, Friedan cannot critique the liberal view that excludes sex from the realm of politics.[19] She is left trying to justify a feminist politics that accepts the public sphere as the realm women must try to enter without calling for a redefinition of the relationship between these two spheres. Although Friedan makes clear that the public sphere of life must be opened to women, it remains much less clear what happens to women's lives within the family and whether this sphere remains woman's domain.

Because Friedan has no theory of sexual power and privilege, which is different from saying that she has no understanding of sexual-class oppression, she is forced to accept the pluralist theory of liberalism. She therefore argues that woman needs representation in the mainstream in order to change society.[20] Women do not need to take power; they need to be included in it. This analysis can make sense only if one views the mainstream as a plurality of groups that are willing to include another group. This pluralist view of politics ignores the relation between power and privilege because it assumes equality of opportunity between groups. The problem for Friedan is not sexual-class oppression, but liberal-legal representation. Liberal feminism, to the extent it accepts this vision of politics, has no understanding of how the privileges of the sexual system of patriarchal society are protected by the political sphere. It does not understand that the state's function is to protect the system of power called patriarchy.

Friedan has no self-conscious theory of woman's oppression based on an analysis of the structural relations of patriarchy and the hierarchical sexual ordering of society. She therefore cannot develop an analysis of why women have not gained equality with men. Friedan knows full well that there is a fight against women's equality, but her liberal view of politics and power cannot explain why this is so.

Friedan rejects an analysis of the system of patriarchy because she rejects its basic thesis: that women are oppressed by men as a sexual class.[21]

> I do not believe that the conditions we are trying to change are caused by a conspiracy for "the economic and social profit of men as a group" as Gloria Steinem sees it. . . . My definition of feminism is simply that women are people, in the fullest sense of the word, who must be free to move in society with all the privileges and opportunities and responsibilities that are their human and American right.[22]

For Friedan, feminism is not a theory about women's oppression but a theory of human rights. It is "a stage in the whole human rights movement"[23] designed to being women into the mainstream.

Friedan interprets the theory of sex-class oppression to mean that all men, individually, hate women. She says this is nothing but man-hating propaganda. She denies the reality of sexual-class conflict between men and women by reducing this theory of patriarchal privilege to a theory about individual men and then dismisses it. She views it in this individualist framework (individual men hating individual women) to avoid having to deal with the question of the patriarchal social structure of society in terms of relations within the family; the segregation of the labor force; or the divorce of home and work, state and family, public and private life. Her individualist interpretation allows her to avoid dealing with the patriarchal organization of society as part of the *political* life of society; patriarchy is merely an individual phenomenon. The conception of women "degraded *as* a sex" stands counter to her liberal individualist view of power. Her pluralist view of politics replaces the theory of sexual oppression. Men and women both appear to suffer from the present system of sexual inequality. "Man is not the enemy, but the fellow victim of the present half-equality. . . . This sense of freeing men as the other half of freeing women has always been there, even in the early writings of Mary Wollstonecraft, Elizabeth Stanton, and the rest. . . ."[24] Nevertheless, there is a difference between Friedan, on the one hand, and Wollstonecraft and Stanton, on the other. Although Wollstonecraft and Stanton never said that man was the enemy, they never said he was not. Neither Wollstonecraft nor Stanton ever tried to deny that men are privileged as men and that they benefit from their privilege. Friedan inadvertently denies male privilege by denying that antagonism exists between men and women as sexual classes.

The problem here is twofold. First, Friedan wrongly interprets the radical feminist analysis of patriarchal class relations. Second, she says she rejects the sex-class theory of woman's oppression at the same time that she implicitly adopts it. All her claims for women—be they equality of opportunity, equality before the law, equal pay—are premised on identifying women as members of a "sexual class" in the first place. As we have discussed in earlier chapters, the demands for liberal rights for women are made on the basis of an individual woman as a part of the social-sexual-class woman.[25]

Friedan herself utilizes this concept of sex class when she demands that woman's ascribed status as a woman within a sex class must be replaced by woman's individual right to the equality of opportunity. Woman must be judged according to her individual achievement, not her unequal sex-class status. Friedan's claim to the rights of woman as an *individual* rests on her rejection of woman being treated as a group, which rests in a sexual-class analysis she says she rejects. Thus, Friedan's feminism is in fact rooted in a theory of sex class even if her liberal priorities do not allow her to recognize its presence. Friedan does not recognize that her own liberal feminist analysis is premised in an understanding of sexual privilege in political terms.

Stanton understood that men had male privilege in relation to housework, sexual reproduction, and the labor force. Although Friedan knows women suffer by virtue of their relegation to the home, domestic labor, and motherhood, she does not discuss this as part of the sexual privilege men have in patriarchy. Friedan reveals the contradictory nature of her analysis in one of her rare acknowledgments of male privilege when she compares men's privilege to that of southern plantation owners.

> A reality we must also face in this revolution is the fact that even the most enlightened of men have got to give up certain things. Just as there were benefits that the Southern plantation owners got out of the slaves, there are benefits that men have gotten out of the prime role. And I don't think it's very realistic to expect any large group of people to voluntarily move over and give up the central place in the sun and by largesse hand it to anyone else.[26]

She quickly adds, however, that the above inequities do not require that women "take the power away from men, but to create institutions that will make possible a real life of equality between the sexes."[27] How one creates new institutions without dislodging the existing power arrangements is unclear. It must be unclear to Friedan, who acknowledges that people do not voluntarily give up their place in the sun and at the same time embraces the pluralist vision of power and social change.

The Liberal Feminist Mystique

Friedan's analysis of women's oppression is best expressed through her discussion of the "feminine mystique." "The feminine mystique permits, even encourages, women to ignore the question of their identity."[28] It defines woman in terms of her femininity, and this is measured in relation to being a mother and a wife, not in terms of being an independent individual.[29] "The problem is always being the children's mommy, or the minister's wife and never being myself."[30] The concept of the autonomous independent self, which originates in liberal thought, appears once again in the feminist demand for selfhood. This time, the conception is not limited to a notion of citizen's rights but takes on a psychological dimension due to the influence of Freudian thinking. As a result, woman's self-identity takes center stage in Friedan's conception of the independent women. She is concerned about woman's loss of identity.[31] She believes that the feminine mystique limits and curtails woman's development as a person, with a separate ego and identity, in much the same way nineteenth-century feminists feared Victorian ideology's impact on woman's sexuality.

Friedan presents this problem, which is particular and specific to the suburban middle-class woman's identity, as though it is woman's problem in general. "It is my thesis that the core of the problem for women today is not sexual but a problem of identity—a stunting or evasion of growth that is perpetuated by the feminine mystique."[32] The feminine mystique is a generalized problem to the degree all women can identify with it as an ideology about femininity that applies to all women across economic class and race lines. Friedan misses the point that in actuality it applies differently to women of different economic classes and races, and that the way one relates to it is not a matter of individual choice. Friedan also seems to accept more of the picture of the nonworking woman presented in the mystique as true than, in reality, it was.

By the time Friedan wrote the *Feminine Mystique,* more than one-third of the nation's workers were women; 54 percent of these women were married, and 33 percent were mothers.[33] Actually, throughout the 1950s, women from middle-income families entered the labor force more rapidly than any other group.[34] By 1956, 70 percent of all families earning between $7,000 and $15,000 had two wage earners in the family.[35] The period from shortly before World War II through the 1960s showed a 34 percent increase in the number of women workers.

In 1945 women already accounted for 36 percent of the nation's labor force. By 1960, 42 percent of the families in the United States had two workers.[36] Since World War II, the majority of women entering the labor force have been married women.[37] Friedan discusses these women workers as if they were holding part-time jobs that were not financially essential to their families.[38] The data do not bear this out.

Most women who worked earned together *with* their husbands between $7,000 and $15,000 a year.

Although the "feminine mystique" presented the picture of woman as a nonworker, woman's wage labor was much more central to the economy than Friedan recognizes, even for middle-class women.[39] If she had recognized this, she would have been able to appreciate the need for connecting her analysis of the "feminine mystique" to woman's actual relation to the public (market) sphere. My criticism of Friedan is not only that she analyzes the white middle-class woman, to the exclusion of the working class and other racial groups, but that she wrongly interprets much of what is actually happening to middle-class women as well. If Friedan had looked at the *reality* of life for black women, working-class women, and the wage-earning working- or middle-class woman, she would have realized that it is not enough to ask for equality of opportunity in the public world without calling for a reorganization of the so-called private world of the family. The double-day of work, which results when the market is opened to women and at the same time the responsibilities of the home remain theirs, is no solution to woman's problem.

Friedan leaves women vulnerable to redefinitions of the feminine mystique because she does not explain the economic and social origins of the "mystique." It is therefore difficult to understand the reasons for the "mystique" and the reasons why it will continually be redefined in terms of the new emerging needs of capitalist patriarchy. As a result, Friedan cannot help women uncover the different and changing forms of the "feminine mystique" or prepare them to fight against changes within the "mystique" that are not in their interest.

She sees woman's acceptance of the feminine mystique, not the system of patriarchy and its economic expression in capitalism, as the greatest obstruction to woman's development. Because she has no structural analysis of woman's oppression, Friedan inadvertently ends up blaming women themselves for their condition. She asks, "Why with the removal of all the legal, political, economic, and educational barriers that once kept woman from being man's equal, a person in her own right, an individual free to develop her own potential, should she accept this new image? . . ."[40] Instead of asking what the origins of the feminine mystique are, Friedan asks only why women accept it.

Although the cultural oppression of women is seriously harmful, Friedan makes it seem as though these ideas about femininity alone completely create the oppression of women. "I think all of these resistances are not that great. Our own self-denigration of ourselves as women and perhaps our own fears are the main problem."[41] The "feminine mystique," as a real ideological force, oppresses women in that they internalize these values. It then curtails women's options and by doing so impinges on their daily lives. But ideas do not come from the air. Their life force is not found in themselves or merely within those who believe them. There must be real needs in the society that reproduce these ideas and give them new life. The human mind plays a part in the process of reproducing ideas, but its part is affected by the cultural, economic, and sexual relations of society. Without connecting the "feminine mystique" to its ideological role—its political purpose in reproducing the relations of patriarchy—it is impossible to understand how it functions as part of the sexual oppression of patriarchy.

But Friedan lacks this understanding and therefore misconstrues the impact woman's liberation would have on both men and women. She thinks women fear it for what it will demand of them and thinks men support it for the freedom it will bring them.[42] This belief shows that Friedan does not see women's liberation involving a struggle for power. According to her view, men have nothing to lose and women have only to take the risk. Woman must question her own self-image and then act on this newly found independence. According to Friedan, there appear to be no constraints upon woman except the limitations she places on herself.

Although the conception one has of oneself makes activity possible, changing the conception of woman is not merely an individual matter. After all, one's conception of oneself as a woman is part of the larger reality of one's definition as a member of the sex-class woman. One's actual daily life activity affects the way one can think about oneself. To perceive oneself as active, independent, and creative, it helps, in fact, to be involved in creative activity. Thinking and acting affect each other. Friedan helps us understand that how we think about ourselves is important, but she does not help us understand that individual yearning is not enough. Individual activity is racially, economically, and sexually ordered with limitations and constraints. Woman does not have the freedom to act in the way Friedan assumes she does within this unequal structuring of patriarchal society. A woman may not have the education; she may have children to care for; she may not be able to earn a living wage.

Friedan envisions woman's problem as "a massive crisis of identity."[43] According to her, the attitudes of the 1950s caused women to seek the comfort of home and children. "After the loneliness of war and the unspeakableness of the bomb, against the frightening uncertainty, the cold immensity of the changing world, women as well as men sought the comforting reality of home and children."[44] Friedan's discussion of the feminine mystique suffers from an idealism that treats social reality as though it were made up of only ideas. In this view, social change requires only a change of ideas and consciousness. Therefore, when Friedan speaks of the dependence of the housewife created by the feminine mystique, she speaks of her dependence as though it were primarily a problem for woman's mind. "They are chains made up of mistaken ideas and misinterpreted facts, of incomplete truths and unreal choices."[45]

I do not mean to argue that women are merely passive subjects within a system of sexual oppression. Neither are they the free actors, which Friedan has made them. Given Friedan's lack of a power analysis, she thinks men have something to gain in women's equality. I would agree. But they also have much to lose—the sexual privilege they enjoy within the sexual hierarchy that divides home and work. Once men lose their male privilege, they will have to share the burdens and responsibilities of childrearing and domestic labor. They will lose privileges and freedoms that have existed as a result of patriarchal oppression. The destruction of a system of power and oppression does not result in everyone gaining equally and in the same way.

Because, for Friedan, so much rests in the realm of ideas (disconnected from the social structures they protect), she can believe that education is a major vehicle of social change. To free women from their secondary status, men will have to accept equal responsibility for the rearing of children. How this happens, or specifically what this means, is never made clear. However, she does see this first of all as a challenge to education.[46] She does not view the reorganization and rearrangement of the care of children as involving a question of power and privilege, although in *The Feminine Mystique* she often demonstrates that this is in fact the case. She therefore thinks education can substitute for the struggle necessary to rearrange power relations. In speaking of the need to educate men to their childrearing role, she writes: "Man and society have to be educated to accept their responsibility for that role as well. And this is first of all a challenge to education."[47]

Although educating people to a new consciousness is part of social change, Friedan has not gone any further than Wollstonecraft here. A serious challenge to the ideas must *include* a challenge to the social structures they protect. Although Friedan does address the exclusionary nature of the female-centered parenting family, she does not discuss its fundamental reorganization as necessary to creating equality for women. It is not enough to ask men to help rear children without understanding that one is speaking of a fundamental reorganization of society. This will involve men in the *equal* sharing in the responsibility for child care. The entire social organization of the way people live their lives, as well as think about them, is involved. The organization of wage labor, the relationship between home and work, the conception of public life, and the definition of masculine and feminine have to be completely rethought and restructured. This is the only way that daily life will be able to reinforce the idea of man as a childrearer. Friedan disconnects the relationship between ideas, social relations, power, and education in ways that merely obscure the way ideology affects and mirrors real life conditions.

It is therefore no surprise that Friedan emphasizes the importance of education as a way to broaden existing choices for women.[48] It would seem that Friedan should know that women are already overeducated for their jobs and for their work in the home. But she still offers individual solutions as political ones. My point is not that education is an irrelevant concern but that there is a difference between educating oneself—and helping others do the same—and accepting this as the political solution to the problem of woman's inequality. This liberal individualist attitude dominates her analysis.

As a result, Friedan often thinks that there is no political solution to an individual problem rather than understanding that there are no individual solutions to political problems.[49] The social connections between women are blurred so that Friedan thinks their only choice is to struggle individually. But this is not a totally accurate reading of Friedan because she does understand the necessity of political movement for women. In this sense, both her politics and her discussion of the "feminine mystique" recognize the social nature of woman's oppression, even though she usually reduces this problem to that of an individual's dilemma.

Friedan reflects these two tendencies when she argues that the educational attempts at social change must be backed up by women's struggle for political equality. Her conception of political equality, as I have noted, is narrow. It involves woman's equality within government, law, and the public arena in general. The problem that remains is that even when women are granted equality before the law, this does not necessarily create equality in their everyday lives. Woman's inequality, rooted in her responsibility for rearing children, is not addressed (directly) by the law. Hence, equality before the law sidesteps this issue.

There are times when Friedan makes statements that beg for a fuller analysis. "It certainly did not occur to any of us then, even the most radical, that companies which made a big profit selling us all those washing machines, dryers, freezers and second cars, were overselling us on the bliss of domesticity in order to sell us more things."[50] But these insights remain underdeveloped in both It Changed My Life and her most recent article "Feminism Takes a New Turn."[51] In this article, she writes of the economic purposes the family fulfills for capitalist society. The problem is that there is little, if any, understanding on her part of the family as a unit of sexual oppression functioning in the interests of patriarchy. When Friedan asks, "Can American capitalism accommodate a strengthened, evolving American family?" she answers, "Why not? despite the rhetoric, the family has never ranked high on the American political agenda, except as a unit to which to sell things." [52]

In her early writing of *The Feminine Mystique,* she recognized the importance of the patriarchal structure of the family, even if she did not term it as such. She criticizes Adlai Stevenson's commencement address at Smith College in 1955 for relegating woman's role to that of wife and mother and the family sphere. "Modern woman's participation in politics is through her role as wife and mother. . . . Women, especially educated women, have a unique opportunity to influence us, man and boy. The only problem is woman's failure to appreciate that her true part in the political crisis is as wife and mother." [53]

Friedan continued to write about the "feminine mystique," characterizing women as mothers and houseworkers with no independent lives, up until 1979. At this point, she recognized (although somewhat belatedly) that "the mystique" has changed. According to Friedan, the vision of the "super-professional" woman reflects the new cultural oppression of women. The interesting point is that Friedan does not discuss this new vision of woman as a redefinition of the "feminine mystique." She does not make the connections that would allow women to understand how this view of women reflects patriarchal ideology's manipulation of women's lives—their energy and their labor—as part of the same process of the 1950s and '60s. Without understanding that she is really criticizing her own analysis in *The Feminine Mystique,* which demanded woman's right to enter the public sphere, like men, she wrote in 1979:

> Why should women simply replace the glorification of domesticity with the glorification of work as their life and identity? Simply to reverse the roles of breadwinner and homemaker is no progress at all, not for women and not for men. The challenge of the 80's will be to transcend these polarities by creating new family patterns based on equality and full human identity for both sexes. [54]

Friedan is finally acknowledging the fact that the relationship between the family and the market needs discussion. She does not want to accept the relegation of women to the family sphere, but she does not want women to accept the ratrace of the market either. "Women's equality will have been for nothing if its beneficiaries, by trying to beat men at their old power games and aping their strenuous climb into and up the corporate ladder, fall into the traps men are beginning to escape." [55] Putting aside the above assumptions for the moment—that women's equality has been won or that men are beginning to escape the ugliness of the business world or that most working women are allowed to engage in the climb up the corporate ladder—it is not terribly clear what Friedan wants, other than to ease the pressures of the work world on women so that they will be free to choose motherhood if they wish it. "The great challenge we face in the 1980's is to frame a new agenda that makes it possible for women to be able to work and love in equality with men—and to choose, if they so desire, to have children." [56]

By 1979, Friedan argued that this challenge called for the restructuring of home and work life. [57] She defines this partially in terms of "balancing the demands of the workplace and the family" and "reconciling" the demands of family and career. [58] It remains unclear how one balances the demands between men and women within the hierarchical sexual structure of their homes and the workforce. Friedan discusses reorganizing the workplace in terms of innovations like "flex-time," where one can arrange their starting and leaving hours according to their children's needs. [59] It is never clear whether this arrangement is supposed to ease women's double burden (of family and work) or significantly restructure *who* is responsible for child care and *how* this responsibility is carried out.

What happened throughout the 1960s and '70s was that the demands on women's time and for their labor increased. Instead of simply being mothers, as the "feminine mystique" presented women, today women are supposed to be "working mothers." They are to operate within the patriarchal sexual division of labor in both the public and private spheres. Although women have gained access to the public domain, they have done so while remaining responsible for the private life of their family members. Women are still defined by the sexual-class structure of their lives. As mothers, they have the added responsibility today to work for wages—to help feed, clothe, and educate their children. Unlike Friedan's description of the career and professional woman, well over two-thirds of the women in the labor force are wage laborers, not professionals climbing the corporate ladder. They are simply "working mothers"; the "mystique" of the 1970s and '80s in new form. This time, instead of criticizing the mystique, Friedan ends up servicing it.

A Conception of Individuality vs.
Liberal Individualism for Feminism

In the late 1960s and early 1970s feminism revealed that a woman's problem was not merely a personal one; it was shared by many other women, in similar ways. Consciousness raising was an effective political strategy because of the social nature of woman's oppression. It helped unmask the social nature of woman's individual existence. [60] Becoming conscious as a feminist meant understanding that one was socially related to other women. A woman's feminist consciousness of herself as an individual was connected to her understanding of herself as part of a sexual class, women. Friedan discusses this reality when she says, "We identified as woman, with every woman."[61] She does not, however, see this statement as proof of the sex-class structure of society. Nor does she see the contradictions between her liberal individualism and the following statement: "But none of us could have found the power to organize a movement in ourselves alone."[62]

Whereas liberalism itself denies the connectedness and relatedness of individuals, liberal *feminism* cannot fully accept this view because its feminist priorities reflect an understanding of the social nature of woman's oppression. Although Friedan says she rejects the sex-class theory of woman's oppression, she cannot completely do so and remain a feminist. Without understanding woman's position qua other women, she would be unable to make the demands she does on behalf of women as a group. Liberal feminism, by dint of speaking of women as a group, is in contradiction with "the principles of liberalism," which do not see people as groups, only individuals. Therefore, her implicit acceptance of woman as part of a sexual class contradicts her explicit denial of it and her adherence to the liberal individualist theory of power.

The liberal individualist conception of human life disconnects one person from another and from the economic, sexual, and racial relations that define *his* (or her) life. Instead of seeing connection and relatedness between people, between politics and economics, between ideology and actual social constraints, they separate all these. The view of people or things as separate supports the dichotomized view of male and female worlds, public and private life, and politics as government, disconnected from the power relations of patriarchy, capitalism, and racism. This is the individualist view of liberalism that one must transcend as a feminist if one hopes to create the real equity between men and women.

At the same time that we can learn from Friedan that the ideology of liberal individualism is insufficient for a theory of women's liberation, we can recognize the necessity of a theory of individuality within Western feminism. This recognizes the individualist nature of Western liberal societies and the necessity that feminist theory must first recognize this before it can transcend it. I am writing of a feminist individualism that recognizes the necessity of independence and autonomy within women's (and men's) lives. Feminist politics requires a social collectivity that recognizes the independence and the interconnectedness of women. *This theory of individualism must recognize the individual character of our social nature and the social nature of our individuality.*

An understanding of the interconnection of power relations and the relatedness of human beings, each to the other, is also necessary to develop a social theory of feminist individuality. Once one understands that woman is embedded in a series of social relations, one sees the necessity of mapping out the relationship between one's individual life and the social and political structure that defines it. Only in this way can the real limitations of sex, race, and economic class on one's individuality be specified. In this way, a conception of woman's individuality will recognize her social and individual self.

Friedan sees the question of individualism for women as requiring "free choice" about decisions that affect their lives, such as abortion and day care. Woman must be free to choose motherhood or abortion.[63] Child-care centers and maternity leaves are necessary for women to freely choose motherhood.[64] Friedan herself recognizes the social needs women have if they are to achieve individuality, even if she seems limited to the ideology of liberal individualism most of the time. She sees abortion as "the final essential right of full personhood for women"[65] and knows it is a social as well as a personal question. Abortion raises the issue of women's individual right to self-determination, but it is also a social decision in that one does not decide how to exercise one's individual right to self-determination in a vacuum.

The social nature of woman's oppression shows that it is not an individual problem, but oppression is rather a socially constructed reality of which the individual is only a part. In other words, one can understand woman's oppression only by seeing woman's position in relation to other women, in relation to men, in relation to housework, in relation to childrearing. Being aware of the oppression of woman is understanding the social relations that define the total existence of being a woman. To the extent that feminism requires the recognition of woman's life within a sex class (however implicit and unformulated this understanding is), feminism lays the basis for the move beyond *liberal* individualism. And to the degree feminism requires a recognition of the individuality of women (and men), it assures a place for the individual in the social collectivity.

The Practice of Liberal Feminism and the Politics of NOW

The National Organization for Women, founded in part by Betty Friedan in 1966, is the largest feminist organization in the United States today. It is difficult to discuss such a large and varied organization as NOW because there is significant political diversity within its different state and local chapters. There is also a difference between NOW's national statement of purpose and its actual political practice. NOW appears to be moving away from Friedan's mainstream individualist politics of the 1960s. Individuals within the leadership of NOW reflect a growing awareness of the interconnections between the economy, the family, economic and sexual-class structure, and racial oppression.

Eleanor Smeal, president of NOW, may well have ended her organization's collaboration with the state for the 1980s when she announced NOW's decision not to endorse President Carter for reelection. On national television she stated that NOW would no longer allow Carter, or politicians in general, to *use* women's issues for their own political purposes. The next week, when Carter held a meeting on "women's issues for the eighties" and invited heads of numerous women's groups, NOW was not invited.

I want to introduce this discussion of NOW with a cautious statement of intent. I mean to present the diversity within NOW, particularly the radical forces within it that are aware of the contradictions within liberal feminism. At the same time, I think it is important to recognize that NOW as a national organization adopts a *liberal feminist* analysis. Its statement of purpose, first formulated in 1966, remains unchanged: ". . . take action to bring women into full participation in the mainstream of American society NOW, exercising all the privileges and responsibilities thereof in truly equal partnership with men. . . ." [66] A similar statement can be found in the New York State NOW By-Laws, 1979.

> NOW's purpose is to take actions to bring women into full participation in the mainstream of American society now, exercising all privileges and responsibilities thereof in truly equal partnership with men. This purpose includes, but is not limited to, equal rights and responsibilities in all aspects of citizenship, public service, employment, education, and family life, and it includes freedom from discrimination because of age, marital status, sexual preference and parenthood.

I want first to analyze the liberal feminist commitment to bringing women into the mainstream, and then I will examine the changes NOW underwent in the 1970s. The question is whether its theory informs and directs its political practice adequately or whether it is time to develop a new theory that better reflects NOW's present involvements and priorities. Interestingly enough, NOW's feminist politics seem to be ahead of its liberal theory in understanding the relationship between the public and private lives of women. This is a case in point in which theory limits a fuller practice, and one in which feminist practice needs to inform the theory. In other words, it is time to reject Friedan's piecemeal, pragmatic politics of the state and fight for a politics that is in the interests of women. This means that feminist practice will have to be more informed by a feminist theory that comprehends the impact of patriarchy, capitalism, and racism on women's lives. First, NOW must become conscious of its own liberal roots and the problems inherent in this.

The liberal roots of NOW are stated explicitly. In its statement of purpose, it speaks of the worldwide revolution of human rights. That women must "advance the unfinished revolution of women toward true equality, now." [67] Hence, its commitment to ending sexual discrimination in all areas of life. NOW wishes to end "conditions that now prevent women from enjoying the equality of opportunity and freedom of choice which is their right as individual Americans, and as human beings." [68] The goal of NOW is to fight for woman's equality of opportunity. [69] The commitment is to creating an equal partnership with men. [70] This primarily involves the struggle for woman's equality within the law.

Equal partnership with men also includes the reorganization of housework and the rearing of children. Men, as well as women, are to become responsible for these realms. There is still no theoretical discussion of the way patriarchy will make these demands difficult. NOW has no discussion in its statements of purpose about the sex-class system or the questions of power that emanate from this realm. Equality with men in conceptualized both in terms of equality before the law and equality within the home, but there is no recognition of the conflicts that exist between these two realms. Nevertheless, NOW's progressive politics derive from its attempts, however limited, to deal with woman's life as it crisscrosses between male and female domains. A politics and theory for NOW have yet to be defined that will allow this progressive dimension of feminism to continue to grow. Without a recognition of the relationship between woman's life in the home and in the market, between her life as a mother and a wage earner, woman can never gain equality with men. After all, it is by understanding these relationships that one comes to comprehend the nature of power in patriarchy. NOW must push for an understanding of this. It can no longer depend on merely extending liberal rights to women. "The crux of the ideology and the actions was simply the concept of 'equality' and the value of the individual: dignity, self-fulfillment, self-determination—which seem like no ideology because they are simply the values of the American Revolution (of all human revolutions basically) applied to women." [71]

The extension of liberal ideology to women is no longer enough. The commitments to individuality, equality, and self-determination have to be seen for their particular liberal quality and their ideological value as well. As liberal rights, they exclude women's equality with men by accepting the liberal division between public and private life. Woman's starting place in the "race of life" is unequal to begin with. Even though many of the demands around child care and abortion rights reflect this understanding, there is no coherent political strategy that coordinates these different efforts.

NOW needs to recognize that it is guided by liberal theory so that it can self-consciously evaluate it. Until women in NOW begin to explore the economic class and patriarchal bias of liberalism itself, they will not be able to see why they must move beyond it. Friedan does not agree. She believes the commitment to every man's birthright to equality must be the guide in the struggle rather than the "later apocalyptic rhetoric of overthrow of male dominion." [72] Apocalyptic rhetoric aside, the understanding of the sexual class, economic class, and racial privilege of society must be politically understood before equality is a possibility.

NOW has been through some changes in the past decade. In 1970 and 1971, NOW was confronted with its heterosexual bias and its oppressive position toward lesbians. It now supports the issue of sexual preference and lesbian rights.

Initially in 1966, NOW was hesitant to take a stand on the abortion issue, and now it leads a major assault against anti-abortion, pro-life forces.

NOW still predominantly holds the position that it is a nonideological group; but in 1973, the NOW chapter in Boulder, Colorado, asked and agreed to form a special committee to study the "economic, social and political philosophy of our society to determine how or whether NOW's goals can be effectuated within the present framework." [73]

The changes taking place in NOW can, perhaps, best be seen in a listing of a few of the New York State resolutions submitted for consideration and possible adoption at the October 1979 national NOW meeting held in Los Angeles, California. It is clear that the political orientation of NOW is more diverse and radical than a reading of the NOW statement of purpose leads one to believe. Here is a sampling of the New York State resolutions:

1. . . . that the homemaker's Bill of Rights calls for the *equal division* of property and assets, instead of the "equitable" division of it.
2. . . . that NOW establish a committee on Women and Nuclear Technology to (a) provide NOW members with information on the health dangers and economic implications of the continued explosion of nuclear technology, (b) serve as a liaison between NOW and the antinuclear movement, and (c) evaluate federal legislation on nuclear issues.
3. . . . that a national NOW Future of Feminism Committee be established in order to (a) prepare a description of the utopia that is our eventual goal, (b) study the influence of nonfeminist, corporate, patriarchal, hierarchical societal models on the operation of NOW, and make suggestions for change,

(c) "That this committee will make suggestions for the issues which will be our highest priorities in the future, but which are now too radical for us, as lesbian and gay rights, abortion and the ERA were thought to be in the past." [74]

Several resolutions adopted at the national convention recommitted NOW to a massive national campaign in support of the Equal Rights Amendment; a support of the passage of a comprehensive reproductive rights plank, abortion legislation being only a part of this; take steps toward eliminating sexual harassment in the workplace; and strengthen organizational efforts on behalf of lesbians. [75]

What is not clear is on what basis these changes in priority can be made within NOW. Its national programs, especially its statement of purpose, still reflect a liberal-legalistic view of politics, although the understanding within some state and local chapters, as well as some members in the national leadership, seem to be critical of this. Without a careful examination of the theory that underlies the basic commitments and goals of NOW and a rejection of its outworn liberal-individualist-legalist view, I think it will be impossible for NOW to fully *act on* its own progressive forces.

NOW's heavy emphasis on legal reform must connect this struggle with the struggle to dismantle the state. Most of the issues of law reform involving abortion, discrimination in employment, child care, marriage, and lesbian custody suits have significant effect on all women's lives. These laws, however, in and of themselves, cannot change women's lives. It is time to move beyond the vision that equality of opportunity and freedom of choice can be created by legal reform alone. It must be reinforced by structural changes as well. NOW must move beyond the liberal-individualist conception of self and power in order to tap its most progressive forces. This requires a recognition of the liberal individualist *and* radical feminist strains within feminism, a recognition of the patriarchal base of liberalism itself, and a political strategy that moves beyond liberalism.

Liberal feminism today has a different problem before it from what it faced in the nineteenth century. Whereas Wollstonecraft and Stanton had to push liberalism in terms of their feminist insights, Friedan tries to accommodate her feminist insights to liberalism. Friedan utilizes the groundwork they laid, but as a pragmatic politician. Although Stanton and Wollstonecraft were unable to see many of the connections and relations between power that Friedan is able to—through the advantage of time—Friedan does not think it is feasible to tackle them.

The question remains whether liberal feminism will continue to work together with the state to mediate the conflicts between liberalism and feminism, as it did in the 1960s, or if it will develop the feminist critique of liberalism that reemerged in the later part of the 1970s. I argue that there is a strong tendency in the latter direction. Proof of this point is that Friedan remains the single significant example of liberal feminist theory of the second wave. Most feminists seeking to develop a theory of women's oppression have been radical feminist, socialist feminist, anarchist feminist, radical lesbian feminist, or black feminist. This reflects a greater consciousness among feminist activists of the contradictory nature between liberalism and feminism.

Even though the contradictions between liberalism and feminism are becoming more apparent, many women are still forced to turn to the liberal reforms that can affect their lives in dealing with their everyday problems. This accounts for much of the hold liberal feminism still has on many women. What is needed for the 1980s is a revolutionary feminist theory that will connect to these everyday reform struggles.

NOTES

1. Many analyses of the second wave of the women's movement focus on the liberal faction of it as though it were indicative of the politics of the women's movement as a total. These studies often mark the beginning of the contemporary women's movement with President Kennedy's appointment of the Commission on the Status of Women in 1961; the Equal Pay Act of 1963, which was the first federal legislation passed prohibiting discrimination on the basis of sex; Title VII of the 1964 Civil Rights Act, which prohibits discrimination on the basis of sex; and the founding of the National Organization for Women. For a fuller account of this interpretation of the beginnings of the women's movement, see Maren Lockwood Carden, *The New Feminist Movement* (New York: Russell Sage Foundation, 1974); Jo Freeman, *The Politics of Women's Liberation* (New York: Longman, 1975); and Judith Hole and Ellen Levine, *Rebirth of Feminism* (New York: Quadrangle, 1971). For a very different and important account of the role of radical feminists in instigating the second wave of the women's movement, see Redstockings, eds., *Feminist Revolution* (New Paltz, N.Y.: Redstockings, 1975; reissued by Random House, 1978). Also see Sara Evans, *Personal Politics, The Roots of Women's Liberation in the Civil Rights Movement and the New Left* (New York: Knopf, 1979), for a much needed account of the historical relationship between the civil rights movement, the New Left, and the women's movement.

2. This distortion of the radical feminist position by the state and Friedan was made somewhat easier because much of the earliest radical

feminist theory emphasized sex class as a theory about individual men's hatred of women. The individualist conception of patriarchy made it easy for the liberal state to manipulate this point. The structural analysis of patriarchy's control over the private life of women via the public male control by men was less well developed by radical feminists in the early 1970s. This is much less true today. In other words, the takeover of the discussion of patriarchy, which Redstockings criticizes liberal feminists for doing, was *partially* rooted in the liberal strains within radical feminism. In order to fight such cooptation, radical feminists need to recognize their own liberal origins. For a fuller discussion of the radical feminist criticism of liberal feminism, see Carol Hanisch, "The Liberal Takeover of Women's Liberation," in Redstockings, *Feminist Revolution.*

3. Betty Friedan, *The Feminine Mystique* (New York: Dell, 1963), p. 37.

4. Betty Friedan, *It Changed My Life* (New York: Dell, 1977), p. 229.

5. Betty Friedan, "Our Revolution Is Unique," in *Voices of the New Feminism,* ed. Mary Lou Thompson (Boston: Beacon, 1970), p. 33.

6. Ibid., p. 34.

7. Ibid., p. 42.

8. Ibid., p. 43.

9. Friedan, *Changed My Life,* p. 225.

10. Ibid., p. 15.

11. Ibid., p. 341.

12. Friedan, "Our Revolution Is Unique," p. 38.

13. Friedan, *Changed My Life,* p. 234.

14. Ibid., p. 186.

15. Ibid., p. 187.

16. Ibid., p. 334.

17. See Robert Dahl's, *Who Governs? Democracy and Power in an American City* (New Haven: Yale University Press, 1961), for a classic example of this view.

18. For a critique of the liberal theory of politics, see Peter Bachrach and Morton Baratz, *Power and Poverty: Theory and Practice* (New York: Oxford University Press, 1970); William Connolly, ed., *The Bias of Pluralism* (New York: Atherton, 1971); William Domhoff, *The Powers That Be, Processes of Ruling Class Domination in America* (New York: Vintage, 1978); idem, *Who Really Rules? New Haven and Community Power Reexamined* (Santa Monica, Calif.: Goodyear, 1978); Richard Gillam, ed., *Power in Post-War America* (Boston: Little Brown, 1971); C. B. MacPherson, *The Real World of Democracy* (Oxford, England: Clarendon, 1966); and Michael Parenti, *Democracy for the Few* (New York: St. Martin's, 1974).

19. Kate Millett's *Sexual Politics* (New York: Avon, 1971) argued the political significance of the sexual arrangements of social life.

20. Friedan, *Changed My Life*, p. 244.

21. Ibid., p. 316.

22. Ibid., pp. 316–17.

23. Ibid., p. 317.

24. Friedan, "Our Revolution Is Unique," p. 38.

25. For a discussion of the concept of woman as part of a sexual class, see Ti Grace Atkinson, *Amazon Odyssey* (New York: Links, 1974); Simone de Beauvoir, *The Second Sex* (New York: Bantam, 1952); and Shulamith Firestone, *The Dialectic of Sex* (New York: Bantam, 1970).

26. Friedan, *Changed My Life*, p. 162.

27. Ibid.

28. Friedan, *Feminine Mystique*, p. 64.

29. Ibid., p. 41.

30. Ibid., p. 23.

31. Ibid., p. 312.

32. Ibid., p. 69.

33. Hole and Levine, *Rebirth of Feminism*, p. 18.

34. Evans, *Personal Politics*, p. 8.

35. Ibid., p. 9.

36. Congressional Quarterly, *The Women's Movement, Achievement and Effects* (Washington, D.C.: Government Printing Office, 1977), p. 37.

37. U.S. Department of Labor Employment Standards Administration, Women's Bureau, *Handbook on Women Workers, 1975* (Washington, D.C.: Government Printing Office, 1975), p. 10.

38. Friedan, *Feminine Mystique*, p. 13.

39. Friedan frankly admits that she is speaking about the middle-class woman because it is this woman, according to Friedan, who is facing an identity crisis. For a discussion of some of these issues, but from a perspective that recognizes the married middle-class woman as a worker, see Milton Cantor and Bruce Laurie, eds., *Class, Sex and the Woman Worker* (Westport, Conn.: Greenwood, 1977); *Conference on Work in the Lives of Married Women, Columbia University, 1957* (New York: Columbia University Press, 1958); Jean Curtis, *Working Mothers* (New York: Doubleday, 1976); Ivan Nye and Lois Wladis Hoffman, *The Employed Mother in America* (Chicago: Rand McNally, 1963); Ann Oakley, *The Sociology of Housework* (Bath, England: Pitman, 1974); idem, *Woman's Work, The Housewife, Past and Present* (New York: Pantheon, 1974); Sheila Rowbotham, *Woman's Consciousness, Man's World* (London: Penguin, 1973); and Robert Smuts, *Women and Work in America* (New York: Columbia University Press, 1959).

40. Friedan, *Feminine Mystique*, p. 61.
41. Friedan, *Changed My Life*, p. 103.
42. Ibid., p. 40.
43. Ibid., p. 23.
44. Friedan, *Feminine Mystique*, p. 174.
45. Ibid., p. 26.
46. Friedan, *Changed My Life*, p. 163.
47. Friedan, "Our Revolution Is Unique," p. 40.
48. Friedan, *Changed My Life*, p. 43.
49. Atkinson in *Amazon Odyssey* has an excellent discussion of woman's oppression as a political problem needing a political solution.
50. Friedan, *Changed My Life*, p. 31.
51. Betty Friedan, "Feminism Takes a New Turn," *New York Times Magazine*, 18 November 1979, pp. 40–106.
52. Ibid., p. 106.
53. Friedan, *Feminine Mystique*, p. 53.
54. Friedan, "Feminism Takes a New Turn," p. 98.
55. Ibid.
56. Ibid., p. 40.
57. Ibid., p. 92.
58. Ibid., p. 96.
59. Ibid.
60. For an excellent discussion of the radical-feminist and social conception of consciousness-raising, see Kathie Sarachild, "Consciousness Raising: A Radical Weapon," in Redstockings, *Feminist Revolution*.
61. Friedan, *Changed My Life*, p. 110.
62. Ibid.
63. Friedan, "Our Revolution Is Unique," p. 35.
64. Friedan, *Changed My Life*, p. 157.
65. Ibid., p. 167.
66. Carden, *The New Feminist Movement*, p. 104.
67. Friedan, *Changed My Life*, p. 125.
68. Ibid., p. 124.
69. Ibid., p. 127.
70. Ibid., p. 123.
71. Ibid., p. 120.
72. Ibid., p. 121.
73. Carden, *The New Feminist Movement*, p. 114.
74. This is a statement taken from the presubmitted resolution to the NOW Convention, October 1979, written by Sheila Molnar Feiger.
75. As reported in the *National N.O.W. Times*, official journal of the National Organization for Women, vol. 2, no. 2 (November 1979): 33–34.

9

The Contradiction Between Liberal Individualism and the Patriarchal Family: The "Working Mother's" Double-Day and Her Sexual Ghetto in the Labor Force

I wish to examine the contradictory nature of women's everyday lives given the increased number of married women wage earners since World War II and their continued responsibility for childrearing and domesticity. I hope this discussion will help explain how patriarchy as an ideology and social structure, and the ideology of liberal individualism (and the structure of capitalism) affect women's lives today. As we have already seen, liberal ideology developed out of the need to rewire the patriarchal division of male and female domains through the differentiation of the home from work, economics from politics, public from private, and personal from political life. Liberal feminism, which developed in reaction to the exclusion of women from liberal "rights," demanded equality of opportunity for women but within the confines of the above patriarchal divisions.

Beginning with World War II, significant numbers of married women entered the labor force. Today a majority of married women work in the market for wages, and as a result women's daily life activity has begun to cut through the patriarchal ordering of separate sexual spheres. A woman, as a wife, mother, and wage earner, no longer can be said to operate within a single sphere. Nor is she often expected to. As married women continue to enter the labor force in unprecedented numbers and also remain responsible for childrearing and the maintenance of the home, their double-day of work is outlined more clearly than ever before. This reality affects a majority of women in the United States for the first time in history.

201

Whereas Wollstonecraft, Taylor, Mill, and Stanton were unable to sufficiently develop a political strategy that addressed woman's oppression within the home and the family, today the structure of a majority of women's lives can help lay the basis for such a politics. Couple this with the fact that there is a widespread acceptance of the extension of the equality of opportunity doctrine to women today,[1] and one can see that there is an important political potential to be understood here.

One cannot understand the full radical potential of feminism as a mass-based movement until one recognizes the contradictions that at present exist in a majority of women's everyday lives[2] as they perform the double-day of work as mothers, wives, and wage laborers. The unprecedented number of married women in the labor force *potentially* undermines the patriarchal controls on women as dependents in marriage and begins to undermine the patriarchal structure of male and female hierarchical relations rooted in the division of the home and the market. It is therefore easier today than it was in the eighteenth and nineteenth centuries to develop such an understanding among women themselves with regard to the oppressive nature of their sexual status because they are required to labor in two domains as a subjugated sexual class. These contradictions, which develop out of the conflict that exists between a woman's role as a mother and her role as a wage earner, can help lay the basis for understanding why the patriarchal roots of capitalism must be attacked to achieve full equality for women. Nevertheless, there is nothing automatic about the development of such a consciousness. Therefore, a feminist politics is needed to address these tendencies in women's lives. Given the necessary struggle of everyday life and a feminist politics to direct it, the connections between patriarchy and capitalism and woman's oppression can be understood.

A feminist politics that can encompass the issues of the "working mother" and the double-day of work will have to move beyond the liberal dichotomization of the family and the market to take account of woman's place in both the patriarchal family and the capitalist market. The use of the term "working mother" reflects the patriarchal bias of the capitalist market to begin with. A "working mother" (from the vantage point of the market) is a mother who works for wages. The assumption is that women, as mothers, do not work. Work is the activity one gets paid for doing. In the analysis that follows the meaning of "working mother" is twofold. Woman is viewed in this instance as working both as (1) a mother, wife and domestic; and (2) as a wage earner in the market. Her double-day of work reflects her responsibilities in the domain of the home *and* the market; her subject status within the family and her relegation to a sexual ghetto in the market. It remains a question for the 1980s whether a feminist consciousness and politics, which moves beyond liberal individualism to an understanding of the structural constraints that define the wage-earning mother's double-day of work and her position in the sexual ghetto, can develop a mass-based feminist politics. The point here is that the everyday life experiences of a majority of women speak to the possibility of such a politics.

It is the reality of the married woman worker and the "working mother" that I explore here. Her married status reflects her supposed dependence on a man. True to this picture, the married woman worker was an exception to the rule before World War II; only 4.5 percent of the women in the labor force in 1890, for instance, were married.[3] Between 1900 and 1940, a majority of the women who worked were unmarried and under twenty-five years old. The married woman of both the working *and* middle classes did not work.[4] In 1911 wives' wages accounted for only 5 percent of the urban working-class family's income. Until World War II ". . . most working-class wives ceded to their adolescent children primary responsibility for supplementary wage earning."[5] After the war, working-class and middle-class women alike increasingly entered the labor force. The similarity between working- and middle-class wives' labor force participation shows the uniformity across economic class lines, enforced on women through the system of marriage. This similarity between working- and middle-class women's labor participation is further documented by Hal Benenson's findings. Using 1970 census data, he finds that 48.8 percent of married women in the middle class earned wages, compared with 52.7 percent of working-class women.[6]

The married woman, considered to be the dependent on man— economically, legally, emotionally—was in the 1970s actually working in the market. The reality of the married woman wage earner becomes a contradiction in terms. Is she dependent as a woman or independent as a worker? By working in both worlds—the family and the marketplace—where contradictory and yet reinforcing rules of behavior operate, women's lives must reflect the tension amid the liberal promises of the capitalist marketplace, the patriarchal values of the home, and the liberal *and* patriarchal dimensions of the market.

There are those who argue that a tension does not exist between the family and the labor force for women who work in both spheres. According to Leslie Woodcock Tentler, women's work experience is a key part in their conservative sex-role socialization. She finds that work experience for working-class women between 1900 and 1930 reinforced, rather than contradicted, their place in the home.[7] Juliet Mitchell argues in *Woman's Estate* that women often work in the service of their family rather than with an idea of personal independence.[8] Realizing that the public sphere can operate to enforce the subjugation of women at home, I want to focus on how the structure of the market *can also* promise equality of opportunity to women. While recognizing that the market has in the past successfully resolved many of the contradictions it poses for itself, I argue that the growing number of married women wage earners challenges the old system of accommodation.

Nevertheless, a significant level of accommodation persists. Commitments to patriarchy structure the hierarchical relations of the workplace, and capitalism infiltrates the home on the most intimate levels. The domains of family and market structure each other. The concern here, however, is to show how the two spheres contradict and undermine each other *in spite of* their mutually reinforcing nature.[9]

The Contradictory Needs of Patriarchy and Capitalism

One has the opportunity today to understand more fully how patriarchy operates politically alongside capitalism. The fit between the two systems of power is not as cohesive as it was in feudalism and early capitalism; conflicts are developing between patriarchy and capitalism due to the differentiation of home and work as specifically female and male spheres and the necessity in advanced capitalism that more than 50 percent of married women work in *both* spheres. An analysis of the two systems reveals that they come into conflict with each other as they try to meet each other's needs. In this process, requisites of patriarchy have been undermined and, as a result, the system of familial patriarchy appears less able to sustain the system of social patriarchy. Capitalism, on the other hand, needs the system of social patriarchy and therefore must try to find supports for the patriarchal ordering of society.

There is an important distinction to be made here between familial patriarchy, which is patriarchy as it appears in family life, and the system of patriarchy expressed within the larger social and political context. Although familial patriarchy structures social patriarchy as a totality, they are not one and the same thing. One should not assume that all changes in the organization of the family reflect a parallel change in the relations of patriarchal power either in the family or in society. Nor should one assume that all changes in patriarchal relations in the family are always paralleled in the system of social patriarchy. In fact, the opposite may occur. As we shall see, when patriarchal relations of the family are undermined, as is done by the married woman wage earner, the patriarchal controls within the labor force itself are used to prop up patriarchal privilege. These two aspects of patriarchy are completely related to one another, but they never should be reduced to the activities of the other. Hence, while it may appear that changes in the family have given women more equality in society, this must be assessed in relation to patriarchy as a total political system.

In order to understand the political totality involved here, it is necessary to examine how the priorities of the system of patriarchy and its structural relations, which maintain the institution of motherhood,[10] and the priorities of capitalism, which involve the economic class rela-

tions of private property and profit maximization, may come into conflict with one another. By focusing on these conflicts, it becomes clearer
that we are talking about two systems of power that have to organize in
relation to each other. The conflicts are proof of the autonomy each
system must have in order to operate in the interests of the other.
Otherwise their respective power bases, which are needed for each
system to function smoothly, are undermined. We shall see that today's
conflicts reflect the undermining of the patriarchal relations of marriage
and the family sphere at the same time that capitalist society needs
them. The most important political dimension of the conflicts between
patriarchy and capitalism is the new level of consciousness that they can
instigate among women.

What, then, are the changes and resulting conflicts that can lay the
basis for this feminist consciousness? The particular conflicts I will examine represent the tensions between the capitalist economy and its
supporting liberal values of equal opportunity and liberal individualism, and the patriarchal structuring of gender relations and their
related protective values. The state's objective is to try and create cohesion between these systems because they need to operate as one, with
one set of priorities—the protection of the capitalist patriarchal order.
But at present the cohesion is weakened by conflicts between the relations of patriarchy and the ideology of liberalism, which is to say that
the narrowly restricted sexually dependent role of women in patriarchy
in the family and in the market is contradicted by the ideology of equal
opportunity. On the other hand, the relations of capitalism and the
ideology of patriarchy, which is to say the need for women wage workers, is contradicted by the patriarchal ideology that woman belongs in
the home. The two ideologies of patriarchy and liberalism come into
conflict as the idea of woman's inequality contradicts and is contradicted by the image of equal opportunity. The diagram that follows
expresses these contradictory relations:

Capitalist Patriarchy

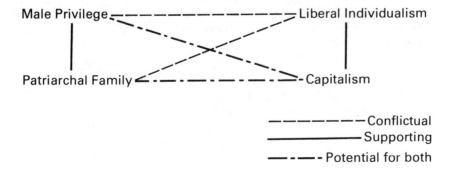

Given the earlier discussion of the family in feudal society, the relations between the family and feudal patriarchy seem to be in greater harmony than those of capitalist patriarchy and the family:

Feudal Patriarchy

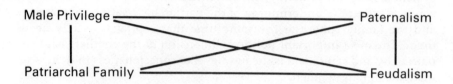

Male Privilege — Paternalism

Patriarchal Family — Feudalism

The conflict between the ideologies of liberal individualism and male privilege seems to develop and heighten in capitalism, as do the needs of capital for a supply of women workers and the family's need for a mother and wife. Within feudalism, the male privilege of the family supports the paternalism of the economic order, whereas in capitalism, the male privilege of the family contradicts both the needs of the market and its ideology of liberal individualism. I argue that the possibility to transform capitalist patriarchy lies in the opportunity to develop and act on a consciousness *of the contradictions between the patriarchal relations of the family and the needs of the capitalist economy for married women workers.*

The "Working Mother" and the Sexual Ghetto in the Labor Force

Conflict arises between the patriarchal values of society, which define woman's responsibility and place in the home as mother, and the growing needs of the capitalist economy for women to enter the workforce. This conflict has a long history of development and accommodation.

In the United States, the reality of the wage-laboring woman and the ideology defining womanhood [11] came into conflict with each other especially during the period from 1890 to 1914. The Victorian image of womanliness excluded the wage-laboring woman from its description of femininity and motherhood. Work for wages was seen to conflict with this feminine role. The woman who worked for wages did so without identifying as a worker. "This meant that she did not force others to recognize that she worked and that she did not identify or think of herself as a 'working woman.' " [12] Although the image of Victorian woman has been updated, the pre–World War I woman, described as mother and wife in the home, applied to women through the 1950s. The ideological shift that has slowly taken place since the mid-1950s is mainly a move from "woman's place is in the home" to the notion of woman as "secondary earner" or "working mother."

The ideology of the "working mother" tries to balance the contradictory nature of woman as a mother and a wage earner. Because the commitment is first to the idea of woman as a mother, most discussions of women workers emphasize that motherhood is their primary duty. This priority can be seen in the following statement made at the Conference on Work of Married Women held at Columbia University in 1957: ". . . I think the fundamental job of the American woman remains what I consider to be the most difficult of all jobs: being a good wife, a homemaker, a mother. She is only secondarily an economic provider." [13] After the appropriate relationship of woman to wifehood and motherhood was stated, woman's individual right to work if she wished was defended: ". . . women who want to work and who must work should be provided every opportunity possible to work." [14] Woman's right to work is defined first in relation to her position as a mother and a wife. Although these statements were made in 1957 and are more cloaked today in that a woman's "right to work" is sometimes emphasized, woman's responsibility remains *first* to her children and her husband; within *this context*, she has the "right" to work.

In spite of the strength of the ideology of motherhood and marriage, "working mothers" have had to enter the labor force in growing numbers as a result of inflation and the proletarianization of white-collar labor, especially clerical work. From 1948 to 1960, "working mothers" of school-age children increased 116 percent, while "working mothers" of preschool children increased 108 percent. [15] Almost one-third of all working women in 1960 were mothers with children under eighteen years of age. [16] Nearly 37 percent of mothers with children under six years of age were in the labor force in 1974. [17] This meant that in 1974, 26.8 million children had wage-earning mothers, and 6.1 million of these children were under six years of age. [18] This was the first year in which there were more mothers than nonmothers in the workforce. The labor participation rate has continued to increase, especially for mothers of preschool-age children.

> In 1977, 51% of mothers with minor children worked, including 41% with children under six and 35% with children under three. The labor participation rate of mothers has increased two times faster than the participation rate of all women, and the labor participation rate has increased even more rapidly for mothers of pre-school-age children than it has for mothers of school-age children. [19]

Maintaining the primary ideology of woman as mother rather than as worker has been achieved through the popularization of the term "working mother," which simultaneously asserts woman's first responsibility to motherhood, and her secondary status as a worker. This may reconcile women's labor outside the home with their (still) primary definition of mother (on the level of ideology), but it is less able to reconcile the conflicts that emerge in women's everyday lives.

The reconciliation between family and market is not merely left to the ideological realm. The market itself tries to reinforce the sexual hierarchy of patriarchy that indirectly bolsters woman's primary role as a mother. Both the choices of work open to her in the market and the wages she can earn keep her in a secondary position to men in the market and to her husband at home. The sexual segregation of the market keeps women's choices and options limited. Woman's disproportionate share of seasonal work and part-time work also reflects her secondary status as a wage earner. Her secondary status within the market, however, openly contradicts the promise of equality of opportunity in the market; her assignment to a sexual ghetto within the market contradicts the emphasis on individual achievement.

Patriarchal privilege is reinforced in the market. Most women do "women's work" in the labor force. The particular work assigned to women has been disproportionately white-collar, although proletarianized labor, and poorly paid. White-collar work for women continues to increase at a much faster rate than employment as a whole.[20] From 1958 to 1974, white-collar jobs increased for women, whereas women's labor participation declined in all other fields.

The major white-collar work developed for women has been clerical labor. The typewriter came into use in 1873 and was advertised by Remington with women using it. In this period, and until 1900, women clerical workers increased against men workers 340 fold.[21] By the late 1920s, more than half of the clerical workers were women.[22] Between 1960 and 1973, the number of women clerical laborers again increased by about 58 percent. By 1973, it was the largest occupational group employing women. In that year, 11 million women, over one-third of all women workers, were employed in clerical work.[23] The number of women secretaries, typists, and stenographers, who account for about three out of eight clerical workers, increased by 90 percent between 1960 and 1973.[24] In 1977, nearly four out of five (78.9 percent) clerical workers in the United States were women; 35 percent (12.7 million women) of all employed women worked in clerical jobs.[25]

Clerical labor represents a particular phenomenon in the history of women's work. It reflects the development of wage work *for* married women in the twentieth century. It is defined as specifically women's work, and part of this requires its presentation as white-collar, as acceptable work for married women to do.[26] This is partially an attempt to reconcile the needs of advanced capitalism for married women workers with the preservation of patriarchy. After all, the patriarchal view of the dependent, nonworking woman in capitalism has been represented through the presentation of the married woman as a housewife. This image can be preserved while requiring her to be in the wage-labor force by presenting the work she does as feminine, ladylike, and wifely.

Although popular views of white-collar labor are that it requires thought and is therefore interesting, that it is of higher status than blue-collar work,[27] and that it is better paid, the large number of white-collar jobs suffer from problems similar to factory labor. Many white-collar jobs are boring, routinized, have little room for decision making, and are poorly paid. The median wage in 1975 for a clerical worker employed full-time, year round, was $7,562. This is 68 percent of the median wage for male factory operatives and 62.3 percent of that earned by male clerical workers.

This conception of "women's work" within the labor force further structures the organization of the labor force. Of the 33 million women working in 1974, sixteen years and older, 62 percent were in white-collar jobs; 21 percent were in service work; less than 16 percent were in blue-collar occupations; and less than 2 percent were in farm jobs.[28] In this same year, 5 percent of employed women were in professional and managerial jobs.[29] In 1973, more than two-fifths of all women working were employed in only ten occupations. These jobs were "secretary, retail trade salesworker, bookkeeper, private household worker, elementary school teacher, waitress, typist, cashier, sewer and stitcher, and registered nurse."[30] Secretaries, stenographers, bookkeepers, schoolteachers, and waitresses headed the list.

Ninety-seven percent of the lawyers and 93 percent of the doctors in this country are male, whereas 98 percent of the secretaries and typists working in the legal field are women; 98.7 percent of all telephone operators and 94.2 percent of all clerical laborers[31] are women; 99.1 percent of the secretaries are women, as are 96.3 percent of the typists.

The existence of the sexual ghetto[32] is reflected in the wages of most women. However, while unequal pay between men and women is often used to try and reproduce the patriarchal relation of female economic dependence on men, it also makes it possible for women to see their second-class status in dollars and cents. Woman's secondary-class position is made explicit when one examines the earnings gap between men and women in the labor force. The wage differential was 75 percent in 1974, compared with a 56 percent differential in 1955. In 1970, only 7 percent of American women earned more than $10,000 a year, compared with 40 percent of American men. Half of the women who worked full-time earned less than $5,000 a year.[33] The median income for women in 1970 was $4,977 and $8,227 for men. The median income of women employed full-time in 1973 was $6,488. Men's was $11,468. In this same year, the median income of minority women, employed full-time, year round, was $5,772, or 88 percent of the $6,488 earned by white women.[34] This wage structure reflects the present sexual and racial restriction of women into the job ghettoes of clerical, service, waitress, nursing, and teaching work.

If women are excluded from skilled jobs by the sexual division of labor in the market, they cannot attain equity. Skilled trade jobs pay twice as much as traditional women's white-collar jobs do.[35] In 1977, 22 percent of the women who worked in the labor force earned between $7,000 and $9,000, whereas 8 percent of the men who worked earned this; 10 percent of the women who worked earned $15,000 and over, whereas 48 percent of the men did.[36] The extension of this sexual division of labor emanating from the home to the labor force contributes to the economic gain for corporate owners. "If in 1970 women who worked had earned the same amount per hour as men who worked, it would have cost employers an additional $96 billion in payroll alone . . . that figure would have risen to $303 billion if hours as well as jobs and pay had been equalized."[37]

Simultaneously, the reinforcement of the sexual division of labor in the labor force protects its operation in the family.

The sexual hierarchy used within the labor force is maintained through the definition of woman as primarily a mother. The sexual job ghetto within the labor force maintains this definition of woman as mother in that it places her in a secondary position within the labor force, reinforcing her primary position within the home. If a woman has limited alternatives for jobs in the world of paid work, and her wages are low, her dependence on a man has not fundamentally changed, particularly if she is married with children. Only 46 percent of all jobs in the economy pay enough to sustain a family at a "reasonable" level. This may explain why 96 percent of the population eventually marries. Even though 38 percent of these people will get divorced, 79 percent of those who divorce, remarry. It is important to recognize that however insufficient job opportunities are for women, and however insufficient the pay, large numbers of women are singly responsible for family households.

Families headed by women are on the increase. By the 1970s, one out of every seven children in the United States lived in a family with a father absent.[38] The family of four, with two children at home and a husband at work, is a picture of the American family that at present fits only 6 percent of the population.[39] In reality, over the past decade, the female-headed households with children have grown ten times as fast as two-parent families.[40] "In March 1977, 7.7 million American families, one in seven of all the families in the population, were headed by women."[41] Almost half of these households are defined as poor and on welfare, which demonstrates that although there has been an influx of married women into the labor force, women are underpaid or cannot find jobs. By 1974, women already accounted for 47 percent of the unemployed.[42]

The woman-headed single-parent family reflects the contradictory nature of woman's existence also expressed in the two-parent family. A woman as a single parent may not be economically dependent on an individual man, although she must contend with the patriarchal limitations on her in the labor force, as well as the lack of alternatives that face her in dealing with the responsibilities of her home and her children. The patriarchal relations of society operate in her life with no man present in that she is defined as a woman, in relation to man, in the workforce, in her wages, in her lack of opportunity. The patriarchal structuring of her work can be understood more readily by her as she crosses between both worlds, the home and market, alone.

This system of sexual hierarchy also sustains a system of domestic labor within the family. In addition to employing women in a manner that increases the profit system for individual corporations, the sexual division of labor maintains a system of domestic labor within the home that reflects woman's primary identity as childbearer and rearer. A Chase Manhattan Bank research report noted that if a housewife were paid for her household labor, she would be worth $257.73 a week. Each housewife therefore performs a job worth $13,391 a year, and the aggregate housewife services would be worth $250 billion a year.[43] This work is done, but it will not be recognized as work by the system of capitalist patriarchy as long as woman is mystified and sentimentalized in relation to the institution of motherhood.

The resolution of this conflict between women as wage earners, as mothers, and as domestic workers has not been as successful as it may first appear. As more women enter the labor force, they expect the ideology of equal opportunity to apply to them. Because of the conflict between the ideology of equal opportunity and women's real lack of equality within the labor force, there is the opportunity for women to see their second-class status more clearly. This has direct impact on how women see themselves as mothers and domestics. Women can become more conscious of the work they do in the home against the backdrop of their wage labor. They can realize the importance of the work they do in the home if they recognize the similarity between their domestic activity and the labor they perform at work for wages. Also, when women work outside the home, like their husbands, they are more apt to question their husband's lack of help in the home. In studies made of women in the labor force, it has been found that their husbands do not share in the work of the home to any substantial degree. Researchers failed to show any real impact a "working wife" has on the amount of time her husband spends on housework.[44]

I argue that the contradiction between performing as a wage earner and thinking of oneself as a mother can help lay the basis for women's questioning the double-day of work. As the double-day of work continues to affect more and more women, of the working and middle classes, the arbitrariness of the sexual division of labor, which assigns women the labor of the home, can become more apparent. Only by addressing this reality can feminists address the question of what constitutes a fair division of labor and a fair day's work.

The "Working Mother" and Feminism

Conflict derives from the changes women's lives undergo as they enter the labor force, while the patriarchal relations and values of dependence both in the home and on the job are maintained. The notion of the "working mother" is the latest attempt to define the consciousness of these wage-earning women. This attempt to adjust ideology, to be more in line with the reality of the "working mother," is partially to protect the patriarchal image of woman as dependent on man. In this view, she is still primarily a mother and therefore needs a man to support her. Her secondary-wage status makes her labor cheaper. But the attempt to reconcile the conflicts between patriarchy and capitalism is only partially successful because the conflicts in woman's individual life continue to intensify.

The interesting phenomenon we are at present experiencing is that the increase in the number of wage-earning women in the United States is not connected to a recognition of women's equality with men or a fundamental reorganization of the mothering process as women's responsibility.[45] In 1900, only 6 percent of women in the United States worked outside the home. In 1970, 48 percent did. In 1977, nearly half of all women age sixteen and over were working or looking for work; approximately 40.5 million women worked in the labor force, compared with 57.2 million men. In 1990 almost 52 million women are expected to be in the labor force, which means approximately a million women a year will enter the labor force until then. These women are expected to be between twenty-five and forty-four years old, married, and a majority will have minor children.[46] But all these women will enter the labor force as secondary citizens. Their entry to the market will be unequal to start with. Their inequality as women in relation to men is maintained by structurally placing women in a ghetto in the market.

The serious challenge to the maintenance of this ghetto is that the market is supposed to be organized around equality of opportunity. The market is supposed to extend the promises of liberal society to those who partake in it. Women who have applied these promises to themselves and who have entered the market as *unequal* members are in a position to understand the patriarchal bias of the economy much in the same way Wollstonecraft and Stanton unmasked the exclusion of women from education and the rights to citizenship. However, the extraordinary potential is that a majority of women, given their everyday lives, can begin to understand this not merely in terms of the public sphere of the market but how this relates to their position in the home. Today's wage-earning mother represents woman's secondary position in the labor force *and* in the home. Because of the nature of women's lives today, especially their double-day of work, a feminist politics can address how woman's sexual oppression and exploitation in the market is rooted in her secondary sexual status in marriage and the family. This is because woman's experience cuts through the spheres of home and market in ways it did not in the eighteenth and nineteenth centuries.

The potential for a mass-based feminist politics focusing on the wage-earning mother and her double-day of work does not end here. It extends to a feminist politics that cuts across race lines. One of the significant differences that has existed between married white women and black women is that married black women have been wage earners in greater numbers than white women. As white married women have entered the labor force, they now share the reality of the double-day of work with the black woman. In 1970, black women's participation in the labor force was only slightly higher than white women's. In 1977, 48 percent of white women and 51 percent of nonwhite women were in the labor force,[47] whereas in 1890, when only 5 percent of married women had jobs outside their homes, "one quarter of black wives and two thirds of the large number of black widows were gainfully employed."[48] Although black women earn less than white women and are found in blue-collar or service jobs more than in white-collar jobs, black and white women share a sexual ghetto in the market. This creates a potential for building a feminist politics that is inclusive of black women's reality.[49]

Working-class and middle-class women share much more in reality than one might think they do on the basis of their economic class differences. This unity, which exists as a result of the large number of married women from both classes in the labor force, makes it possible for women of different economic and racial privilege to understand their common sexual second-class citizenship. The middle-class woman of the 1970s is part of the same sexual ghetto in the market as her working-class and black sister, although this ghetto is hierarchically structured along racial lines. These women share the reality of being "working mothers." Middle- and working-class, white and minority women are in a better position than ever before to understand the commonality of their oppression. This is a first step toward understanding how their sexual oppression is experienced differently as well.

The state seeks to deflect the feminist consciousness of women workers from the cross-economic class and racial nature of their oppression. The more the state can isolate and contain this consciousness, the more difficult it is for feminists to act on these new possibilities. As long as feminist politics remains liberal, it will not be able to resolve the contradictions discussed in these pages. It will not be able to encompass the needs of married working women and minority women alike. This limitation exists because liberalism is not merely politically organized with an economic class and race bias, it is patriarchically structured as well, sexually biased in favor of men. By focusing on the contradictions of the married woman worker and the "working mother," feminist politics can begin to transcend the limitations of liberalism.

NOTES

1. Woman's right to equality with men is understood as part of the "ideology of liberal individualism." It exists alongside sexual hierarchy. The point here is that equal rights, on the level of *ideology*, permeates the political language today even though this language is very often divorced from the *belief* that woman is equal to man.

2. See Nancy Hartsock, "Feminist Theory and the Development of Revolutionary Strategy," in *Capitalist Patriarchy and the Case for Socialist Feminism*, ed. Zillah Eisenstein (New York: Monthly Review Press, 1978), for a discussion of the relationship between feminist politics and women's everyday lives.

3. Ralph E. Smith, "The Movement of Women in the Labor Force," in *The Subtle Revolution*, ed. Ralph E. Smith (Washington, D.C.: Urban Institute, 1979), p. 5.

4. Although the distinction between working class and middle class will be used throughout this chapter, there are significant problems with this distinction. Because there has been little clarification about what these terms specifically mean in relation to individual women's lives, these categories do not encompass woman's particular position in the family structure or the market. It is most often *assumed* that a working-class woman is defined by the blue-collar status of her husband. For a discussion of the problems with a conception of working class based on the equation of blue collar and working class, see Harry Braverman, *Labor and Monopoly Capital* (New York: Monthly Review Press, 1974). For pathbreaking work on the relationship between family structure and class identification, see Harold Benenson, "The

Theory of Class and Structural Developments in American Society: Occupational and Family Change, 1945–1970" (Ph.D. dissertation, New York University, 1980).

5. Leslie Woodcock Tentler, *Wage-Earning Women, Industrial Work and Family Life in the United States, 1900–1930* (New York: Oxford University Press, 1979), p. 138.

6. Harold Benenson, "The Theory of Class and Structural Developments in American Society," chap. 1, pp. 10–11.

7. Whereas I specifically choose to examine the element of conflict (contradiction) between the sphere of the home and the market for wage-earning women, Tentler, in *Wage-Earning Women,* focuses on how these two spheres reinforce each other. Although there is a difference in emphasis in our two approaches, I think Tentler misrepresents the level of conflict that exists *within her own analysis.* She argues that many working-class homes are dominated and controlled by the wives and mothers within them: the mothering role gives women a sense of personal power in this sphere (p. 178), and their domestic role gives them a sense of greater status than their work outside does (p. 179). I therefore question how, in these instances, the work experience of these women merely reinforces their role in the home. If the working-class woman has an element of power in her home, this is actively contradicted by her work (and lack of control within it) in the labor force.

8. Juliet Mitchell, *Woman's Estate* (New York: Random House, 1971). For an alternate interpretation of the importance of woman's participation in the labor force for developing feminist theory, see Joan Kelly, "The Doubled Vision of Feminist Theory: A Postscript to the 'Women and Power' Conference," *Feminist Studies* 5, no. 1 (Spring 1979): 216–28.

9. See Zillah Eisenstein, "Developing a Theory of Capitalist Patriarchy and Socialist Feminism," in Eisenstein, *Capitalist Patriarchy,* for a discussion of the mutual dependence and *reinforcement* of the systems of capitalism and patriarchy. The conflict I discuss in this chapter takes place within the larger context of this mutual support.

10. See the discussion of institutional motherhood in Adrienne Rich, *Of Woman Born, Motherhood as Experience and Institution* (New York: Norton, 1976). Also see Nancy Chodorow, *The Reproduction of Mothering, Psychoanalysis and the Sociology of Gender* (Berkeley: University of California Press, 1978); and Dorothy Dinnerstein, *The Mermaid and the Minotaur, Sexual Arrangements and Human Malaise* (New York: Harper & Row, 1976).

11. The discussion here is indebted to my sister, Sarah Eisenstein. Her "Working Women's Consciousness in the United States, 1890–W.W. II" (Ph.D. dissertation, Columbia University) remains unfinished due to her long battle against cancer and her early death. I hope this

work will be available to the public in the not too distant future. Also see Mary Ryan, *Womanhood in America* (New York: New Viewpoints, 1975).

12. Sarah Eisenstein, "Working Women's Consciousness," chap. 3, p. 42.

13. *Conference on Work in the Lives of Married Women, Columbia University, 1957* (New York: Columbia University Press, 1958), p. 15.

14. Ibid.

15. Ivan Nye and Lois Wladis Hoffman, *The Employed Mother in America* (Chicago: Rand McNally, 1963), p. 8.

16. Ibid.

17. U.S. Department of Labor Employment Standards Administration, Women's Bureau, *Handbook on Women Workers—1975* (Washington, D.C.: U.S. Government Printing Office, 1975), p. 3.

18. Ibid., p. iii. There were only 1 million licensed day-care slots at this time, which meant that 5 million children still needed day care. The need for child care has continued to increase.

19. Rosalyn Baxandall, "Who Shall Care for Our Children? The History and Development of Day Care in the United States," in *Women: A Feminist Perspective*, ed. Jo Freeman (2nd ed.; Palo Alto, Calif.: Mayfield, 1979), p. 140.

20. U.S. Department of Labor, *Handbook on Women Workers—1975*, p. 83.

21. Evelyn Nakano Glenn and Roslyn Feldberg, "Clerical Work: The Female Occupation," in Freeman, *Women: A Feminist Perspective*, p. 318.

22. For a discussion of the proletarianization of clerical work and its transformation to women's work, see Braverman, *Labor and Monopoly Capital;* and Margery Davies, "Woman's Place Is at the Typewriter: The Feminization of the Clerical Labor Force," in Eisenstein, *Capitalist Patriarchy.* For a contemporary analysis of clerical workers, see Jean Tepperman, *Not Servants, Not Machines, Office Workers Speak Out* (Boston: Beacon, 1976).

23. U.S. Department of Labor, *Handbook on Women Workers—1975*, p. 96.

24. Ibid., p. 97.

25. Glenn and Feldberg, "Clerical Work," p. 314.

26. The complicated question of the status of the women in these jobs involves the fact that the ideology describing white-collar labor presents a picture of the work that is different from what it *actually* is. To the degree that most clerical work is alienating and exploitative wage labor, it can be objectively described as working class in nature. It is also, however, true that many of these very workers identify as middle class. One is left with the problem of assessing a situation in which a

woman performs a working-class job and may identify as a middle-class person. This self-definition of her status is not irrelevant and yet it is not the whole story.

27. This presentation of clerical labor as white-collar work reflects significant problems in assessing the nature of this work. For different interpretations of the nature of white-collar work today and its relationship to working-class and middle-class consciousness, see Barbara Garson, *All the Livelong Day* (New York: Doubleday, 1975); Richard Sennett and Jonathan Cobb, *The Hidden Injuries of Class* (New York: Knopf, 1972); E. E. Masters, *Blue Collar Aristocrats* (Wisconsin: University of Wisconsin Press, 1975); Braverman, *Labor and Monopoly Capital*; Richard Hamilton, *Class and Politics in the United States* (New York: Wiley, 1972); and Andrew Levison, *The Working Class Majority* (New York: Coward, McCann, and Geoghegan, 1974).

28. U.S. Department of Labor, *Handbook on Women Workers—1975*, pp. 83–84. For further discussion of women wage earners and their place in the market, see Milton Cantor and Bruce Laurie, eds., *Class, Sex and the Woman Worker* (Westport, Conn.: Greenwood, 1977); Juanita Kreps and Robert Clark, *Sex, Age and Work: The Changing Composition of the Labor Force* (Baltimore: Johns Hopkins University Press, 1975); and Ann Stromberg and Shirley Harkess, eds., *Women Working, Theories and Facts in Perspective* (Palo Alto, Calif.: Mayfield, 1978).

29. Ibid., p. iii.

30. Ibid., p. 91.

31. *Newsweek*, 6 December 1976, p. 70.

32. Not all oppression/exploitation of women derives from the sex-segregated nature of the labor market. Women who do the same jobs as men get paid less, or do not get promoted, or do not receive pay increases, etc. They are also exposed to sexual harassment. They also have to deal with extra family responsibilities. All these things affect working women, including those who work in traditional male occupations.

33. Karen Lindsey, "Do Women Have Class?" *Liberation* 20, no. 2 (January–February 1977): 18.

34. U.S. Department of Labor, *Handbook on Women Workers—1975*, pp. 4–5.

35. Muriel Lederer, *Blue Collar Jobs for Women* (New York: Dutton, 1979), p. 2.

36. Nancy Barrett, "Women in the Job Market: Occupations, Earnings, and Career Opportunities," in Smith, *The Subtle Revolution*, p. 33.

37. *Dollars and Sense*, no. 20 (November 1976): p. 4.

38. Isabel Sawhill, "Discrimination and Poverty Among Women Who Head Families," in *Women and the Workplace*, ed. Martha Blaxall and Barbara Reagan (Chicago: University of Chicago Press, 1975), p.

201. Also see Heather Ross and Isabel Sawhill, *Time of Transition, The Growth of Families Headed by Women* (Washington, D.C.: Urban Institute, 1975).

39. Sawhill, "Discrimination and Poverty Among Women," p. 191.

40. Ibid., p. 201.

41. Francine Blau, "Women in the Labor Force: An Overview," in Freeman, *Women: A Feminist Perspective*, p. 275. The racial breakdown of families headed by women is important to note. In 1977, 36 percent of all black families, 20 percent of all Hispanic families, and 11 percent of all white families were headed by women. See U.S. Department of Labor, Bureau of Labor Statistics, *U.S. Working Women: A Databook Bulletin 1977* (Washington, D.C.: Government Printing Office, 1977), p. 41.

42. U.S. Department of Labor, *Handbook on Women Workers—1975*, p. 66.

43. Gerder Lerner quoting from Sylvia Porter's "What's a Wife Worth," in *The Female Experience: An American Documentary* (Indianapolis: Bobbs-Merrill, 1977), p. 110.

44. Sandra Hofferth and Kristin Moore, "Woman's Employment and Marriage," in Smith, *The Subtle Revolution*, p. 114.

45. For a discussion of these wage-earning women, see Linda Gordon, Rosalyn Raxandall, and Susan Reverby, eds., *America's Working Women, A Documentary History 1600 to the Present* (New York: Vintage, 1976); Nancy Seifer, *Nobody Speaks for Me! Self-Portraits of American Working Class Women* (New York: Simon & Schuster, 1976); Jean McCrindle and Sheila Rowbotham, eds., *Dutiful Daughters* (London: Allen Lane, Penguin, 1977); Jean Westin, *Making Do, How Women Survived the '30's* (Chicago: Follett, 1978); Louise Kapp Howe, *Pink Collar Workers* (New York: Putnam's, 1977); Lin Farley, *Sexual Shakedown: The Sexual Harassment of Women on the Job* (New York: McGraw-Hill, 1978); and David Katzman, *Seven Days a Week, Women and Domestic Service in Industrializing America* (New York: Oxford University Press, 1978).

46. Ralph E. Smith, *Women in the Labor Force in 1990* (Washington, D.C.: Urban Institute, 1979), p. v.

47. Blair, "Women in the Labor Force," in Freeman, *Women: A Feminist Perspective*, p. 276.

48. Ibid., p. 269.

49. Although it is not *sufficient* to build a feminist politics solely on the *common* grounds of woman's oppression, which cuts through the racist structure of society, from this commonality a politics can be created that builds a commitment to understanding the *differences* between black and white women in all its richness. Only then can a feminist politics inclusive of black women's needs be developed. Some work that begins to examine the particular role of black women in

feminism and the system of oppression are Lorraine Bethel and Barbara Smith, eds., *Conditions: Five, The Black Women's Issue* (New York, 1979); Ellen Dubois, *Feminism and Suffrage, The Emergence of an Independent Women's Movement in America, 1848–1869* (Ithaca: Cornell University Press, 1978); Combahee River Collective, "A Black Feminist Statement," in Eisenstein, *Capitalist Patriarchy;* idem, "Why Did They Die? A Document of Black Feminism," *Radical America* 13, no. 6. (November–December 1979): 41–51; Sara Evans, *Personal Politics, The Roots of Women's Liberation in the Civil Rights Movement and the New Left* (New York: Knopf, 1979); Beverly Fisher, "Race and Class: Beyond Personal Politics," *Quest* 3, no. 4 (Spring 1977): 2–15; Herbert Gutman, *The Black Family in Slavery and Freedom, 1750–1925* (New York: Pantheon, 1976); Diane Lewis, "A Response to Inequality: Black Women, Racism and Sexism," *Signs* 3, no. 2 (Winter 1977): 339–61; Margaret Simons, "Racism and Feminism: A Schism in the Sisterhood," *Feminist Studies* 5, no. 2 (Summer 1979): 384–402; Carol Stack, *All Our Kin, Strategies for Survival in a Black Community* (New York: Harper & Row, 1974); *Off Our Backs,* "Special Issue on: Racism and Sexism," 9, no. 10 (November 1979); Michele Wallace, *Black Macho and the Myth of the Super-Woman* (New York: Dial, 1978); and Alice Walker, "Born at Home," *Ms.* 8, no. 8 (February 1980): 67–76.

10

The Capitalist Patriarchal State and the Politics of Liberal Feminism

At this point, we turn to a discussion of how the contemporary state attempts to contain the subversive content of liberal feminist demands, which have the capacity to recognize the sexual-class oppression of women across economic class and racial lines. The subversive quality derives from the feminist assault against the actual patriarchal organization of liberal society. Although the state has actively sought to mediate the conflicts between capitalism and patriarchy through its lip service to the Equal Rights Amendment, the 1978 funding of the Houston Women's Conference, the reversal of the Supreme Court decision to disallow pregnancy disability and its various legislation on abortion, it has been unsuccessful in creating cohesive policy. Part of the reason for this lack of success, as we shall see, are the differences that exist within the state on how best to deal with the conflict between capitalist and patriarchal needs. I also argue that many women who adopt liberal feminist political strategy lead lives that lay the basis for a radical feminist understanding of woman's oppression. They therefore may be less ready to accept state attempts to narrow their concerns as (liberal) feminists and call these victories. As we saw in the last chapter, women's lives have the potential to help them understand the difference between the promise of "equal rights" and the actual options to practice them. This lays the possibility for a feminist politics that builds from liberalism and, in the end, self-consciously moves beyond it.

An exploration of contemporary liberal feminist politics uncovers its complex relationship to the state. Today President Carter tries to present a narrow legalistic "rights" interpretation of liberal feminism as the state's position on women. This position of the state, as supposedly supportive of the equality of opportunity for women, complicated feminist politics for the 1970s and continues to do so in the 1980s. NOW's recent denouncement of Carter's use of the ERA for his own political purposes speaks to the concern that the state manipulates feminist demands for its purposes. However, there is not a unified position among feminists about how best to deal with the state; feminists have yet to figure out how to use the liberal feminist position of the state as progressively as possible for women without being circumscribed by it. Part of this feminist politics involves taking advantage of the lack of unity within the state itself on "reproductive policies."

As I argued in the previous chapter, a progressive feminist politics will have to be guided by the concerns of the "working mother" and her exploitation in the sexual ghetto in the market. By doing so, feminist politics, rooted in a firm understanding of woman's sexual-class oppression within marriage and the market, will cut through the liberal blinders that dichotomize life into male and female, public and private, state and family, home and work spheres. This perspective undermines the ideology of liberal individualism in feminism because it reveals that woman is part of sexual class and that this class definition is part of her individual identity. This recognition of the sexual-class character of woman's oppression focuses on the patriarchal roots of liberalism. It is because of this aspect of liberal feminism—that it demands equality on behalf of women as a sexual class and in order to achieve this must dismantle the patriarchal oppression on which the state is founded— that the state seeks to inhibit the class consciousness of women as women. The point, however, is that the contradiction which exists between liberal individualism and patriarchy or liberalism and feminism cannot be mediated successfully. Even the state's embrace of the narrow version of liberal feminism recognizes and therefore undermines the system of patriarchal privilege. This self-contradictory nature of liberal feminism, its critique of patriarchy, recognizes women as an excluded or oppressed group, against liberal individualism, which makes it potentially subversive to the state. I argue that the crisis of liberalism today is rooted in this crisis of patriarchal control as women have come to question the separate sexual sphere doctrine and as a result have inadvertently questioned the basis of the state (i.e., the formal institutionalization of the separateness of male and female life). Therefore, the state is at present looking for new forms of patriarchal control.

Once one recognizes the state's dual role in trying to mediate and therefore coopt the subversive potential of feminism and its incapacity to do so fully, one must rethink the important role of political reform in this context. Feminists need to reconceptualize the relationship between reform and revolution to better understand how they can use liberal feminist reforms to challenge their oppression while the state's concern is to use the reform process to sustain woman's subordination. Part of understanding this is realizing that many of the demands made by liberal feminists today, like those of the 1978 government-funded Houston conference, require revolutionary upheaval of the society. Further examination is needed about the seemingly contradictory nature of "requesting" revolutionary "demands" from the state. Patriarchy will not "wither away," nor will it be destroyed through liberal reforms alone. But how these assessments are connected to a meaningful revolutionary analysis remains for feminists to articulate.

The contradictory nature of legal reform for feminists lies in this fact that it can deradicalize the potentially subversive nature of feminism by instituting limited gains, and at the same time it challenges woman's oppression by affecting woman's consciousness of herself as a person with certain rights. Only by recognizing that both these aspects exist as consequences of feminist legal reform can women begin to define a politics in their full interests. Women can then know that while they fight for the greatest equality possible in the United States, they will not achieve equality from reform alone; that these fights lay the basis for a revolutionary consciousness and revolutionary action. Reform cannot replace revolution; it is rather an assessment of how feminists must build a revolution from the existing political context.[1]

I argue in this chapter that feminists must push the state as far as it can go toward the equality of opportunity of women to help uncover the patriarchal structure of the state, which cannot actually allow women's equality with men. Juliet Mitchell senses this when she states: "A new society that is built on an old society that, within its limits, has reached a certain level of equality, clearly is a better starting point than one that must build on a society predicated on privilege and unchallenged oppression."[2] By pushing the state in this direction, women will make both formal and real gains. They will also learn that the present state cannot abide woman's actual equality with men. As feminists uncover this reality for themselves in their struggles with the state, they will begin to build a feminist politics that moves beyond liberalism.

The State, Patriarchy, and Capitalism

Legal reform simultaneously deals with the two-sided phenomenon of the power and needs of the state and the needs of feminists. This is not to deny the potential and actual power feminists have in trying to shape the alternatives and choices in their lives, but it is to emphasize that these reform struggles take place within an arena of state power. This arena reflects the antagonistic sex-class relations that exist within patriarchy, capitalism, and racism. Proof of this conflict and women's potential power is the actual system of oppression that organizes their lives. If there were not differing needs and interests within the sex-class system of patriarchy and liberal society, the state would not need laws to reinforce patriarchal privilege.

The major purpose of patriarchy, besides actualizing its system of power, is mystifying the basis of this power so that it cannot be recognized by the oppressed. Although this is true of capitalism as an economic system, it is more complex in patriarchy in that patriarchy initially structures the contours of political life. This mystification process presents the ideology of public and private life as part of bourgeois life and as an aspect of the liberal state, rather than as a patriarchal distinction between male and female domains, which is preliberal. Today, in bourgeois society, the distinction has been further developed through the political differentiation of the state as public and the family as private. At the same time that the state's activity reaches into all spheres of people's everyday lives, the state makes concrete the distinction between public and private life.[3] The state sets itself up as the public sphere, and life within the family is then defined as private in relation to the state. Nicos Poulantzas states this clearly: "For it is not the 'external' space of the modern family which shuts itself off from the state, but rather the state which, at the very time that it set itself up as the public space, traces and assigns the site of the family. . . ."[4] This ideological structuring of the public and private worlds by the state opens up private life to the encroachment by the state by supposedly closing off this realm from state power, which, in actuality, leaves it vulnerable to state interference.

Because of the patriarchal origins of this distinction, the state is identified as the male and public world, and the family is defined as the female and private world. The rule by men is formalized by the state because this division of public and private life is at one and the same time a male/female distinction. On the basis of this distinction, ideology identifies the realm of female, family, private life, as outside political life and the domain of the state. As such, patriarchy has no political identification on the state level. The division between public and private life, when it is identified, is spoken of as reflecting the development of the bourgeois liberal state, not the patriarchal ordering of the bourgeois state.

When liberal feminists adopt the liberal theory of politics and the state, they are therefore unable to deal with the question of patriarchy as it operates on the state level. As a result of their pluralist view of governmental politics, they have been unable to deal with the question of economic class and racial privilege either. Until feminists are aware of the state's involvement in protecting patriarchy as a system of power, much in the same way as it protects capitalism and racism as systems, feminists will be unable to see why a reform politics, though necessary, is insufficient. A feminist theory of the state is necessary to understand why this is so.

How does one begin to understand the state's role in the maintenance and reproduction of patriarchy? The state is actively involved in protecting the hierarchical sexual structuring of society through its laws and ideology. In other words, there is nothing natural about the way life is structured sexually; it is a historical and political phenomenon. It reflects conscious organization and protection. Lévi-Strauss has stated that "the structure of the family always and everywhere, makes certain types of sexual connections impossible, or at least wrong." [5] Legitimacy of children becomes part of the system of control. "The important thing is that every society has some way to operate a distinction between free unions and legitimate ones." [6] The organization of such relations is most definitely a concern of the political order and as such is a concern of the state. The political nature of sexual hierarchy derives from this fact that it involves conscious organization to maintain and reproduce it on its massive scale. Today, these concerns involve the state in trying to salvage the nuclear family, trying to mediate the conflicts between woman as mother and wage earner, trying to control women's struggles for reproductive freedom.

All these questions address the issue of woman as a reproducer of the species. As such, she has potential power. The state's concern is with controlling this power. This conception of patriarchy, the struggle to control women's reproductive activity and the limiting of her choices related to the institution of motherhood, reflects the centrality of patriarchy to Western society. The successful control of the struggle lays the basis for the survival of patriarchal society. The state's investment in protecting the institutions and structures that maintain patriarchy and the ideology that continues to reproduce it follows. The state is continually involved, therefore, in questions of reproductive control (childbearing) and motherhood (childrearing): abortion, contraception, sterilization, the nuclear family, pregnancy disability payments, and so forth. Through these policies, patriarchal control tries to deny reproductive control to women in both the bearing and rearing of children. [7]

The state's interest in these matters is also reflected in repeated discussions of public policy, although references are piecemeal and fragmentary. This fragmentation reflects the policy that exists, rather than the lack of a policy. It also reflects the fact that the state's policies on the reproductive control of women are often contradictory and inconsistent. President Carter, for example, has made well known his aversion to abortion. In 1976 he stated in the *Washington Post:*

> Georgia had a very strict law on abortion prior to the Supreme
> Court ruling in 1973 which I favored. . . . The Georgia Law . . .

only permitted abortion when the mother's life was considered to be in danger or if the pregnancy was a result of rape and the rape had been proven in court. And it only permitted abortions under those circumstances in the first trimester. That was my preference.[8]

He has stated his support of the Hyde Amendment, even though, as he says, he knows it is unfair to poor women.

I do not think that the federal government should finance abortions except when the woman's life is threatened or when the pregnancy was a result of rape or incest. . . . There are many things in life that are not fair, that wealthy people can afford and that poor people can't. . . . I don't believe that the federal government should take action to try to make these opportunities exactly equal, particularly when there is a moral factor involved.[9]

Through his stand on abortion, Carter wishes to reaffirm the values of nuclear family life. He hopes to stabilize woman's role within the family by doing so. "There can be no more urgent priority for the next administration, than to see that every decision our government makes is designed to honor and support and strengthen the American family."[10] Carter's faction of the state is actively involved in seeking policies that will reaffirm the order of the nuclear family amid the various social and economic changes that have created the "working mother." This concern will continue to occupy the state in the 1980s, until the challenges to the nuclear family[11] are absorbed by shifts within the present formulation of patriarchal family life. Carter's desire to accommodate the new family forms to the needs of capitalist patriarchy underlies his version of liberal feminism.

Toward a Feminist Theory of the State

The government is an arena of state power that is institutionalized, visible, overt, and legitimated. Liberals think government is equivalent to the state and the multiple relations of power it represents. It sits above the conflicts of society and is not seen as a part of them. It rather regulates society, the family, the economy, and so on, from the outside. The state is separate and apart; it regulates public life and is separate from private life.

Instead of viewing the state from this liberal vantage point, feminists need to understand that the state is a part of the struggles within society. The activity of the state actually grows out of the irreconcilability of conflicts[12] within society. Its commitment is to the creation of order and political cohesion by mediating these conflicts.

Nicos Poulantzas has defined the state as "not a theory but a relation, more exactly the condensation of a balance of forces." [13] But this Marxist and neo-Marxist conception of the state has yet to define patriarchy as one of the major forces the state must reinforce and mediate. It is to this question that feminists must turn in order to understand how the state represents not only capitalist class interest but patriarchal class interests as well.

The state deals with the arising conflicts between the needs of capital and the needs of patriarchy in terms of the political relations and purposes that define the state in the first place: the hierarchical relations that structure both the relations of capital and patriarchy. The (a) governmental apparatus with its relatively autonomous [14] relation to (b) the economic class structure, (c) the sexual class structure, and (d) the racist division of labor, protect the capitalist patriarchal system as a whole. However, the choice of how to go about creating political cohesion, while conflicts arise between the needs of capital and the needs of patriarchy, reflects the relative autonomy of the state. Within this limited realm of choice (i.e., the protection of capitalist patriarchy), conflicts internal to the state appear. In other words, the state does not merely reflect the interests of the capitalist class or patriarchy. Because there are conflicts within the capitalist class and between the actual needs of capitalism and patriarchy, the state cannot merely be an instrument of one or the other. This is because there are conflicting and unresolvable conflicts that the state first has to attempt to mediate, within capitalism, within patriarchy, and between the two systems.

By understanding this "relative autonomy" of the state, one focuses on conflict within the state. In other words, different power interests that the state represents often have different sexual and economic needs. In these instances it is necessary for the state to balance the needs of society as a whole against these particular interests. Conflicting demands cannot be met equally, and it is the role of the state to decide in these instances. These demands are part of the *political struggles within* the state and form the state. A particular example of the above would be the present conflict between the oil companies and the auto companies over high oil prices, which affect these sectors of the ruling class differently. Another example is the conflict between the proabortion forces and the Right-to-Life movement on the ERA. The state as a "thing" does not stand above these conflicts. These conflicts instead create state policy out of the different interests within the ruling class, which is both patriarchal and capitalist.

The relative autonomy of the state means that "the" state does not merely do what "the" capitalist class wants, because there are intraclass conflicts within the capitalist class. When the capitalist class disagrees among itself, its interests cannot be represented in the state as a unified whole. This is not to deny the economic class relations of the state, it is just not to oversimplify them. As Ralph Miliband states: "As was already noted earlier, the relative independence of the state does not reduce its class character: on the contrary, its relative independence makes it possible for the state to play its class role in an appropriately flexible manner." [15] As well, the relative autonomy of the state from the capitalist class cannot be fully understood until the state's relationship to patriarchy is also understood. The patriarchal foundations are older and more durable. They also structure the foundation of the state more intimately than capitalist class relations do, because the state in and of itself institutionalizes patriarchy. As a result, the relative autonomy of the state derives from conflicts that are internal to the capitalist class but exist on the question of patriarchy itself. Therefore, there is no more cohesive state policy on patriarchy than on capitalist class relations, in practice, although it may seem as though there should be, at least in theory.

The conflicts the state must address are not merely those of intra- and intereconomic class conflict but intra- and intersexual class conflict as well. In other words, the state is not unified on a position on abortion in the same way the Trilateral Commission and southern rim cowboy forces conflict over aiding the flow of capital to the Southwest. Although it may be in the interest of General Electric, in a purely economic sense, not to pay disability benefits to pregnant women, it is in the interests of capitalism and patriarchy to mediate this conflict within wage-earning mothers' lives. Although it may not be in the economic interests of the capitalist class to pay for childbirth and the related costs for welfare women rather than for abortions, which are much cheaper, it is perceived by some within this class to be in their political interest. The state has to formulate cohesive policy out of contradictory needs. This is particularly difficult in terms of balancing the needs of patriarchy and capitalism because of the disparate way patriarchy operates on the state level.

There is no parallel to the capitalist ruling class for patriarchy as a separate system, which is different from saying that there is no representation of patriarchal needs on the state level. Commitments to patriarchal power underline all realms of the state and cannot be condensed. However, the medical profession, the capitalist class itself, and trade unions form key centers of patriarchal power in the state realm. [16]

The medical profession (the American Medical Association) has emerged in the twentieth century as having intimate connections with business and legislative bodies. This has been evident in the AMA's fight against a national health insurance plan and is also evident in the abortion debate. As I shall argue, the latest Supreme Court decision involving a woman's right to an abortion has given the power of decision to the medical profession, not to women. As such, the power remains within the confines of the state, with the priorities of patriarchy and capitalism. The AMA shares the state's interest in monopolizing and concentrating medical knowledge in its own hands, which denies women reproductive freedom. This is one of the basic tenets of patriarchy.

Part of the state's process in mediating conflicting, particularly in terms of the public's acceptance of the state, is through the use of ideology. This involves mystifying the power relations of the state and, by doing so, obfuscating power. In this way the structural aspects of society, through individual consciousness, are supported by ideology itself. The ideological apparatus involve the media, which includes newspapers, journals, magazines, television, radio, movies, theater; the church, as it operates as organized religion; the educational system, defined as formal cultural training through the schools; and the law.[17] The social relations involved in these networks, which are primarily responsible for the presentation, maintenance, and reproduction of patriarchal ideology, reflect the state's involvement and investment in patriarchal relations.

The system of law organizes the above relations as it regulates them. The law acts as an ideology in that it presents a picture of woman's place through marriage law, domestic law, laws relating to prostitution, abortion, birth control, rape, homosexuality, day care, welfare, employment. The law as ideology, though, does not merely mystify reality; it structures real options at the same time. It points to the complicated role of law as an ideological tool in patriarchal control. The law both mystifies what women are and what they can do at the same time that it sets up real constraints and options. In other words, the law presents a picture of reality that is often not true; it also can effectively constrain one's real options; and it can positively note formal rights. This contradictory nature of the law, that it cloaks woman's oppression while it promises her equality and actually gives her actual "rights," gives the law its ideological power.

Because the state is so active in reinforcing the structures of patriarchy through ideology, patriarchy is often wrongly construed as merely an ideological phenomenon. If it were, the state would be able to resolve the conflicts that are partially created by the contradictory nature of liberal and patriarchal ideology by merely changing patriarchal ideology. This option is not open to the state because this ideology is needed to protect and reinforce the structural relations of woman's oppression. This is why the state is so preoccupied with maintaining the vision of the "working mother" and the sexual hierarchy of society this implies. It also needs the ideology of liberal individualism to help cloak the economic class relations of society. However, it is just this vision of liberal individualism that uncovers the unfair sexual relations of society at the same time. The best the state can do in these instances is try to mediate the real conflicts that exist between liberal individualism and feminism. It partially does this through the inversion of patriarchal reality in liberal ideology professing its commitment to woman's equality. Hence, the state searches for a presentation of liberal feminism that will mediate these conflicts. Nevertheless, the state produces ideologies that often create greater conflict rather than cohesion. Douglas Kellner has written of the contradictory nature of ideology:

> Although hegemonic ideology tends to legitimate dominant institutions, values, and ways of life, nonetheless it is not monolithic. Instead in advanced capitalist societies, hegemonic ideology tends to be fractured into various regions (the economy, politics, culture, etc.). There is no one unifying comprehensive "bourgeois" ideology; hegemonic ideology is saturated with contradictions.[18]

In the analysis put forward in this chapter, a major contradiction today to liberal ideology is patriarchal ideology. Therefore, the shifting of patriarchal ideology may reflect formal rather than real gains for women as the state attempts to accommodate the tensions between liberalism and feminism. This accommodation is done in the interest of maintaining woman's sexual subordination with public life. Hence, in the past, reforms of patriarchal law have meant an undermining of patriarchal privilege [19] rather than its elimination. However, each time an accommodation is sought between feminist demands and liberal patriarchal needs, it becomes more possible to examine the real purposes of the state. Because the demand for woman's equality even in the purely legal-formal sense has the subversive quality of questioning the male domination of public life, liberal feminists are in a better position today to understand how patriarchy operates as part of the state.

Contemporary Liberal Feminism

Today liberal feminism is a mix of several orientations. Although all liberal feminists adopt the ideas of freedom of choice, individualism, and equality of opportunity, they differ on how self-conscious they are about the patriarchal, economic, and racial bias of these ideas. By differentiating between several different tendencies within liberal feminism, I hope to clarify the differences that exist within liberal feminist politics.[20] My purpose is to identify the radical feminist tendencies that exist within significant sectors of liberal feminist politics and by so doing clarify the basis for building a revolutionary feminist politics.

The set of ideas identified as liberal feminist has remained strikingly similar in both its nineteenth- and twentieth-century formulations. What is interesting to note is that the position this set of ideas holds within the political spectrum of alternatives has changed considerably, especially in relation to the state. Whereas the feminist demands of Wollstonecraft, Mill, Taylor, and Stanton stood as radically liberal in their day, they are now part of the established ideology of the state. Whereas these early feminists were utterly progressive in demanding education, the vote, and property rights for married women, today these formal legal equalities exist. As a result, those who narrowly define women's equality in terms of these citizen rights believe women have attained equality with men.

The Feminist Political Spectrum

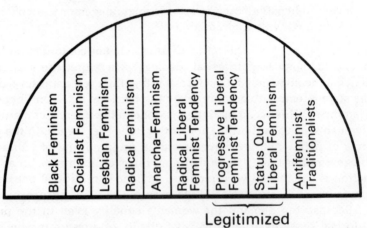

Legitimized
Liberal Sector

Antifeminist traditionalists do not believe in women's equality to begin with. The Right-to-Life movement cuts through this group and the status quo liberal feminists. Both antifeminists and status quo liberals operate as reactionaries today. Those like Phyllis Schlafly, who argue against the ERA, believe that woman is already equal to man in the judicial and political sense. Schlafly contends that it is up to the individual woman whether she takes advantage of the opportunities she has or not. Such a rendering of liberal feminism is expressed as a defense of the status quo. In this sense liberal feminism is used to protect the status quo from women's demands. Those adhering to this view make up a much smaller group than the liberal feminists who remain progressive by insisting that their legal reform demands have not yet been met. Their demands for the ERA and other legislation committed to women's equality of opportunity continue to undermine the patri-

archal privilege on which the liberal state is y with men but does not
of these feminists do not fully recognize the ierarchical organization of
their demands. Therefore, although their pol
sive to the state, they do not always recogniic reform, although in this
This progressive liberal feminist tendenl gains against the Right-
is the aspect of liberal feminism the state seek in general. Even though
does so at the same time it tries to undercvrect impact on women's
privilege. This orientation within liberal er woman's present posi-
struggle for formal equality between men anm. The ERA presents this
central to woman's liberation. This view oh be used by the state as a
liberal rights theory as sufficient for creatirty, and on the other hand,
man with little recognition that "rights" reco This predicament reflects
structure of sexual, economic, and racial inenist reform. Nevertheless,
tendency within liberal feminism has not monto clearer focus from the
Mill, and it may have backtracked in terms agitation that have been
craft's radical feminist understanding of thewould be a political deba-
version of liberal feminism argues that the jory.
structure can accommodate woman's equalittroduced to Congress in
The issue left unresolved in this view isninists in the 1980s. The
equal to. One hardly believes women are fig
coal miners of society or the male industria
plant who were sterilized by the chemicals th 1e law shall not be denied
lem is that when these liberal feminists sa y any state on account of
men, they gloss over the fact that men are
class structure. This points to the way these f he power to enforce by
equality of opportunity. They wish to be ec 1s of this article.
sense that all men can rise according to the a effect two years after the
gence, and energy they have. However, this
in actuality does not exist. Feminists need that "the ERA is an attack
ions in order to see how they operate in the i sees society as organized
women. In the end, women will be less thare ERA argue that it "will
place they occupy until the sexual-class stru increase their perception
Some liberal feminists today seem to un
demands as a result, but still adopt the li supposed to highlight the
structure their feminist strategy for social chaThe liberal individualist
women are subversive to the state, although e demand for the ERA as it
make this clear. This radical liberal feminisnton's demands. The pur-
versive to the state in that it specifically addrson is treated as an indi-
a "working mother" in a sexual ghetto and. "In many ways, the ERA
sexual-class identity across economic class 1 treating each person as
men for this viewpoint focus on the exploita1 in the eyes of (liberal)
the sexual segregation of women in the wf the laws" guaranteed by
right of women to reproductive choice, and he Constitution have not
to the survival of the species. I argue that thigainst women as a sexual

class, within the law. Women are not recognized as individuals; they rather are discriminated against as a sexual class. The law recognizes women as a sexual class, but does not recognize that women are discriminated against as such.

Several recent U.S. Supreme Court rulings show this to be the case. The Court has repeatedly denied that discrimination is practiced against women on the basis of sex: indeed, 1971 was the first time a plaintiff complained of sex discrimination under the constitutional guarantee of equal protection and *won*. The Supreme Court most recently denied the reality of sex discrimination when it decided in the *Feeney* case, in June 1979, to uphold the Massachusetts law giving veterans absolute preference over nonveterans in state civil service jobs. This ruling denies that sexual discrimination was a factor. Discrimination, the Court held, was on the basis of the category veteran, not woman. The Court also used this same reasoning when it ruled against pregnancy disability payments in *Geduldig* v. *Adiello*, June 1974, and in *General Electric Co.* v. *Martha Gilbert et al.*, 1976, holding that such a policy does not discriminate against women. The Court decided the policy was discriminatory toward pregnant persons per se, not women. On the basis that pregnancy is defined as a gender-neutral condition, the Court justices argued that no sexually discriminatory violation was found.

Although the theoretical underpinnings of the ERA are radical feminist in that they recognize woman's oppression as a sex class, much of the commitment to the ERA remains liberal. Although there is a recognition of woman's exclusion as a sexual class from the free rights of society, the liberal pluralist, nonstructural view of politics prevails. "If we view society as a natural and constant struggle of values, we see the ERA as a strong statement of pluralism—of freedom *for* diversity." [26] In this view, ideas are represented as separate from the structural relations they protect. I argue, instead, that the sex-class theory of power has to void the liberal pluralist representation of equality as sufficient. The definition of woman's problem is still understood in the pluralist view as a problem of identity more than of social structure. Friedan's liberal feminist assumptions remain valid for these feminists who believe that the ERA will change their lives because it will present a different view of womanhood. The focus remains on the ideological role the ERA plays in representing woman's equality as the norm. However, since liberal ideology operates in the interest of the capitalist patriarchal state, feminists need to know how the ERA functions as an ideology in the interests of the state as well. In other words, feminists must realize that the ERA challenges the ideological statements of patriarchy but not the actual patriarchal organization of everyday life. [27] It will be left to feminists to fight for this actual equality. At this stage of struggle, when women's equality is not left to theory but fought for in practice, women will be involved in the revolutionary process of struggling for their liberation.

At issue here is the question of the role liberal law plays in the patriarchal subordination of women and the impact this relationship has on the question of the necessity of reform legislation like the ERA. The relationship between liberal law and women's lives is different from the relationship between liberal law and men's lives in that the law protects men's domination and woman's subordination, although often indirectly.[28] To this extent, when women begin to challenge their sexual status within the law, their challenge to liberal law is far more subversive than reform legislation could be for a white male. It is this element—that women as liberal feminists seek to be recognized within the system of liberal rights and challenge the patriarchal underpinnings of these rights at the very moment that they demand them—that lays the complicated base for discussing the political significance of liberal feminist reform. After arguing that all feminist attacks on liberal law are at least potentially subversive, in that they question the structural foundations of (patriarchal) rights, I think it is important to distinguish between legal reforms that address the cross-economic class and racial identity of women as a sexual class, and those that envision women as isolated individuals. Because feminist reforms of the law have the capacity to subvert and protect the state, it is important to clarify both aspects of feminist reform activity.

Feminist law reformers are often unclear about the contradictory nature of liberal feminist law reform. They argue on the one hand that changes in the law will structure new options for women, and on the other hand that the law lags behind society and needs to catch up. Both these arguments are used in defense of the liberal-legal-political strategy. However, reformers also say that ". . . the law must sometimes acknowledge social change in order to preserve its influence as an institution,"[29] because law lags behind actual social changes. It then becomes unclear how the law can affect actual changes in women's lives, or their consciousness for that matter. The problem is that the law functions as a part of ideology (and lags behind actual social conditions), yet certain changes in the law actually create greater equality for women. The struggle for the ERA has the ability both to reflect and to instigate progressive change to the degree it recognizes its own radical feminist orientation and the necessity to subvert the state.

This is why I think the ERA should be understood as a first step in building consciousness about the necessity of the destruction of male supremacy and capitalism as systems of power. The ERA as a demand for equality can be used to uncover the built-in inequality of the economic class structure and patriarchal system we live in. In this sense, the ERA as a demand for reform can lay the basis for revolutionary consciousness. The ERA as a reform move will help lay the basis for restructuring the society because equality between men and women is not possible under the power structures of patriarchy and capitalism. As liberal feminists come to see how their feminism cannot supply equality or equality of opportunity between men and women (either economically, racially, or sexually), there is the potential for their further radicalization. Struggling for the ERA can move feminists out of the simple reform/revolution dichotomy and involve them in the process of their liberation.

Let women learn from the American feminists of the nineteenth century, who were clearly liberal, yet radical for their time. Let feminists learn from these early mistakes. Wollstonecraft and Stanton understood that they were individually, personally powerless as women, but they never could fully integrate this into their political platform and strategy. The problem, then as now, is that the liberal, legalistic notion of social change cannot recognize the sexual-class oppression of women.

This is not to say we should abandon the legal struggle for greater equality of opportunity, but these struggles must be connected to the process of showing how and why these demands are fought against. We must use this to build consciousness about how women are exploited and oppressed within the structures of capitalism, racism, and patriarchy. As I have argued, women's everyday lives help lay a basis for this understanding. I am writing of a sexual, racial, and economic structure of power. Although the legal structure protects parts of this system, it does not encompass it in its totality. If anything, it mystifies the real system of power by making only parts of it visible. If the law is focused on as solely representative of the system of oppression, the total structure is missed.

Reproductive Rights: Pregnancy Disability and the Politics of Abortion

Just as the state seeks to mediate the conflicts between liberal individualism and feminism through the ERA to try and control the politics of feminism, it more directly seeks control of all women through its ability to control women's choices about bearing children. The state does this directly through sex discrimination, abortion, and sterilization laws, and more indirectly by maintaining a heterosexual system that defines woman's primary purpose as childbearing. Nevertheless, there is a difference in the way the ERA functions as a symbolic generalized statement of woman's equality and the specific state policies that directly seek to mediate the conflict between liberal individualism and feminism on particular issues like pregnancy disability leave, abortion law, and day-care policy. The recent reversal by Congress of the Supreme Court decision disallowing pregnancy disability payments in *Geduldig* v. *Adiello* and in *General Electric Co.* v. *Martha Gilbert et al.*, reflects the way the state seeks specifically to mediate conflicts between patriarchy and capitalism.

The Disability Amendments took effect in October 1978 and allow women to decide when they will take their pregnancy leave, rather than be forced to quit their jobs in the third month of pregnancy. Employers can no longer set arbitrary time limits on when the woman must return to work. Future corporate medical plans cannot apply a different standard of medical benefits to pregnant women.[30] This legal reform, which recognizes women's needs as a sexual class, applies to all women, especially wage-earning women who can ill afford to give up the income from their jobs during pregnancy. Actually, a majority of women today cannot afford to give up their earning power during pregnancy. Neither the patriarchal or capitalist interests within the state can give women up, either as mothers and wives or as wage earners. Pregnancy disability pay is a recognition of this need for "working mothers" by certain sectors of the state.

This issue of pregnancy disability is an instance when the Court and Congress disagreed about how to smooth out the real conflicts between capitalism and patriarchy, given the increasing number of "working mothers." In this instance, a policy has actually addressed the discrimination of women as women; pregnant women can no longer be summarily fired or lose their seniority if they take time off during or after pregnancy. Their reproductive capacities cannot be used against them in the workplace in this particular way any longer. On the other hand, the residual conservative aspect of this reform is that it still expects women to take the disability leave. The next step here should be a push for paternity leave, which would have to be granted on the basis that childbearing and childrearing are male as well as female concerns.

State policy on reproductive issues is not a cohesive whole. This can be seen most clearly in the instance of abortion policy. There are conflicts within the state over how to deal with present feminist demands. The state's desire to control women's possibilities surrounding reproductive choice puts different elements within the state in conflict with feminists on specific abortion legislation. The issue of a woman's right to choose whether she shall have an abortion was as central to feminist politics in the 1970s and is now in the 1980s as a woman's right to an education and the vote was central to nineteenth-century feminism. Today feminists claim that it is their individual right to control their own bodies. They argue that the decisions surrounding pregnancy and abortion are theirs to make as independent, autonomous beings. The move to legalize abortion was initiated by this liberal feminist view of woman's individuality.[31] Many radical, socialist, lesbian, and anarchist feminists hold this liberal view as well.

The contradictory nature of liberal patriarchal politics and this feminist individualism appears in the struggle to legalize abortion. A feminist individualism requires women to fight for and only accept a reproductive rights plank that recognizes their "right" to reproductive freedom and the free choice of abortion. Yet, for all women to be free to choose abortion or childbirth, they have to have the actual freedom from economic want, sexism, and racism. This "right" applies to all women equally as an individual right and at the same time operates differently in practice for poor women and/or black women than it does for a middle-class-white woman.

The capitalist patriarchal state has still not recognized woman's right to reproductive freedom. The 1973 decision in *Roe* v. *Wade* and *Doe* v. *Bolton* legalized abortion but did not recognize abortion as an individual right of women based on the right of reproductive freedom. Instead, the state has granted woman the right to an abortion based on her right to privacy. The abortion law "protects the woman from unduly burdensome interference with her freedom to decide whether to terminate her pregnancy."[32] Women are thus limited by this liberal patriarchal formulation of "the right to privacy," which is really something quite different from a right to an abortion. As we shall see, the Hyde Amendment, which amended the Medicaid statute and prohibited the use of federal medicaid funds for elective abortions, defined woman's privacy in such a way as to limit a woman's right to an abortion along economic class and race lines.

Concern with abortion is relatively recent in the United States. Its history expresses part of the struggle of the state to control the options around sexual reproduction. There were no laws on abortion until 1800. Until then, a woman was free to have an abortion until quickening.[33] The first wave of abortion law occurred between 1821 and 1841, but it was not difficult to get an abortion until the 1880s and 1890s. Indeed, the Catholic church's present position on abortion did not take form until 1869[34] under Pope Pius IX. Until then, the church's stand was that abortion was a question of individual privacy. Nadean Bishop writes that the church believed that "the right to privacy and the autonomy of the individual are basic doctrines that are violated by governmental interference in matters of family planning."[35] By the end of the nineteenth century, however, abortion laws existed in most states and remained unchanged until the 1960s. According to James Mohr's analysis, the medical profession was primarily responsible for the growth of abortion law in their quest to control its practice. Licensed doctors wanted the abortion market for themselves, and until the late 1900s, they faced the competition of nonlicensed persons who performed abortions. Many of the new laws applied to the person performing the abortion more than they did to the woman seeking it.

This process of monopolizing control of abortion must be understood as an attempt to control women's choices in relation to pregnancy in a period when abortion was on the increase and the birthrate had dropped among middle-income women. The medical profession played its role, in terms of the interests of the state, by taking the decision surrounding abortion out of the hands of women and putting it into the hands of doctors. Expertise, knowledge, and medical technology must be kept out of the hands of women and controlled by doctors if the state is to win the struggle for reproductive control.

It therefore should be no surprise that when abortion was legalized by the 1973 ruling of the Supreme Court in *Roe* v. *Wade* and *Doe* v. *Bolton*, the ruling once again gave a greal deal of power to the medical profession. According to attorney Kristin Glen, ". . . the Supreme Court was not upholding a *woman's* right to determine whether to bear a child. . . . Instead it was upholding a *doctor's* right to make a medical decision."[36] In the decision of *Roe* v. *Wade*, it is clearly stated that "the abortion decision in all its aspects is inherently, and primarily, a medical decision. . . ."[37] As such, the right to an abortion is not conceived as a woman's right to selfhood. She, rather, on the basis of the right to privacy, can choose to have an abortion. Her right to privacy, not her individual rights to her body, lay the foundation for the legalization of abortion. Blackmun's position in the case states this explicitly: "This right of privacy whether it be found in the Fourteenth Amendment's concept of personal liberty and restrictions upon state action, as we feel it is, or as the District Court determined, in the Ninth Amendment's reservation of rights to the people, is broad enough to encompass a woman's decision whether or not to terminate her pregnancy. . . ."[38]

The woman's right to be free from unwarranted governmental intrusion is not an unqualified right. It must be considered against the interests of the state. The state's interest in the health of the mother begins after the first trimester. Within the first trimester, elective abortions are allowed. Increased regulations exist for abortions within the second trimester, and abortions are prohibited in the final trimester. The reason given for this schedule is the concern for the woman's health. Although abortions in the later months of pregnancy are more dangerous, this is not the only concern operating here. If woman's health in its narrow biological definition were all that were involved, the Hyde Amendment could have never been passed, because it may not have been in the health interests of poor, undernourished women to bear their children. It also may not have been in their interests to be sterilized. The state's view of children as a public resource, of welfare mothers as state wards or hirelings, and their concern with population control (and eugenics) all play a role in the state's articulation of abortion policy.

The Hyde Amendment, passed in 1976, now awaits a Supreme Court ruling on its constitutionality.* In 1977, the House banned all Medicaid abortions except those that were necessary to save a woman's life. The Senate said it would allow abortion in cases of rape, incest, and when deemed medically necessary. In 1977, 4.6 million U.S. women of reproductive age were eligible for Medicaid. Approximately 427,000 had unwanted pregnancies they wished to terminate. There were 133,000 women on welfare unable to obtain Medicaid-funded abortion services in 1977 before the Hyde Amendment took effect. This number was expected to rise to 340,000.

Women on welfare cannot pay for an abortion out of their monthly welfare payments. An abortion costs $285, and the monthly AFDC payment for a family of three is $241. The cost of an abortion is equal to a family's food allocation for three months and their clothing budget for nine. Initially, the Supreme Court said these women were free to find private funding, which reflects the deficiencies of the abortion law in the first place: that women, in short, are *free from* the interference by government in their decision to have an abortion. This right does not require that government "interfere" by making public funds available to them. The *right to privacy* in the case of welfare women is just what they do not need. An abortion law based on this right actually denies women the state aid they require.

To the extent that to date the abortion law has been based on the right to privacy rather than a woman's right to self-determination and reproductive freedom, it has been a limited victory for women. In the state's version of liberal feminism, poor and welfare women are separated from all other women, and their rights are denied. The right to privacy is an exclusionary right because you have to be self-sufficient and self-supporting before the right can actually protect you. This version of liberal feminism, rooted in women's right to privacy from interference and not woman's right to self-determination and reproductive freedom, in actuality gives no woman the right to an abortion. Present abortion law shows how formal "rights" are vacuous in the absence of the material means to make their exercise possible. In this instance, it becomes clear that a fully socialized health-care system, available to all, is necessary (although not sufficient) as a condition of reproductive freedom.[39] The state, which is unable to recognize the full utilization of liberal ideology for women, whittled the feminist version of pro-choice reproductive freedom down to its liberal expression. Such a definition cannot apply to all women equally because of the economic class and racial bias of liberalism. What we also see here is that it cannot recognize a full statement of feminist individualism either, because of its

* After this book went to press, the Supreme Court ruled the Hyde Amendment constitutional.

patriarchal base. Liberal feminists accepted the state's 1973 ruling as a victory, whereas now a more critical social analysis reveals that it was a limited one. It is politically important to make clear to women that their right to control their bodies has not been accepted as a tenet of the state. This understanding must be rearticulated as a pro-choice reproductive rights platform that will extend the right to abortion to all women. But it must also extend to guarantee them the material preconditions (a living wage, abortion services, and so on) if their "right to control their bodies" does not remain a formal vacuous "right."

When one examines abortion policy further, it becomes clear that there is considerable internal conflict within the state on how best to mediate the conflicting needs of patriarchy and capitalism. The decision in *Danforth* v. *Planned Parenthood* is a case in point of the contradictory nature of state policy. In July 1976, the Supreme Court ruled that a husband does not have the right to veto his wife's decision to have an abortion: a woman does not have to have her husband's consent for an abortion. Judge Dooling's decision in *McRae* v. *Harris* is another case in point. In January 1980, Dooling declared the Hyde Amendment ban on the use of federal Medicare funds for abortions unconstitutional. Dooling ruled that it was unconstitutional to deny medical funds for medically necessary abortions while defining "medically necessary" broadly by including a woman's mental and social well-being within the definition. He also argued that the Hyde Amendment was a violation of a woman's right to privacy and to religious freedom. These decisions represent a significant move forward for the reproductive-freedom movement and a setback for the Right-to-Life forces. These cases also reflect the conflict within the state over how best to mediate conflicts between feminists and the patriarchal needs of liberal society. Although there is *a* state need to stabilize patriarchy, there are multiple and conflicting conceptions of what this need is.

Current Political Struggles: New Right vs. Feminists

I have argued thus far that state intervention is used today for the purpose of smoothing out the conflicts between the ideology of liberal individualism and the ideology and reality of male dominance. Factions within the state are trying to reassert patriarchal control by challenging existing abortion rulings, publicly funded day care, the ratification of the ERA, and homosexual rights. These four policy areas represent the arena for conflict between the New Right and the Center liberals, inside and outside the state apparatus. The Right-to-Life and STOP ERA groups are a part of the New Right, which includes groups like the Ku Klux Klan, the Birch Society, and Goldwater and Wallace supporters. Anita Bryant and Phyllis Schlafly have become spokeswomen for the New Right on the ERA, homosexual rights, and abortion policy. But the

New Right is controlled by men. Sean Morton Downey is the chairman of the Life Amendment Political Action Committee (LAPAC), which is sponsoring an antiabortion amendment to the Constitution. Richard Vigueric is the New Right's chief fund raiser, and Paul Weyrich is head of the Committee for the Survival of a Free Congress (CSFC). This committee claimed that 15 percent of the victors in the 1974 congressional races were supported by them. By 1976, it is said that the New Right had helped to elect almost 35 percent of the U.S. House of Representatives,[40] and they claim to have won several upset victories in 1977 by using abortion as a key issue. According to Sasha Lewis, "In 1978 the New Right raised more money than either labor or big business. It scored several key upset victories and backed nearly 40% of the successful candidates in the U.S. House of Representatives."[41] New Right forces operate within the state, fighting for an antifeminist position on women's rights.

The Center liberals, who Carter often aligns himself with, support a liberal feminist program, narrowly defined. This program includes pro-ERA, pro-nuclear family, and anti-Medicaid abortion politics. Carter's problem is to figure out how to maintain the least radical version of liberal feminism, given the real conflicts that exist within the state itself between the "center" and the "right," often headed by Reagan, and the level of liberal-feminist awareness in the country. The state's activity grows out of the conflicts between the New Right, Center liberals, and liberal feminists, and the irreconcilability of these conflicts. The contradictory nature of state policy, as in abortion policy, reflects the irreconcilable nature of these conflicts.

Carter's support of the ERA can be understood and, hence, reconciled with the political mobilization against it when one sees that he is trying to mediate the conflicts between the patriarchal bias of liberalism and feminism by presenting a particular interpretation of liberal feminism. After all, the ERA does not address the issue of patriarchal control or sexual hierarchy, but rather legitimizes present structural arrangements in liberal equal opportunity terms. As I argued earlier, the ERA presents the formal equality between men and women as a symbolic gesture; it does little to affect actual substantive changes in the way women live on an everyday basis. Therefore, women as wives, "working mothers," and wage earners in a sexual ghetto are given the equal right with men for opportunity. But these rights are assigned them abstractly and do not take into account their unequal starting point (in the home, in the market, and so on) in the "race of life." Carter understands this and therefore supports the ERA in the hopes of demobilizing the subversive elements within the liberal feminist movement that are demanding actual, concrete social reforms.

The Center liberals in the state realize that women's equality before the law is an adjustment the state has to make in order to stem the tides of liberal feminist struggle, which otherwise might lead to more radical indictments of society. Carter understands that a law cannot make equality or *by itself* change dominant social relations. Representatives of the state know this, although they disagree among themselves how best to manipulate the pro-ERA feeling of the liberal feminists who believe real equality can be won through the law. They therefore support a narrow reading of the ERA, as Carter does.

If feminists recognize the state's purpose in trying to demobilize the most radical and subversive elements of liberal feminism, it cannot succeed. Instead, women, knowing that the ERA is an insufficient gesture, can fight to apply it in specific cases. Then the ideological content of the ERA—its recognition of woman's equality—can be effectively used by feminists for their own purposes. And in trying to make the promise of equality real, they will realize the necessity of structural change.

Joyce Kolko's point—rulers never believe the ideology they use—rings true here. It is only people who internalize the ideology as their own values who really believe in it. Richard Nixon could one day espouse anticommunist rhetoric and the next day push for détente with the Soviet Union. Carter has switched once again, back to cold-war rhetoric. He also supports the ERA while he does nothing to aid its ratification. Carter's choice to support the registration and eventual drafting of women into the armed forces is another attempt at giving lip service to the idea of woman's equality. He is quoted in the *New York Times* as stating: "My decision to register women is a recognition of the reality that both women and men are working members of our society. . . . It confirms what is already obvious throughout our society— that women are now providing all types of skills in every profession. The military should be no exception."[42] His statement confirms the need of the state to recognize the role of women in the workforce without any recognition of the double burden of labor entailed for a majority of women wage earners. Carter presents the extension of women's right to the draft as a statement of her equality. But there is no substance to this claim. The registration and possible drafting of women merely extends woman's right to be drafted alongside her unequal position in the sexual ordering of society. She will be drafted as a cook or a clerk. Without the ERA, women will have little legal basis in which to challenge this sexual hierarchy. Carter may even see women's registration for the draft as a tradeoff in an election year—instead of the ERA, he will support the draft. Both serve the same purpose for him, and the draft without the ERA may be more effective for his needs in an election year. He can present himself as supportive of woman's equality while giving women little in actual fact.

The public often internalizes the ruling patriarchal ideology in a more intimate and static way than politicians do. Factions in the public internalize the ruling patriarchal ideology of society and therefore are slower to change their political position than politicians are. As a result, sections of the public may be in conflict with the ruling class when it begins to embrace a new form of patriarchal ideology. The case of Phyllis Schlafly is an example of this. Her political views have become unrealistic in the face of societal and feminist demands. Her reaction to Carter's position on drafting women is a case in point. She argues that "President Carter stabbed American womanhood in the back in a cowardly surrender to women's lib . . . if this administration can't stand up to women's lib, they can't stand up to the Russians." [43] Elements of the antifeminist backlash do not accept the ideology or practice of the "working mother," or a further extension of equal rights doctrine to women. Nor do they understand why elements of the state support these changes. This is why the antifeminist campaign, supported and led by the New Right both inside and outside the state, is working at cross purposes with some factions of the Center liberal sector of the state.

Antifeminist activity heightens the conflicts that elements of the Center liberal sector of the state wish to mediate. The New Right obviously believes it needs to reassert patriarchal control by denying many of the feminist gains made by woman for abortion, day care, and equal rights. Many of the liberal Center know that these gains are also related to women's ability to work in the labor force and remain responsible for childrearing. While all in the Center liberal sector purport liberal feminist commitments, they differ on how to deal best with the conflicts between the New Right and the demands of feminists. Sometimes it appears that elements within the Center liberal sector gain from the New Right offensive against feminist demands in that the state can do much less for feminists and still appear supportive of liberal feminism. In this sense, conservative forces serve as a brake on radical feminist demands. Sometimes this is to the advantage of the liberal Center and sometimes it is not.

Liberal Feminism and the State: The Houston Women's Conference and Abzug's Dismissal

From the vantage point of this discussion of the state, feminists need to reassess the political importance of the government-funded 1978 Houston Women's Conference. Obviously the state's purpose in funding the conference was different from that of the feminists who organized and attended it. If one believes that the state reflects the irreconcilable conflicts between capitalism and patriarchy, liberalism, and feminism, a whole set of questions emerge about the real purpose of the Houston conference.

The government defined the purpose of the conference to explore woman's condition and needs. I argue that its purpose was rather to attend to the growing instability created by the conflict between feminist demands and the New Right, even though this conflict has been put to use by other sectors of the state. The state's interest in the Houston conference by segments of the Center liberal sector reflects in part a concern that the New Right (who already are well funded) be countered by a public hearing of liberal feminism, narrowly defined. To the extent that the reactionary New Right position that woman belongs in the home is not helpful to a society that requires a majority of its women to be "working mothers," it was necessary to publicly reinforce the position of "working mothers" by recognizing several limited demands of liberal feminists that address this reality. By trying to legitimize liberal feminism and the notion of the "working mother," the state tried to weaken liberal feminism as a protest movement and radical feminist politics. However, the demands articulated at the Houston conference defeated this purpose to a significant degree in that they moved beyond the narrow liberal feminist position of equal-rights doctrine. In this sense, the state did not remain in control of the outcome of the meeting. As we have seen, several demands called for an end to the double discrimination against minority women, an end to sexual harassment on the job, and the establishment of reproductive freedom and an end to involuntary sterilization.

What remains to be examined is how the Houston conference was only a limited victory in terms of the needs of feminists. In other words, how did the structure of the conference itself, which presupposed the benevolence and reason of the state, compromise the demands and the autonomous identity of those making them? At issue here is the prevalence, once again, of the liberal conception of power that locates power in the governmental realm, a view less valid today than ever before in American history. Even though many of these women know that the reason they do not have what they want for themselves and their families is not because their interests have not been heard in the pluralist arena of politics, their participation in the conference allows this view renewed legitimacy. The point is not that these women should not have taken part in the conference but that they should have made public the actual antagonistic needs that exist between the U.S. government and feminism. In this sense, the demands sent to Carter should have directly stated how they could actually be put into practice rather than be left to the state to ignore or articulate them in equal-rights fashion. Then when the state did not act in accordance with these guidelines, feminists could have organized around their plan for implementation. They would have kept the energy from the conference mobilized.

Houston was a beginning, but it is necessary to be clear about what was begun. Feminists need to be ready to fight for what they want as they continue to take advantage of the reformist politics of a liberal society. In the end, feminists need to understand that for equality to exist between men and women, the structure of patriarchy must be destroyed; and for this to happen today, they must also dismantle capitalism. Reform is not sufficient, but neither is it irrelevant if one believes that you build revolutions through struggle and do not call for them from above.

Intrastate Conflict: Carter and Abzug

It is important at this moment in our history to understand that Carter is now actively trying to demobilize the radical faction of the liberal feminist movement. The firing of Bella Abzug was part of this tactic. Abzug's firing reflects the high level of internal conflict that is present within the state over woman's role in society. Part of this conflict originates in the state's different solutions for the salvaging of the troubled nuclear family. The problem also now centers on how the state can demobilize the radical factions of the liberal feminist movement, which seek to focus on creating change in a majority of women's everyday lives by focusing on women's sexual-class identity across economic class and racial lines.

Most of the reporting on Abzug's dismissal as co-chair of the National Advisory Committee on Women explains it as a personality clash between her and the President. It is said that she (as well as her committee) overstepped the bounds of legitimate criticism. The controversial report by the committee questioned Carter's antiinflationary program as ignoring women's particular needs and their role in the economy; it criticized the large expenditures in military and defense as extravagant; and it requested a firmer commitment toward the ERA from the administration. It also condemned the administration for the ban on Medicaid abortions.

In several interviews after her firing, Abzug said that what really angered Carter was that women spoke out on economic issues, that women had strayed from women's issues as they had been narrowly defined by the administration. They had entered the male domain. Her committee made clear that the economy is a woman's issue when women earn 58 cents for every dollar earned by a man. Inflation hits women harder, and present state policies do not recognize this inequity. It criticized Carter's antiinflation program for imposing "additional and disproportionate burdens upon women because of possible increases in unemployment rates, slashing social and other human needs programs . . . absence of child care programs, so urgently needed by women, and the failure to address the widespread poverty and the financial plight of our cities, where a majority of women and all Americans live."[44]

The major fear the administration had was that women were beginning to connect the relationship between the economic class and sexual subordination in their lives. This is what Carter had to stop: the radical elements within the liberal feminist movement that identify the sexual-class nature of women's oppression across economic class and racial lines.

Abzug was held responsible for the subversive report as a co-chair of the National Advisory Committee and was quickly fired. Not only was she fired, but her dismissal coming moments after her public denial about supposed conflict with the President was to make her look like a fool. Part of the attempt to make Abzug look like a fool was to make the issues she has come to represent look ridiculous to the public.[45]

Abzug thinks Carter judged wrongly by dismissing her and that he angered women when he, in effect, told them that the economy is not a "woman's issue." She thinks he misjudged women's consciousness about what they think their rightful place is and what their concerns are. Speaking in an interview, Abzug said of Carter's staff: "Their staff had as much information on the women's movement as they had on Iran."[46]

Abzug's dismissal was an effort by Carter to further legitimize the narrow legal-liberal interpretation of the ERA rather than its broader view which connects women's rights to questions of the economy, abortion, and homosexuality. His position once again was an effort to reify the division between public and private life in women's lives. Whether Abzug was actually any more progressive than her temporary replacement, Marjorie Bell Chambers, is irrelevant. She had come to represent these broader political issues to the public. Whatever else Marjorie Chambers was, she was not connected to the more radical elements of liberal feminism. The *New York Times* reported that while she had been active in fighting for improvements in the legal status of women, she generally stayed away from controversial issues like abortion and lesbian rights. At the time of her temporary appointment, she was instructed by Carter to stick to women's issues and that the economy was not considered a woman's issue. Abzug's permanent replacement, Lynda Byrd Robb, further documents this effort by Carter. She is to represent the narrow concerns of liberal feminism, as opposed to Abzug's concern with poor women and Medicaid abortion or wage-earning women and questions of inflation.

Carter has to reassert the narrow interpretation of liberal feminism and the ERA against pressure from the right within the state. He did it with the dismissal of Abzug. The motive of the state, via liberal feminism, is to keep women in their place as secondary wage earners and as mothers. If feminists understand this, then they can begin to understand, as a women's movement, that their feminism cannot be met by the liberal state, which has no commitment to women's liberation. Radical and socialist feminists know this,[47] but unless they are a part of the struggles with liberal feminists against the state, they have little ability to fight for this radical political understanding. What becomes very clear is that if feminists are to be a part of the struggles with the state on questions of the ERA, abortion rights, welfare payments, and the like, they need to develop a strategy that fully utilizes the subversive content of feminism. As women continue to become more conscious of themselves as an oppressed sexual class, they will be able to develop a political strategy which recognizes this. This is in essence the real difference between liberalism and liberal feminism: feminism is potentially subversive to liberalism and the capitalist patriarchal state.

NOTES

1. See Rosa Luxemburg, "Reform or Revolution," in *Selected Political Writings,* ed. Dick Howard (New York: Monthly Review Press, 1971), for her discussion of the relationship between reform and revolution. Her concern with the economic class relations of society and the particular historical-political context in which she wrote allowed her to make a simple and clear distinction between the two activities. I argue that a feminist theory of the state, as well as an assessment of the present political situation in the United States, reveals the inadequacy of this model for our present purposes.

2. Juliet Mitchell, "Woman and Equality," in *The Rights and Wrongs of Women,* ed. Juliet Mitchell and Ann Oakley (London: Penguin, 1976), p. 399.

3. Nicos Poulantzas, *State, Power, Socialism* (London: New Left Books, 1978), p. 66.

4. Ibid., p. 72.

5. Claude Lévi-Strauss, "The Family," in *Family in Transition,* ed. by A. Skolnick and J. Skolnick (Boston: Little Brown, 1971), p. 63. Also see Claude Lévi-Strauss, *The Elementary Structures of Kinship* (Boston: Beacon, 1969).

6. Lévi-Strauss, "The Family," p. 57.

7. State involvement in all facets of reproductive policy is recurrent. President Kennedy approved in 1963 federal support to increase

research on new contraceptives. Former Presidents Harry Truman and Dwight Eisenhower were co-chair of Planned Parenthood–World Population in 1965. In 1967 President Johnson approved a $20 million budget for contraceptive programs. Nixon cut back this budget and was outspoken against the legalization of abortion, although the Supreme Court had four Nixon appointees in 1973, when the court legalized abortion. For further discussion of the politics of birth control and reproductive issues, see Linda Gordon, *Woman's Body, Woman's Right, A Social History of Birth Control in America* (New York: Grossman, 1976).

8. *Abortion: Freedom of Choice and the Right to Life* (New York: Facts on File, 1978), p. 75.

9. Ibid., p. 105.

10. *The Women's Movement, Achievement and Effects* (Washington, D.C.: Congressional Quarterly, 1977), p. 10.

11. For interesting discussion of the recent politics of the family, see Wini Breines, Margaret Cerullo, and Judith Stacey, "Social Biology, Family Studies, and Anti-Feminist Backlash," *Feminist Studies* 4, no. 1 (February 1978): 43–69; "The Family," *Daedalus* 106, no. 2 of the Proceedings of the American Academy of Arts and Sciences; Susan Dworkin, "Notes on Carter's Family Policy—How It Got That Way," *Ms.* 7, no. 3 (September 1978): 61–96; Barbara Easton, "Feminism and the Contemporary Family," *Socialist Review* 8, no. 39 (May–June 1978): 11–36; Rayna Rapp, Ellen Ross, and Renate Bridenthal, "Examining Family History," *Feminist Studies* 5, no. 1 (Spring 1979): 174–201; and Kenneth Woodward et al., "Saving the Family," *Newsweek*, 15 May 1978, pp. 63–90.

12. Lenin's theory of the state recognized the irreconcilable conflicts generated by the economic class structure. Patriarchy had no identity on the state level for him, nor did it play a part in creating irresolvable conflict for the state. However, I intend to use the conception of irreconcilable state conflict to better understand the relationship between patriarchy and capitalism on the political level. See V. I. Lenin, "State and Revolution," in *Selected Works*, vol. 2 (Moscow: Progress, 1970). For further discussions of Marx's and Marxist theories of the state, see Hal Draper, *Karl Marx's Theory of Revolution*, part I: *State and Bureaucracy*, vol. 1 (New York: Monthly Review Press, 1977); Frederick Engels, *The Origin of the Family, Private Property and the State*, ed. Eleanor Burke Leacock (New York: International Publishers, 1972); Alan Hunt, ed., *Class and Class Structure* (London: Lawrence and Wishart, 1977); Karl Marx, *The Eighteenth Brumaire of Louis Bonaparte* (New York: International Publishers, 1963); Karl Marx and Frederick Engels, *The Communist Manifesto* (New York: International Publishers, 1948); idem, *The German Ideology* (New York: International Publishers, 1947); Goran Therborn, *What Does the Ruling Class Do When It Rules?* (London: New

Left Books, 1978); and Erik Olin Wright, *Class, Crisis and the State* (London: New Left Books, 1978).

13. Nicos Poulantzas, *Classes in Contemporary Capitalism* (London: Verso Editions, 1974), p. 161.

14. See Ralph Miliband, *Marxism and Politics* (Oxford, England: Oxford University Press, 1977), for a clear discussion of how the conception of the relative autonomy of the state is distinguished from the instrumentalist view, which sees the state as a mere instrument of the capitalist class. His view elaborates the way the state mediates conflicts within the capitalist ruling class, rather than merely being an instrument of the dominant class. For further clarification of the noninstrumentalist, noneconomistic theory of the state, see Louis Althusser, *Lenin and Philosophy and Other Essays* (New York: Monthly Review Press, 1971); Sally Hibbin et al., *Politics, Ideology and the State* (London: Lawrence and Wishart, 1978); Annette Kuhn and Ann Marie Wolpe, eds., *Feminism and Materialism* (London: Routledge and Kegan Paul, 1978); Gary Littlejohn et al., *Power and the State* (London: Croom Helm, 1978); Ralph Miliband, "The Capitalist State: Reply to Nicos Poulantzas," *New Left Review* 59 (January–February 1970): 53–60; idem, "Poulantzas and the Capitalist State," *New Left Review* 82 (November–December 1973): 83–92; Poulantzas, *State, Power, Socialism;* idem, "The Problem of the Capitalist State," *New Left Review* 58 (November–December 1969): 67–78; and idem, "The Capitalist State: A Reply to Miliband and Laclau," *New Left Review* 95 (January–February 1976).

15. Miliband, *Marxism and Politics,* p. 87.

16. Even though these three sectors of the state interest are centers of patriarchal power, they are themselves clearly divided on what a reproductive-rights policy should look like. The Rockefellers' and the Hunts' conflict over abortion policy; and powerful male unions, like the Steelworkers, have come out in support of reproductive leave policies for men and women alike.

17. Poulantzas, in *Contemporary Capitalism* (p. 25), develops this important discussion of the ideological role of the state. Also see Althusser, *Lenin and Philosophy;* Stuart Ewen, *Captains of Consciousness, Advertising and the Social Roots of the Consumer Culture* (New York: McGraw-Hill, 1976); Antonio Gramsci, *Selections from the Prison Notebooks* (New York: International Publishers, 1971); Douglas Kellner, "Ideology, Marxism, and Advanced Capitalism," *Socialist Review,* 8, no. 42 (November–December 1978): 37–67; and idem, "TV, Ideology and Emancipatory Popular Culture," *Socialist Review* 9, no. 45 (May–June 1979): 13–54.

18. Kellner, "Ideology, Marxism and Capitalism," p. 13. His discussion of cultural hegemony and ideological conflict remains limited in

that it does not examine how the patriarchal needs of the state are central to this conflict.

19. Kate Millett captured this reality when she stated in *Sexual Politics* (New YORK: Avon, 1971), "Patriarchy, reformed or unreformed, is patriarchy still: its worst abuses purged or foresworn, it might be actually more stable and secure than before" (pp. 121–22). Although one can stabilize patriarchy by modernizing its expression and thereby decrease potential conflict, I also argue that feminist reform can destabilize patriarchy. Feminist reform creates new levels of conflict as well as state cohesion. Millett tends to play down the subversive content of feminist reform struggle and, as a result, presents a somewhat static notion of patriarchal domination.

20. These tendencies that I label "progressive" and "radical" reflect the different orientations and political understanding of liberal feminists. These two tendencies, which presently coexist within liberal feminist politics, often lead to an oversimplified and incorrect view of the complexity of liberal feminism and its radical feminist orientation. The equation drawn between liberal feminism and its "progressive," rather than its "radical," faction leads to a much more limiting view of liberal feminism than actually exists. This is the picture of feminism the state seeks to legitimize.

21. *An Official Report to the President, the Congress and the People of the United States, March 1978, The Spirit of Houston* (Washington, D.C.: National Commission on the Observance of International Women's Year, 1978), p. 15.

22. Ibid. See the entire report.

23. Hazel Greenberg, "The ERA in Context: Its Impact on Society," in *Women's Rights and the Law: The Impact of the ERA on State Laws,* ed. Barbara Brown et al. (New York: Praeger, 1977), p. 10.

24. Equal Rights Amendment Project of the California Commission on the Status of Women, *Impact ERA, Limitations and Possibilities* (Millbrae, Calif.: Les Femmes, 1976), p. 4.

25. Greenberg, "The ERA in Context," p. 2.

26. Ibid., p. 10.

27. It can be argued that the ERA affects everyday life by affecting the consciousness of women. This argument involves the larger epistemological question of the relationship between consciousness (subjective) and material life (objective). If one thinks that these two realms have significant impact on each other and do not exist completely separate from one another, feminist reform activity that affects woman's consciousness of her oppression can be said to begin to change her objective condition as well. This, however, does not lessen the burden for bringing about substantive changes in her actual status. It rather is to connect the different processes involved in creating social and politi-

cal change. To the extent the ERA affects consciousness, it is a part in the process of addressing woman's subordination.

28. See Albie Sachs and Joan Hoff Wilson, *Sexism and the Law* (New York: Free Press, 1978). For the related issue of woman's status in terms of her constitutional rights, see Leslie Friedman Goldstein, *The Constitutional Rights of Women* (New York: Longman, 1979).

29. Greenberg, "The ERA in Context," p. 6.

30. Peg Simpson, "A Victory for Women," *Civil Rights Digest* 11, no. 3 (Spring 1979): 14.

31. For a fuller discussion of the liberal roots of abortion policy and reproductive rights, see Rosalind Petchesky, "Reproductive Freedom: Beyond a Woman's Right to Choose," *Signs* (forthcoming, Summer 1980).

32. Kristin Glen, "Abortion in the Courts: A Laywoman's Historical Guide to the New Disaster Area," *Feminist Studies* 4, no. 1 (February 1978): 13.

33. James Mohr, *Abortion in America, The Origins and Evolution of National Policy, 1800–1900* (New York: Oxford University Press, 1978), p. 4. Quickening was defined as the point when the pregnant woman began to feel the fetus move and was taken as the only actual proof of pregnancy.

34. See Lawrence Lader, *Abortion* (Indianapolis: Bobbs-Merrill, 1966); and idem, *Abortion II, The Making of the Revolution* (Boston: Beacon, 1974). For other important discussions of the history of abortion, see Barbara Ehrenreich and Deirdre English, *Witches, Midwives and Nurses: A History of Women Healers* (New York: Feminist Press, 1973); idem, *For Her Own Good: 150 Years of the Experts Advice to Women* (New York: Anchor, 1978); Gordon, *Woman's Body, Woman's Right.*

35. Nadean Bishop, "Abortion: The Controversial Choice," in *Women: A Feminist Perspective*, ed. Jo Freeman (2nd ed.; Palo Alto, Calif.: Mayfield, 1979), p. 67.

36. Glen, "Abortion in the Courts," p. 9.

37. Ibid.

38. *Abortion: Freedom of Choice and the Right to Life*, p. 75.

39. For an excellent analysis of the politics involved in state policies on birth control, sterilization, and population control, see Committee for Abortion Rights and Against Sterilization Abuse, *Women Under Attack: Abortion, Sterilization Abuse, and Reproductive Freedom* (New York: CARASA, 1979).

40. Sasha Lewis, "The Far-Right Plan for 1980," *Seven Days* 3, no. 10 (14 August 1979): 22.

41. Ibid. For further discussion of the New Right, see Andrea Dworkin, "Safety, Shelter, Rules, Form, Love: The Promise of the Ultra-Right," *Ms.* 7, no. 12 (June 1979): 62–76; Linda Gordon and Allen

Hunter, "Sex, Family and the New Right: Anti-Feminism as a Political Force," *Radical America* 11–12 (November 1977–February 1978): 9–25; Michele Magar, "Two Rights Make a . . . The New Right has Wooed and Almost Won the Right-to-Lifers," *Seven Days* 3, no. 12 (26 October 1979): 20–21; and Lisa Cronin Wohl, "Decoding the Election Game Plan of the New Right," *Ms.* 12, no. 2 (August 1979): 57–96.

42. Richard Halloran, "Carter Draft Plan Urges Registration of Men and Women," *New York Times*, 9 February 1980, sec. 1, p. 1.

43. "Plan Is Given Cautious Approval by Women's Groups," *New York Times*, 9 February 1980, sec. 1, p. 9.

44. Mim Kelber, "What Bella Knew," *Ms.* 12, no. 10 (April 1979): 98.

45. Further proof of this argument can be found in Gloria Jacobs and Jane Melnick, "Bella Speaks Freely," *Seven Days* 3, no. 1 (23 February 1979): 6–8. According to this article, Carmen Delgado Votaw was at the meeting that discussed the press release that so angered Carter, while Abzug was not. However, it was Abzug who was fired. I argue that Abzug was fired because she had been the vocal representative of the radical faction of liberal feminism, whereas Carmen Delgado Votaw had been virtually ignored by the media. Therefore, the firing of Abzug could function as a public display against these radical forces, whereas firing Votaw could not.

46. Ibid., p. 8.

47. The issue that radical and socialist feminists have not paid sufficient attention to is the subversive content of feminist reforms and therefore the ability to build a mass-based feminist movement from these struggles.

Index

Abolitionists, 148–49
Abortion, 3, 8, 17, 19, 192, 194–96, 220, 224–28, 247, 250, 252; politics of, 236–44
Abzug, Bella, 176, 232, 244–48, 253
Alexander, Sally, 143
Althusser, Louis, 250
American Medical Association, 227
Anarcha-feminism, 230, 238
Anderson, Michael, 143
Anna Karenina, 154
Anthony, Susan B., 128, 145, 148, 155, 160, 167, 169, 170–73
Antifeminist traditionalists, 230–31, 241–44
Anti-Slavery Convention (London, 1840), 148
Arden, Jane, 100
Aries, Phillippe, 86
Aristocracy, 90–93; of sex, 149–52
Aristotle, 23, 34
Astell, Mary, 110
Atkinson, Ti Grace, 7, 12, 199–200
Autobiography, The, 114, 115, 123
Aylmer, Bishop, 35

Bachrach, Peter, 198
Baratz, Milton, 198
Barber, Elinor, 83, 84, 85, 87
Barker, Ernest, 30, 51
Barrett, Nancy, 217
Beauvoir, Simone de, 7, 12, 199
Beechey, Virginia, 28
Bell, Daniel, 11
Benenson, Hal, 203, 214, 215
Berg, Barbara, 172
Berman, Marshall, 83, 86
Bethel, Lorraine, 219
Bishop, Nadean, 238, 252
Black(s): enfranchisement of, 147–49; feminism, 230; women, 185, 213, 218–19
Blanchard, William, 83, 84
Blatch, Harriet Stanton, 168, 170, 171, 172, 173

Blau, Francine, 218
Bliss, W. D. P., 142
Blue-collar status, 214–15
Bluhm, William, 83
Bodin, Jean, 51
Bolingbroke, Lord, 50
Bourgeois society, 23, 33–34, 43–44, 48–49, 92, 127, 223; marriage in, 37–38; motherhood in, 99–102; rationality and, 93–96; Rousseau on, 55, 70–74
Bradlaugh, Charles, 128
Bradley, Rose, 51
Branca, Patricia, 130, 143
Braverman, Harry, 214, 216
Breines, Wini, 249
Bridenthal, Renate, 249
Bryant, Anita, 241
Buhle, Mari Jo, 169
Butler, Melissa, 50

Cantor, Milton, 199, 217
Capitalism, 5, 9–12, 20–21, 28, 51, 180, 185, 188, 202; ERA and, 234–36; feminist theory of, 226–28; individual liberty within, 123–26; needs of, 204–6, 208–9; politics of liberal feminism and, 222–25; Stanton on, 166–67; wage-labor system in, 23–26, 96–97, 120–22, 124, 129–32, 168–69, 184–85, 206–12. *See also* Patriarchy
Carden, Maren Lockwood, 197, 200
Carter, Jimmy, 193, 220–21, 224–25, 232, 242–48, 253
Cerullo, Margaret, 249
Chambers, Marjorie Bell, 247
Childbirth, 7, 14–17, 224
Child-care centers, 192, 194, 196, 216
Childrearing, 14–17, 78, 99–100, 135–38, 187–88, 194, 201, 224, 236–41
Chodorow, Nancy, 15, 27, 84, 215
Christian Oeconomie, 36
Citizen rights, 91–92, 115, 127, 132, 148, 151–53, 163, 213

Civil Rights Act (1964), 197
Civil rights movement, 177, 197
Clark, Alice, 35, 37, 51, 52, 97, 110, 111
Clark, Robert, 217
Clerical Labor, 208–10
Cobb, Jonathan, 217
Collectivity, social, 5, 115–16; individuality and, 122–25, 127
Collier, Jane, 27
Commendacious of Matrymony, 36
Commission on Status of Women, 197
Committee for the Survival of a Free Congress, 242
Confessions of Rousseau, The, 61
Connolly, William, 198
Consciousness, women's, 8, 10–11, 14–15, 177–78, 186–88, 190–91, 202–3
Cornford, Francis, 29
Cott, Nancy, 168, 169
Cranston, Maurice, 50, 83
Cromwell, Oliver, 36
Cropsey, Joseph, 83
Crow, Duncan, 130, 143
Curtis, Jean, 199

Dahl, Robert, 198
Daly, Mary, 18, 27
Danforth v. Planned Parenthood, 241
Davies, Margery, 216
Davis, Paulina, 170, 171, 172
Delphy, Christine, 7, 12
Dependence: economic, 9, 76–77, 80–84, 133–34, 136–37, 159, 165; sexual, 92–93, 101, 103, 186–88
Dinnerstein, D., 15, 27, 84, 215
Discrimination, rulings on sex, 234
Divine-right theory, 34; feminist critique of, 40–44; liberal attack on, 37–40, 91
Divorce, 36, 159–60, 210
Doe v. Bolton, 238, 239
Domestic work, women's, 7, 9, 24, 36–37, 96–97, 146–47, 158–59, 187–88, 194; economic value of, 172, 211; in Victorian age, 129–32, 135
Domhoff, William, 198
Double-day of work, 8, 185, 201–19
Douglas, Ann, 168, 173
Downey, Sean Morton, 242
Draper, Hal, 249
Draft, military, 3, 8, 243–44
Dubois, Ellen, 11, 138, 170, 171, 172, 173, 219
Duncan, Graeme, 141
Dunn, John, 52
Dworkin, Susan, 249, 252

Easton, Barbara, 249

Economic class, 12, 57–58, 184; inequities, 126; interests, 120–22; work and, 96–99
Education, 47–48, 70–71, 80, 117–18, 121; of women, 48, 93–94, 100, 110, 133–34, 153, 165, 187–88
Ehrenreich, Barbara, 28, 252
Eisenhower, Dwight, 249
Eisenstein, Sarah, 215–16
Eisenstein, Zillah, 12, 29, 51, 214, 215
Elizabeth I (queen), 35
Emile, 68–70, 79, 80, 81
Engels, Friedrich, 120, 141, 143, 249
English, Deirdre, 28, 252
English Domestic Relations, 36
Equality, sexual, 103, 107–8, 109, 180, 212–13; and natural law, 77–80, 150–51
Equal Pay Act (1963), 197
Equal Rights Amendment (ERA), 8, 19, 196, 220, 226, 230, 246–48, 251–52; New Right and, 241–43; as strategy for feminists, 232–36
Extraordinary women, 137–38
Evans, R. J., 143
Evans, Sara, 11, 197, 199, 219
Ewen, Stuart, 250

Family, 181; child-centered, 68, 86; crisis of, 3; feudal, 20, 24–25, 36; Friedan on, 188–90; liberal individualism and, 47–49, 201–19; Locke on, 33–34, 37–44, 47–49; nuclear, 224–25; patriarchal, 24–25, 201, 204–6; radical feminism and, 177; Rousseau on, 58–60, 79–80, 82; Stanton on, 156–60, 165; in Victorian age, 134–39
Family, Sex and Marriage, in England, 1500–1800, The, 19–20
Farley, Lin, 218
Father-right, 18–19; vs. political rule, 37–44. *See also* Male privilege
Feiger, Sheila Molnar, 200
Feldberg, Roslyn, 216
Female-headed households, 210–11, 218
Feminine Mystique, The, 175, 177–200
Feminism. *See* Anarcha-feminism, Black feminism, Lesbian feminism, Liberal feminism, Radical feminism, Socialist feminism
Feudalism, 18–20, 23–25, 36, 38–39, 68–69
Figes, Eva, 83
Figgis, John Neville, 52
Filmer, Robert, 33, 38, 39, 40, 41, 50, 51, 52, 59
Firestone, Shulamith, 7, 12, 199

Fisher, Beverly, 219
Flax, Jane, 84
Flexner, Eleanor, 108, 169, 172
Flex-time, 190
Forster, Robert, 83
Foucault, Michael, 84
Freedom, 56, 73, 90–91; and contradictions of patriarchy, 76–84; political, 74–76; Wollstonecraft on, 94–95
Freeman, Jo, 197
Friedan, Betty, 3, 4, 175, 176, 177–200; feminine mystique, 184–90; individuality and, 190–92; liberal theory of power, 179–83
Fussell, G. E. and K. R., 30, 51

Gage, Matilda J., 169, 170–73
Garforth, Francis W., 141
Garson, Barbara, 217
Geduldig v. *Adiello*, 234, 237
General Electric v. *Martha Gilbert et al.*, 234, 237
George, Margaret, 89, 108, 109
Gies, Frances and Joseph, 28, 53
Gillam, Richard, 198
Gitlin, Todd, 13
Glen, Kristin, 239, 252
Glenn, Evelyn Nakano, 216
Godwin, William, 100, 106
Goldstein, Leslie Friedman, 252
Goldstrom, J. M., 143
Gordon, Ann, 169
Gordon, Linda, 27, 218, 249, 252
Gramsci, Antonio, 12, 250
Greece, classical, 22, 66, 74, 163
Greenberg, Hazel, 233, 251
Greer, Germaine, 12
Griffin, Susan, 12
Grimes, Alan, 172
Grimke, Sarah, 148
Gutman, Herbert, 219

Hacker, Andrew, 83
Halloran, Richard, 253
Hamilton, Richard, 217
Hamilton, Roberta, 30, 51
Hanisch, Carol, 198
Harkess, Shirley, 217
Harper, Ida Husted, 169, 171–73
Harrington, William, 36
Harrison, Rachel, 13, 15, 27
Hartsock, Nancy, 3, 11, 214
Havelock, Eric, 29
Hayek, Friedrich, 144
Hegel, G. W., 44
Hewitt, Margaret, 132, 143
Hibben, Sally, 250
Hill, Christopher, 36, 50–54

Himmelfarb, Gertrude, 139, 140, 142
Hoare, Quintin, 12
Hoffman, Lois Wladis, 199, 216
Holcombe, Lee, 143
Hole, Christina, 30, 51
Hole, Judith, 197, 199
Holtzman, Elizabeth, 176
Homosexuality, 19, 195, 241
Houston Women's Conference, 220, 222, 232, 244–46
Howe, Louise Kapp, 218
Hufton, Olwen, 57, 83, 84, 86
Hunt, Alan, 249
Hunter, Allen, 252–53
Hyde Amendment, 225, 239–41

Identity, loss of, 184–88
Ideology, liberal, 13, 20; criticism of, 90; of equal rights, 214; new femininity and, 146–49; Rousseau and patriarchal, 55–88; state's use of, 228–29; usage defined, 10
Idleness, women's, 97–98, 130–31, 132, 146
Independence: economic, 94–99; Rousseau on, 76–84; Wollstonecraft on, 89, 91–92, 94–99
Individualism, liberal, 5–6, 44–47; family and, 47–49; feminism and, 152–55, 190–92; individuality and, 114–22, 190–92; new feminism and, 146–49; and patriarchal family, 201–19; Rousseau on, 56, 73–74, 82–83; and social collectivity, 122–25; Wollstonecraft on, 94; women and, 127–29, 153; and working class, 119–22
Inflation, 246–47
Interdependence, social, 82, 146
Interrante, Joseph, 28
It Changed My Life, 188

Jacobs, Gloria, 253
Johnson, Lyndon, 249

Kamm, Josephine, 139, 142
Katzman, David, 218
Kelber, Mim, 253
Kellner, Douglas, 12, 229, 250
Kelly, Joan, 29, 215
Kennedy, John F., 197, 248
Keohane, Nannerl, 29
Koedt, Anne, 12
Kolko, Joyce, 243
Kraditor, Aileen, 172
Kramnick, Isaac, 50, 53, 86, 109
Kramnick, Miriam Brody, 98
Kreps, Juanita, 217

Kuhn, Annette, 12, 27, 28, 250

Labor force: economic class and, 96–99; property and, 45–47; sexual ghetto in, 206–12; sexual harassment in, 217; "women's work" in, 208–10
Lader, Lawrence, 252
Lamphere, Louise, 29
Larkin, Paschal, 54
Laski, Harold, 39, 50, 52, 53
Laslett, Peter, 35
Lasser, Carol, 28
Laurie, Bruce, 199, 217
Lederer, Muriel, 217
Lenin, V. I., 249
Lerner, Gerda, 168, 218
Lesbian(s), 17, 195, 196; feminism, 230, 238
Levellers, the, 46
Levine, David, 52
Levine, Ellen, 12, 197, 199
Levison, Andrew, 217
Lévi-Strauss, Claude, 224, 248
Lewis, Diane, 219
Lewis, Sasha, 252
Liberal: assault against male right, 90–93; theory of power, 179–83; usage defined, 4–5. See also Individualism, liberal
Liberal feminism, 3–13, 127, 230; contemporary, 229–32; and enfranchisement of women, 162–67; historical origins, 31–174; as mainstream, 4; mystique of, 184–90; New Right and, 241–44; patriarchal bias of, 132–39; politics of, 220–53; and politics of NOW, 192–97; spectrum, 230; state and, 177–200, 222–25, 244–48; theory of power, 179–83; "working mother" and, 212–14
Liberalism, 3, 6, 11–12, 20, 149; criticism of, 89–112; family and, 47–49; Locke on, 40, 44, 48–49; middle-class bias of, 108–9; rationality and, 44–49, 109; Rousseau on, 73–74; usage defined, 5; vs. radical feminism, 102–8. See also Individualism, liberal; Liberal feminism
Life Amendment Political Action Committee (LAPAC), 242
Lindsey, Karen, 217
Littlejohn, Gary, 250
Lochhead, Marion, 143
Locke, John, 5, 19–20, 33–54, 74; biographical note, 49–50; family and liberalism, 47–49; paternal vs. political power, 37–44, 59; power and rationality, 44–47, 93
Lutz, Alma, 168
Luxembourg, Rosa, 144, 248

McCrindle, Jean, 218
McDonough, Roisin, 13, 15, 27
Macfarlane, Alan, 52
MacPherson, C. B., 11, 44, 53, 54, 198
McRae v. Harris, 241
Magar, Michele, 253
Mahowald, Mary Briody, 29
Male privilege, 90–93, 182–83, 205–6. See also Patriarchy
Marcuse, Herbert, 141, 142
Marriage, 7, 10, 18–19, 90, 147, 196, 201; in 18th-century France, 57–58; middle-class, 96–102; Puritan doctrine of, 36–37; Rousseau on, 65, 67–70; Stanton on, 156–60, 162; in Victorian age, 129–32, 133, 136–37; and "working mothers," 207–8
Married Women's Property Act, 159
Marx, Karl, 54, 84, 87, 111, 143, 249
Masculine-feminine dichotomy, 23–26, 33–34, 59–60, 65–66, 96, 103–8, 115, 145, 157–58, 162–65, 181, 191, 204, 221, 223; as historical process, 78–80; in Victorian age, 134–39
Masses, the, 115, 117
Maternity leave, 192
Melnick, Jane, 253
Merit-based society, 43, 69–70, 73, 152–53
Middle-class women, 9–10, 89–90, 98, 108–9, 115, 146, 178, 203, 213–15, 216; loss of identity by, 184–88; as mothers, 99–102; in Victorian age, 129–32
Miliband, Ralph, 250
Mill, John Stuart, 3, 6, 20, 28, 113–44, 152, 157; individuality and liberal individualism, 114–22; liberal individualism and women, 127–29; patriarchal bias of liberal feminism, 132–39; on private property, 125–27; on socialism, 122–27; women's work, 129–32
Millett, Kate, 83, 199, 251
Mink, Patsy, 176
Mitchell, Juliet, 203, 215, 222, 248
Mohr, James, 238, 252
Moral society, 56, 60, 75, 80–84
Morgan, Robin, 12
Motherhood, 27, 58, 90, 192, 224; institutional, 14–17, 204–5; middle-class, 99–102; pension, 172; Rousseau on, 67–68; Stanton on, 160–62; in Victorian age, 137–38; and

Motherhood (*cont.*)
"working mothers," 207–8
Mott, Lucretia, 145, 148, 158

National Advisory Commission on Women, 232, 246–47
National Organization for Women (NOW), 176, 177, 180, 192–97
National Woman's Rights Convention (1858), 164
National Woman Suffrage, 165
National Women's Political Caucus, 179
Natural law, 77–80, 150–51
Natural right, property as, 34, 44–47
New femininity, 146–49
New Left, 177, 197
New Right, 241–44, 245
New York Times, 243, 247
Nixon, Edna, 108
Nixon, Richard, 243, 249
Nouvelle Heloise, La, 56, 68
Nye, Ivan, 199, 216

Oakley, Ann, 143, 168, 199
Okin, Susan Moller, 30, 83
O'Neill, William, 169, 172
One Woman's Situation, 89
On Liberty, 114, 115, 117
On the Subjection of Women, 113, 115, 127, 132, 134, 136, 137
Opportunity, equality of, 43–44, 109, 126–28, 132–35, 146–47, 179, 203, 214, 220
Ortner, Sherry, 29
Osbourne, Martha Lee, 29

Parenti, Michael, 198
Pateman, Carole, 29
Paternal authority, 37–44, 59–60
Patriarchy, 5–7, 10, 28; ahistorical, 27–28; antipatriarchalism in, 33–54; bias of liberal feminism and, 132–39; contradictions of, 76–84, 204–6; ERA and, 234–36; "feminine mystique" and, 178–79; feminist theory of, 226–28; Friedan on, 181–83, 185–86; historical, 18–22; motherhood and, 14–17, 66–70; needs of, 204–6; as political system, 26; and politics of feminism, 222–25; public-private life and, 22–26; Rousseau and ideology of, 55–88; Stanton on, 166–67; usage defined, 8–9, 18; "working mothers" and, 201–19
Paulson, Ross Evans, 172
Petchesky, Rosalind, 140, 252

Peters, Richard, 83
Phillipps, Wendell, 148
Pinchbeck, Ivy, 96, 110, 111
Pirenne, Henri, 53
Pius IX, Pope, 238
Plamenetz, John, 83
Pluralism, 120, 123, 181–83, 234
Pocock, J. G. A., 30, 53, 168, 172
Poland, 68–69, 72
Political rule, 75–76; father-right as basis, 19–20; liberal theory of, 179–83; vs. paternal rule, 37–44
Pomeroy, Sarah, 22, 30, 85
Porter, Sylvia, 218
Poulantzas, Nicos, 223, 226, 248
Powell, Chilton L., 51, 52
Power, Eileen, 29, 58, 84
Power: liberal theory of, 179–83; and rationality, 44–47; women's sexual, 56, 62–64
Principles of Political Economy, 113, 115, 125
Property, private, 44–47, 71, 73, 76, 79, 120–21, 125–27, 166–67
Public-private life, 5–6, 16, 33–34, 59–60, 65–66, 96, 103–8, 115, 145, 157, 162–65, 181, 189–91, 193–94, 221, 223; as historical process, 78–80; patriarchy and, 22–26, 204; in Victorian age, 134–39
Puritan doctrine, 36, 50

Race, 147–49, 184, 218–19, 222–23
Radical feminism, 7–8, 11, 12, 27, 230, 238, 251; as antifamily, 177; Friedan on, 178, 180; liberalism vs., 102–8; Stanton and, 155–62
Rand, Benjamin, 54
Rank, rule by, 90–93; graded, 169
Ranum, Orest, 83
Rationality: bourgeois society and, 93–96; power and, 44–47; women and, 35–37, 42–43, 48, 93–96, 109
Raxandall, Rosalyn, 218
Redstockings, 11, 177, 197
Reform Bill (England, 1867), 128
Reform: politics, 221–24; vs. revolution, 221–22, 236
Reiter, Rayna Rapp, 25, 29, 249
Reproductive rights, 17, 192, 194–96, 224–25, 236–41
Reverby, Susan, 218
Revolution, 155
Revolution vs. reform, 221–22, 236
Rich, Adrienne, 15, 18, 27, 215
Right-to-Life, 226, 230, 233, 241
Robb, Lynda Byrd, 247
Roe v. *Wade*, 238, 239

Roosevelt, Theodore, 151, 172
Rosaldo, Michelle, 27, 29
Ross, Heather, 218
Rossi, Alice, 139
Rousseau, Jean Jacques, 5, 23, 55–88, 152; ambivalence toward women, 60–62; bourgeois market, 70–74; family and state, 58–60; independence, 76–84; liberal values, 68–70; motherhood, 67–68; political freedom, 74–84; power of women, 62–64; sexual dependence, 80–84; virtuous woman, 64–67, 93–94
Rowbotham, Sheila, 29, 144, 199, 218
Rubin, Gayle, 21, 29
Ryan, Mary, 147, 168, 169, 216

Sabine, George, 83
Sachs, Albie, 252
Salper, Roberta, 139
Salzman, L. F., 53
Sarachild, Kathie, 200
Sargent, Lydia, 12
Sawhill, Isabel, 217, 218
Schlafly, Phyllis, 230, 241, 244
Schochet, Gordon, 50, 52
Schroeder, Pat, 176
Schwartz, Henry, 23, 29, 30
Scott, Joan, 110, 111
Sée, Henri, 84
Seifer, Nancy, 218
Seneca Falls Convention, 145, 157
Sennett, Richard, 217
Sex-class system, 6–9, 11, 12, 21, 28, 37–38, 103–7, 115, 140, 194, 221; Friedan on, 178–79, 181–83, 191–92; Stanton on, 154–56, 159, 163
Shklar, Judith, 68, 85, 86
Simons, Margaret, 219
Simpson, Peg, 252
Single-parent families, 210–11
Smeal, Eleanor, 176, 193
Smelser, Neil, 144
Smith, Adam, 92
Smith, Barbara, 219
Smith, Daniel S., 169
Smith, Geoffrey N., 12
Smith, Ralph E., 214, 218
Smuts, Robert, 199
Social Contract, The, 58, 78, 81
Socialism, 118, 122–27, 180
Socialist feminism, 11, 230, 238
Stacey, Judith, 249
Stack, Carol, 219
Stanton, Elizabeth Cady, 3, 6–7, 128, 145–76; "aristocracy of sex," 149–52; enfranchisement of women, 162–67; liberal individualism, 152–

55; new femininity, 146–49; as radical feminist, 155–62
Stanton, Henry, 160
Stanton, Theodore, 169
State: ERA and, 234–36; feminist theory of, 225–29; liberal feminism and, 222–25, 244–48; Locke on, 33–34, 37–47; right to property and, 44–47; Rousseau on, 58–60, 75–76; Stanton on, 166–67
Steinem, Gloria, 182
Stevenson, Adlai, 189
Stone, Lawrence, 19, 27, 110
Strauss, Leo, 83
Strayer, Joseph, 52
Stromberg, Ann, 217
Suffrage: black, 147–49; women's, 128, 132, 145–46, 162–67

Tawney, R. H., 50
Taxes, 71–72
Taylor, Harriet, 3, 6–7, 113–44. *See also* Mill, John Stuart
Taylor, John, 114
Tentler, Leslie W., 203, 225
Tepperman, Jean, 216
Theory of Moral Sentiments, 92
Therborn, Goran, 249
Thompson, E. P., 8, 12, 30, 110
Tilly, Louise, 110, 111
Tomalin, Claire, 108
Truman, Harry S, 249
Trumbach, Randolph, 27, 28
Two Treatises of Government, 34

U.S. Constitution, 149–51, 165, 233
U.S. Supreme Court, 220, 227, 237–41

Victorian era, 98, 114–15, 129–32, 169, 206
Vigueric, Richard, 242
Vindication of the Rights of Man, 91
Vindication of the Rights of Woman, 91, 98, 106, 107
Virtuous woman, 64–67, 93
Votaw, Carmen Delgado, 253
Voting: black, 147–49; plural, 118–19; women's, 128, 132, 145–46, 162–67

Wage-labor system, 23–26, 39, 57–58, 80, 96–97, 102–3, 121, 129–32, 136, 168–69, 184–85; sexual ghetto is, 206–12; "women's work" in, 208–10, 217
Walker, Alice, 219
Wallace, Michele, 219
Wardle, Ralph, 108, 110, 111, 112
Weber, Max, 50

Welfare mothers, 239–41
Wexler, Victor, 61, 83, 84
Weyrich, Paul, 242
White-collar jobs, 208–10, 216–17
Whitford, Richard, 36
Wilson, Joan Hoff, 252
Wohl, Lisa Cronin, 253
Wollstonecraft, Mary, 3, 6–7, 9, 57, 65, 89–112, 150, 187; liberalism vs. radical feminism, 102–8; male right, 90–93; middle-class mothers, 99–102; rationality, 93–96; work and economic class, 96–99
Women('s): black, 185, 213, 218–19; as childbearers, 7–8, 14–17, 78, 99–100, 135–38, 194; consciousness, 8, 10–11, 14–15, 177–78, 186–88, 190–91; domestic work, 7, 24, 36, 96–97, 129–32, 146–47, 158–59, 168, 172, 187–88, 194, 211; dependence, 9, 57–58, 76–77, 80–84, 101, 103, 133–34, 136–37, 159, 165, 186–87; double-day, 8, 185, 201–19; education, 48, 93–94, 100, 110, 133, 153, 165, 187–88; extraordinary, 137–38; as heads of households, 210–11; idleness, 97–98, 130–31, 132, 146; loss of identity, 184–88; middle-class, 9–10, 89–90, 98–102, 129–32, 146, 178, 184–85, 203, 213–15, 217; natural, 80–81, 134–36; rationality, 35–37, 42–43, 48, 92–94, 109; reproductive rights, 17, 192, 194–96, 224–25, 236–41; Rousseau on, 60–68; as sexual class, 6–9, 11, 12, 28, 92–93, 103–7, 115, 140, 154–46, 159, 163, 178–79, 181–83, 221; sexual power, 56, 62–64; suffrage, 128, 132–33, 145–49; in Victorian age, 129–39, 169; virtuous, 64–67, 93; wages, 57–58, 96–97, 129–32, 136, 184–85, 203, 209–10; working-class, 98, 132–33, 146, 203, 213–15, 216; as "working mothers," 8, 10, 190, 201–19, 221, 245
Woodward, Kenneth, 249
Working-class women, 98, 132–33, 146, 203, 213–15, 216–17
"Working mothers," 8, 10, 190, 201–19, 221, 245
World War II, 8, 184, 201, 203
Wright, F. A., 30
Wright, Martha, 148